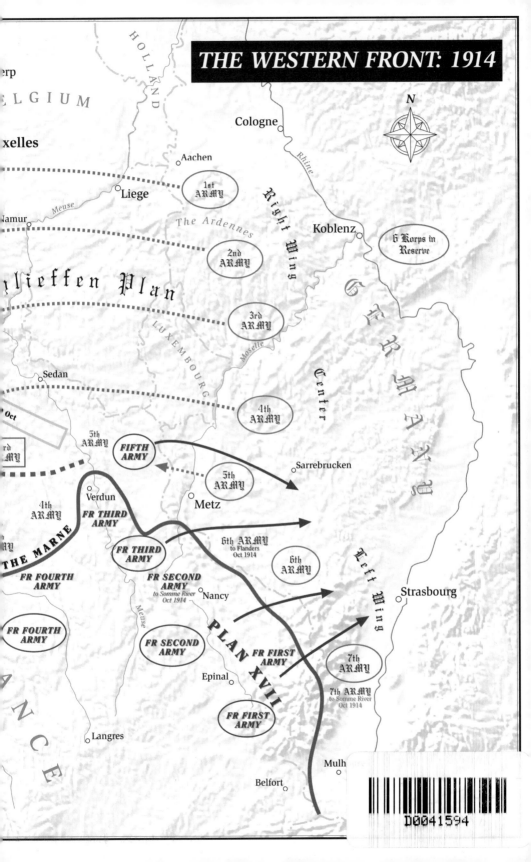

A Storm in Flanders ★

A Storm in Flanders ★

The Ypres Salient, 1914–1918:
Tragedy and Triumph on
the Western Front

Winston Groom

Atlantic Monthly Press
New York

This book is dedicated to Carolina Montgomery Groom, age three.
—from Papa

Published simultaneously in Canada
Printed in the United States of America

FIRST EDITION

Library of Congress Cataloging-in-Publication Data
Groom, Winston, 1944-
   A storm in Flanders : the Ypres salient, 1914–1918 : tragedy and triumph on the
Western Front / Winston Groom—1st ed.
      p. cm.
   Includes bibliographical references and index.
   ISBN 0-87113-842-5
   1. Ypres, 1st Battle of Ieper, Belgium, 1914.   2. Ypres, 2nd Battle of Ieper, Belgium,
1915. 3. Ypres, 3rd Battle of Ieper, Belgium, 1917.   4. Ieper (Belgium)—History, Military.
5. World War, 1914–1918—Campaigns—Belgium—Ieper.   I. Title.
D542.Y5 G76 2002
940.4'144—dc21   2002019433

Atlantic Monthly Press
841 Broadway
New York, NY 10003

02 03 04 05 10 9 8 7 6 5 4 3 2 1

Introduction ★

The Ypres Salient in Belgian Flanders was the most notorious and dreaded place in all of the First World War, probably of any war in history. Typical was this British infantryman's reaction on being told that his battalion was to go there: "I mentioned Ypres and he cursed the place. Rumors of what waited ahead of us had disturbed everyone." This was said between men who had just gone through the ordeal of the Battle of the Somme, where more than 50,000 British soldiers became casualties on the first day.

From the autumn of 1914 to the autumn of 1918 Flanders was, in effect, a gigantic corpse factory. Hundreds of thousands died there for ground where gains were measured in mere yards. It was where, in 1914, the British professional army was virtually annihilated, though it had stopped the German drive to capture control of the English Channel. It was where, in 1915, the Germans first introduced the hideous novelty of poison gas. It was where the horrors of the flamethrower were unleashed. It was where, in 1917, during the most infamous battle of the war, Passchendaele, thousands fought and drowned in mud sometimes waist deep. And it was where, in 1918, all the ground gained over the previous bloody years was first lost in a great German assault and then, in an electrifying turnabout with the aid of newly arrived American divisions, was not only regained but precipitated the final destruction of the German war machine.

What people most remembered about the Salient was the smell: the ever-present odor of rotting humans, horses, mules, rats, and food mixed with the stench of excrement, lingering poison gases, the repulsive aroma of quicklime used to decompose the dead, and the acrid stink of high-explosive artillery shells. It was said that you could smell the battlefield miles before you ever reached it. It was where the poppies grew in Flanders Fields while a million men lived like troglodytes in slimy underground trenches and from 1914 to 1918 fought and died with such consistency that even on "quiet days" casualties ran into the thousands—every day, for four long and grisly years. Almost every British army battalion at one time or another fought in Flanders. Although for purposes of continuity historians have catagorized events at Ypres into three or four major battles, in fact the fighting there was continuous. In short, it was Hell on Earth.

It might seem surprising, even odd to some, that since I am chiefly known as the author of *Forrest Gump*, and an American, that I would undertake to write a story about the fighting in Flanders, which was primarily between the British and the German armies. Despite the fact that I am no stranger to writing on historical subjects, it still seems a little far afield, so I will try to explain why.

Many years ago following a lunch at my grandparents' house I was roaming through the bookshelves when I came upon one of the Michelin Guide books on Europe printed in 1920. The famous tire maker had begun these publications some years earlier as a way of encouraging Europeans and foreign tourists to get out on the road and see the country (and, presumably, in the process burn up more tire rubber). The guide was entitled *Guides to the Battlefields: Ypres,* and even then the cover was fading and the ink blurred on the handwritten price tag of seven francs.

It piqued my curiosity because not only had I never heard of Ypres, I had no idea even of how to pronounce it. Skimming through, I was captivated by the pictures, graphic photographs depicting a landscape torn by war almost to the extent of ground zero at Hiroshima. Growing up in the post–World War II era I had become used to photographs of destruction—Berlin, Dresden, Monte Cassino—but this was different. Naturally

I knew of World War I, the great conflict fought more than forty years earlier in Europe, which "we," meaning the Americans, had won (though subsequently I have learned that the British and French see it somewhat differently). I recall as a young boy that on Armistice Day, November 11 (now renamed Veterans Day), over the public address system at school a student or teacher would always read the poem "In Flanders Fields," while on the streets downtown men would buy little red cloth poppies from vendors and wear them in their lapels to commemorate the armistice and peace. The poppy, which grew profusely in the fields of Belgian Flanders, at least at the war's beginning, had become the international symbol of the Allied victory over Germany and her associates.

As I pored over the Michelin Guide book the photographs stood out starkly, and struck a chord. By the time they were taken the Great War had been over for nearly two years, yet the landscapes remained unreclaimed. Men in dark suits and homburgs and women with long black dresses and white shirts strolled down streets that had been cleared amid a sea of rubble that had once been their residences and businesses. The photographs revealed an almost total obliteration of old—in many cases medieval—cities, towns, and villages, yet had it not been for the grotesqueness of their surroundings the people in the pictures might have been out for a normal Sunday afternoon outing.

Even in panorama, few objects stood higher than half a chimney and there were virtually no trees where whole towns had once flourished. In some of the pictures a person on a bicycle could be seen, or the occasional motor car. Moreover, the vistas shown beyond the towns strained the imagination—they looked if nothing else like the landscape of the moon, so pockmarked by tens of millions of artillery-shell craters that if any one section were taken out of perspective it would appear that someone had just plowed a field or spaded up the earth for miles around for an enormous garden plot.

The captions told the story: "All that remains of the Great Cloth Hall," "Remains of the Cathedral of Ypres," etc. The guide informed me that Ypres (pronounced "*Ee*-pra") was in Belgium, in a region called Flanders, named for an ancient land that ran along the North Sea from northern France into northern Belgium. It was the scene of the bitterest fighting of the war.

I asked my grandfather about the guidebook; he told me that he had bought it and others on a tour of World War I battlefields many years before. He himself had fought in the Great War as a soldier in the American First Infantry Division—though he fought in France and had not before been to the battlefields of Belgium. He was quite elderly then and I knew that he did not like lightning and thunder; my father told me it was because of his experiences in the war.

He gave me the book, which I have kept in my own library for many years. I learned subsequently that it is now considered one of the classic documents—especially for its photography—on the Flanders battles. It is ironic that the last history I wrote began with my discovery in the attic of my parents' house of an old strongbox containing the Civil War papers of my great-grandfather (from another branch of the family). This led to the 1995 publication of *Shrouds of Glory: From Atlanta to Nashville: The Last Great Campaign of the Civil War.* Much inspiration in my life seems derived from musty attics and dusty bookshelves.

Over the years I became fascinated by the images of the fighting in that part of Belgium. I would read about Flanders whenever I could find material, but all the "war talk" in those days was of the Second World War, not the First; in college there were courses devoted to World War II—mainly because a number of the professors had fought in it—but none on World War I.

Not long afterward I had my own war to fight (Vietnam), and when I returned in 1968 I was in no mood to "study war." Several years later, however, while a journalist in Washington, I found myself at the library in Georgetown and came across a book on the Flanders battles far more detailed than the Michelin Guide. Again I became curious about how and why so many millions of soldiers, British, German, and all their allies, could have stood the wretchedness of trench warfare for four ghastly years. What is more, having then recently returned from the much lamented American war in Southeast Asia, I wondered how many in the American armed forces then (or now) would have put up with the daily subhuman slaughter and deprivation that went on at Ypres or, for that matter, on practically all the battlefields of the so-called War to End All Wars. I expect I might not have put up long with it myself.

Likewise, I was intrigued by the similarities in the two wars: the soldiers of the First World War had no helicopters, planes dropping napalm, or chemical defoliants (they accomplished defoliation anyway, though, by methodical artillery fire). On the other hand, we in Vietnam did not have to contend with cavalry horses, poison gases, or trenches. However, both became wars of apparently pointless attrition. World War I began as a war of mass movement; each army tried to turn the flank of the other and score a quick victory on the principles of military science as it was understood at the time. After three bitter months of fighting, the war turned into a stalemate and the so-called strategy then devolved into "attrition," the crude notion of simply wearing down the enemy by brute force and superior resources—in other words, killing for killing's sake. In Vietnam it was believed in the beginning that airborne strikes against enemy formations—thousands of men descending from the sky in helicopters—would quickly outposition and defeat an earthbound enemy. Several years later it, too, had sunk into a war of attrition, and the repugnant term "body count" became a household word.

I began to read more on World War I, particularly about the fighting in Flanders, and even published a (rather shallow) piece on it in my newspaper. During more than twenty-five years since then, I have strived to become a student of the subject and often entertained the notion of writing a book on the Ypres battles. Not the kind of book that would entail a daily, blow-by-blow account of the entire four-year episode, but rather one that would give Americans a picture of what it must have been like in that most dreadful and deadly of conflicts in which we, too, participated. The French army, of course, suffered throughout the war even more than the British, and their heroic ordeals at the Marne and at Verdun are well recorded. Likewise, the Germans. This book, however, is not about the French or Germans. It is written *for* Americans. Therefore I have tried to unravel the idiosyncrasies of our common language, in which unfamiliar terms and historical personages and events so familiar to the British are illuminated for American readers.

I am also aware that in certain quarters in Great Britain, Americans and other foreigners are sometimes greeted with skepticism if they write about the First World War. The literary historian Paul Fussell, author of

The Great War and Modern Memory, experienced something of this twenty-five years ago, and compared it with the way "an American person of letters [might] react to an interpretation of American literature by, say, a citizen of Papua, New Guinea." If that is still so, I beg forgiveness for any presumption; but again, this book is written for an American audience and it seemed to me that Ypres was the only constant cauldron of battle throughout the entire four-year conflict. It would be wrong to leave an impression that most of the war was fought in Belgian Flanders; it was not (though much of it was). Still, the Ypres fighting provides a unique opportunity to tell a narrative, anecdotal history of the First World War by utilizing it as a single centerpiece upon which the issues of strategy, tactics, politics, literature, the home front, and the experiences and sufferings of the participants could be hung.

The fighting in Flanders is in many ways metaphoric of what most Americans recall of the First World War, if they recall it at all: the sense of the utter futility of massed infantry attacks, the grim life in the trenches with its daily bath of blood, the stubbornness of the high command, condemned as "donkeys" or as "butchers and blunderers," sacrificing the flower of their nation's manhood on those savage killing fields. And yet there was far more to it than that, as we shall see: the political intrigues and infighting between the military and the civilian governments of the belligerents, lost opportunities, failed intelligence, and, above all, the hardships, courage, victories, and failures of so many undaunted men on both sides of the murderous Flanders "no-man's-land."

By the third year of the war people in all the warring nations had come to recoil against the slaughter on the Western Front, yet few were prepared to do anything about it. Major General J.F.C. Fuller, chief of the British Tank Corps General Staff in 1917 and later a scathing critic of his country's conduct of the war, stated, in 1957, forty years after the German capitulation, that the year 1917 would have been an excellent time to stop the war, for the Allies to have pursued a negotiated peace with the Germans. He shared the view with others that a policy of unconditional surrender was ridiculous and unnecessary and that, even in lieu of peace negotiations, the British blockade of Germany ultimately would have starved them out.

Somehow, though, General Fuller ignored in this theory the lessons later learned by those same Allies against Nazi Germany and Japan.

While Americans have largely forgotten the First World War, the British nation dwells on it—some say they are obsessed by it—since a great part of an entire generation of their menfolk lie buried beneath Belgian and French soil. (Not long into the war, an administrative decision was made to not send back the bodies of those killed, even though they were barely a stone's throw across the English Channel. The reasoning was that it was impossible to send back everyone—not only because there were so many "missing" but because it would create a huge logistical nightmare. One suspects it was also because so many funerals might have had a chilling effect on British resolve.)

Even today the Flanders battlefields are crowded with tour buses filled with Englishmen and -women, much in the way Gettysburg is in this country, perhaps even more so. The war of 1914–1918 was a different time from what we know now, with another, more horrid war past, the prospect of atomic destruction still looming in the air, the Cold War subsided but threats of deadly terrorism presently on people's minds. There is every probability—as most historians persuasively argue—that if the First World War had not been fought, then the Second World War would not have been either; that the rise of Hitlerism and communism would have been only a frightful dream. But the war *was* fought, and when it was over more than four years after it began, 9 million soldiers, sailors, and aviators were dead and countless more maimed for life, four great empires were erased from the earth, and the course of the twentieth century was changed forever.

Author's Note on Unit Sizes and Designations

The numerical composition of the various units in World War I can be confusing, since various nations employed different numbers of people in their designations. It is useful, though, to look first at a breakdown of the British Army, unit by unit, to get a general feeling for the nomenclature of troops involved. Here is a simplified table:

       Platoon: 60 men commanded by a lieutenant
       Company: 240 men commanded by a captain
      Battalion: 1,100 men commanded by a lieutenant-colonel
        Brigade: 4,400 men commanded by a brigadier-general
       Division: 12,000 to 14,000 men commanded by a major-general
    Army corps: 36,000 to 40,000 men commanded by a lieutenant-general
           Army: 180,000 to 240,000 men commanded by a general.

The disparities in numbers as the units merge larger is because that in addition to the infantry—the core of all fighting units—various support troops are invariably added: artillery, quartermaster, supply, cavalry, ordnance, engineers, medical, and other technical personnel. The French and German armies were roughly equivalent to the British model. The Americans, however, had quite larger divisions, often totaling 24,000 men. These, however, proved unwieldy in battle.

Regiments were an entirely different matter, and can also be confusing. Regimental designations were a somewhat old-fashioned and quaint way to identify a unit, but one which evoked a tremendous esprit de corps: The Scots Guards, The Black Watch, The Green Howards, The King's Royal Rifles, The Irish Rifles, and on and on. Regiments could number anywhere from 1,000 to 5,000 men and, while they were technically incorporated in the unit divisions enumerated above, they retained their historic names, although after the battles of First Ypres, when most of the old professional army had been wiped out, the honor often meant something less to replacements in the line.

It should also be remembered when trying to understand how many men were actually involved in a battle, that most times units were well below their designated strength because of casualties, men on leave, sick, or detailed elsewhere. Thus, a battalion which would have ideally contained 1,100 men, would often go into battle with 600 to 800 and, considering the horrific losses during the First World War, be happy if that many were available.

Chapter One ✭

Forests have been sawed down for the paper to explain the origins of the First World War; historians argue and debate it still. A precise truth can never be divined because of the fallibility of the human factor—in the tortuous process who, on which side, in their darkest thoughts, understood or believed what, and at which moment? It is almost as if mischievous gods dropped a gigantic jigsaw puzzle from the sky in which some of the pieces will always be missing and others do not exactly fit the places for which they were designed. One thing generally agreed on is that the long and terrible path began in 1870, when Germany united itself into a nation.

Prior to then, Germany had been a collection of twenty-five kingdoms and principalities loosely governed by the state of Prussia, which was presided over by Kaiser William (Wilhelm) I. In the 1860s, at the advice of Germany's revered statesman, Prince Otto von Bismarck, the Prussians set about to gather up all these entities into a Greater Germany, thus becoming the largest and most powerful state in Europe. She then quickly assailed and subdued her neighbors Denmark (1864), Austria (1866), and France (1871). It was the French conquest that caused the trouble. After encircling Paris and reducing the inhabitants to a diet of cat meat, the Germans demanded and received the two longtime French provinces that constituted Germany's border with France: mineral-rich Alsace and

Lorraine. This humiliation galled the French down to the last peasant, creating a bitter animosity that lasted generations and helped lead to the outbreak of the First World War.

Led by William I, who now became the kaiser (emperor), Germany suddenly became the most threatening state in Europe. With the exception of republican France, at that time Europe was ruled by monarchies. To the east of Germany lay the vastness of czarist Russia, which also controlled part of Poland as well as the Baltic states; to the south was the Hapsburg empire of Austria-Hungary, governed by Emperor Franz Joseph and including what is now Czechoslovakia, Croatia, Bosnia-Herzegovina, Galicia, and Transylvania. South of this were the turbulent, angry, and emerging states of Serbia, Romania, Bulgaria, Albania, and Montenegro. To the north were the Scandinavian countries Norway, Sweden, Finland, Denmark. To the west along the Atlantic and North Sea coasts were France, Spain, Portugal, Belgium, Holland. And out in the ocean lay the island kingdom of Great Britain.

At the time of the German unification Great Britain was the most formidable industrial power in the world. Soon Germany began to challenge her, aided by an influx of iron and coal from the conquered French provinces. For the remainder of the nineteenth century, the industrious Germans made giant leaps in modern technologies and economics: steel production, mining, chemicals, education, finance, transportation, electronics, and, of course, the most up-to-date military armaments, while much of continental Europe, especially France, seemed content to languish as agricultural nations.

On a visit in 1878, the venerable Mark Twain described Germany this way: "What a paradise this land is! What clean clothes, what good faces, what tranquil contentment, what prosperity, what genuine freedom, what a superb government!" In a way it was true; the Germans were a proud people and within the space of a few years had created much to take pride in. By the end of the nineteenth century the German public school system had eliminated illiteracy, the German economy was booming, and, in terms of equipment and overall effectiveness, she had the mightiest army in the world.

On balance, the last quarter of the century was a time of world peace; the prosperous Gilded Age saw the development of the telephone, electric lights, automobiles, motion pictures, manufacturing advances, vast railway systems, and luxury transatlantic shipping—all products of the so-called Second Industrial Revolution. It was also a time that saw enormous improvements in weapons and weapons systems—the invention of high-explosive gunpowder, rapid-fire rifles, and, of course, the machine gun. Perhaps the most important—and certainly the most important during World War I—was the development of long-range artillery. In warfare until almost the close of the nineteenth century, the guns had to be fired basically by "line-of-sight," which meant that the gunners had to actually "see" the target. But with the invention of high-tensile steel and the manufacture of larger and larger guns and howitzers, as well as the application of precise trigonomic calculations, artillery could be hidden away far from a battle area, protected by ridges or other terraine features, and preregister fire over almost every square yard of the field. The effect of this would prove to be devastating in the coming conflict.

Winston Churchill summed up thusly the great advances in technology during the latter part of the nineteenth century: "Every morning when the world woke up, some new machinery had started running. Every night while the world had supper, it was running still. It ran on while all men slept."

Yet amid this new abundance roiled an undercurrent of unrest. There was a dramatic rise of nationalism among many European nations then dominated by the empires of others—particularly in that eternal volcano, the Balkan states. Serbia, Bosnia, Herzegovina, Romania, Bulgaria, and Montenegro all chafed under the harsh rule of Turkey's crumbling Ottoman empire. Added to this were all the old religious fears and hatreds: Muslim versus Christian, Catholic versus Protestant—and everybody against the Jews. Disputes festered over trade and tariffs and envy over colonial possessions engendered an uncommon outbreak of pride, vanity, greed, mistrust, and shortsightedness among both rulers and ruled. Throw in the rising creed of socialism and one can see how the kettle had begun to heat. This was especially true in Russia, ruled by the iron-fisted czar Nicholas, who, quite naturally, had outlawed the preaching of socialism in all its various facets. Still the philosophy flourished among large numbers of workers in Russian cities. There they kept alive their utopian dream of a classless society where everyone got his fair share—a world without poverty or suffering or political oppression. Time was running out for the empire of the czars.

This was no less true in Germany. There, despite the rosy picture painted by Mark Twain and others, dissatisfaction among the laboring classes had produced the largest socialist party in the world, constantly plotting to overthrow the government and the capitalist system. The German right to vote was basically a sham, because the German constitution was so constructed as to leave the principal power in the hands of the kaiser and his cronies in the military. There was a federal parliament of sorts—a Reichstag. Its duties were limited to presiding over minor internal matters involving the various German states. Still, in all things of consequence, including the right to declare war, the kaiser had the last word.

Religious intolerance was pervasive. Most of the aristocracy and upper classes had joined the sixteenth-century Protestant Reformation, and even as the new century dawned Germany's large Catholic population suffered widespread discrimination. Jews even more so. Despite the patina of happiness and prosperity, a good portion of German society seethed.

The continuing enmity of France toward Germany over her lost provinces of Alsace and Lorraine led the Germans to become apprehensive. Fearing that France meditated a war of revenge, Helmuth von Moltke, chief of the German General Staff who had guided the victory over France in 1870–71, remarked, "What we have gained by arms in half a year, we must protect by arms for half a century." Yet Bismarck, Germany's "Iron Chancellor," desired no war and set about making alliances with other powerful empires to ensure Germany's security against France, Russia, and to a lesser extent England. It must be understood that, unlike the United States, Germany did not have two huge seacoasts to protect her, nor friendly or weaker nations at her borders. She had been in conflict with her neighbors almost since time immemorial. The treaty with Russia was crucial because of her vast border on the eastern frontiers of Germany. England—which had been fighting with the French from the time of the Norman Conquest up through the Napoleonic Wars at the beginning of the century—was sought after as a hedge against French aggression. In 1879 Bismarck also forged an alliance with Austria-Hungary. In 1883 Italy was brought into the pact, which later included Romania under a secret agreement.

What chilled Bismarck's bones was the notion that France would make her own alliance with behemoth Russia, hemming Germany in between the two of them. His apprehension was heightened in 1887 when Russia and Austria-Hungary (hereafter referred to as Austria) collided in a dispute over control in the Balkans, during which it seemed as if Russia and France might unite in a pact of their own. But in a brilliant piece of German diplomacy, Bismarck, playing off fears of external and internal threats, managed to cobble together the League of the Three Emperors: Germany, Austria-Hungary, and Russia. This was not only an insurance treaty but a "Reinsurance Treaty," under which Germany and Austria promised not to undermine Russia in the Balkans and Russia, for her part, agreed not to form an alliance against Germany-Austria with France. That stratagem more or less kept the European peace until old Kaiser William I died in 1888. His son Frederick succeeded him as kaiser but he died, of cancer, after only three months. Then *his* son took the throne as William II. The first thing this brash young autocrat did was to get rid of the venerable Bismarck and repudiate the latter's carefully laid diplomacy.

The new kaiser had long had his own ideas about how Germany's future in world affairs should progress. Kaiser William II was a strange figure; born with a withered arm, he grew up chafing while his grandfather and Bismarck dallied in the odd assortment of mutual defense treaties to ensure Germany's security. Even before his ascension to the throne William was writing letters advocating a preventive war against France and Russia on the time-worn theory that they were conspiring against Germany. This was not altogether paranoia; France was, as ever, still furious over her humiliation in the Franco-Prussian War and the loss of Alsace and Lorraine, and Russian diplomats had made it clear that they were anxious about Germany's intentions and military might. Neither wanted war with Germany, however, and in fact feared her.

One of the remarkable things about European diplomacy prior to World War I was the intimate family relationships between rulers who would ultimately become the belligerents. It all began with Great Britain's Queen Victoria, granddaughter of King George III (ruler of England during the American Revolution). In 1837, at the age of eighteen, she became Queen of England.

Victoria and her husband, Prince Albert, a German, had nine children, who married into practically all the royal houses of Europe. Her eldest son, Prince Albert Edward, married a princess of Denmark and became England's King Edward VII when Victoria died in 1901. His son—Victoria's grandson—George V, succeeded his father as king of England just in time for World War I.

One of Victoria's daughters married a German prince and their daughter—Victoria's granddaughter—became the wife of Czar Nicholas II of Russia. Not only that, but another of Victoria's sons had married the czar's aunt. Also, Queen Victoria's firstborn daughter married the German kaiser Frederick and their eldest son became Kaiser William II, who ascended to the German throne in 1888.

Thus, England's George V, Russia's Nicholas II, and Germany's William II were all cousins, either directly or through marriage, descendants of England's Queen Victoria.

The new German kaiser was something of a military nut, especially with regard to the navy, at that point a relatively small part of the German armed forces establishment. He appointed himself a field marshal, as well as an admiral (a title that had also been bestowed on him by his cousins in England), and decreed that henceforth the regular dress at his court would be the military uniform. The kaiser, though he could be cranky, was not stupid. He was particularly impressed with a gift some years earlier by his cousin George, the future king of England, of a Gatling gun, and insisted that the German Army embrace with vigor this new automatic weapon. By the time World War I broke out, the German Army had not only mastered use of the Gatling's successor, the machine gun, but incorporated nearly 12,000 of them into their fighting battalions—nearly triple the numbers the Allies possessed. (The British Army, on the other hand, was still talking about the advantages of the cavalry charge and the French, the "Spirit of the Bayonet").

In 1890 the League of the Three Emperors alliance lapsed. The kaiser made no move to renew it; instead, he virtually slammed the door in Russia's face, refusing to continue financial loans to them and otherwise giving them the cold shoulder. As the historian Donald Kagan points out in *On the Origins of War*: "There was considerable pressure, especially among the younger elite surrounding the young Kaiser, for change, almost any change. From the Kaiser's point of view, how could he rid himself of the dead hand of the past and establish his own place as leader of his people if he merely walked the paths paved by his predecessors. What was the point of dismissing Bismarck only to be ruled by his system and his policies?"

This "change for change's sake," or "I did it because I'm the kaiser and I could," would prove to be a very big mistake.

Not surprisingly, the French instantly saw their opportunity and began courting the Russians, holding out, among other emoluments, the prospect of loans to them from the great House of Rothschild. In 1892, as Churchill put it, "The event against which the whole policy of Bismarck had been directed came to pass," and, though they did not ratify it for two more years, France and Russia agreed to a dual alliance, under which each would come to the other's aid if attacked by Germany or her allies. Thus, if hostilities broke out, Germany now faced the unhappy prospect of fighting a two-front war. Meanwhile, the kaiser had embarked on a foreign policy that some believe was deliberately meant to vex his perceived enemies—which now included Great Britain, even though England had devoted herself to remaining neutral within the increasingly sour disposition of continental affairs. The kaiser's behavior toward England was rooted in one of the world's worst motives for troublemaking: jealousy. William coveted Great Britain's exalted position among the nations of the world. He coveted the great empire upon which "the sun never set." He especially coveted England's magnificent naval fleet's complete dominance of the high seas. "Germany," as the historian Martin Gilbert explains, "united only in 1870, had come too late, it seemed, into the race for power and influence, for empire and respect." The kaiser, however, was determined to rectify this: with the most powerful military machine in the world, he did not intend to play second fiddle to a small island nation such as Great Britain. What he wanted, he said, was for Germany to have "a place in the sun."

Some years earlier, in the mid-1880s, Bismarck—who had always believed that acquiring African colonies for Germany would become a liability—changed his mind, and so Germany began to move into Africa, colonizing Cameroon, Togoland, Tanganyika (East Africa), and German Southwest Africa. The main reason for Bismarck's reversal was that it had become all too apparent that the German population was outgrowing Germany's ability to assimilate them. Consequently, large numbers of young men were leaving the Fatherland to work in other nations and their colonies—in England this resulted in an unusually large number of German table waiters. Unfortunately for Germany, their colonial acquisitions were not particularly profitable. They were located mostly in equatorial Africa—a wild, fetid, unhealthy, and not very prosperous region, either for raw materials or for trade; they were also prone to native uprisings, as the Germans would soon find out. However, these were all that were left since Britain, France, and other countries had long since secured the more desirable northern and southern parts of the continent. Nevertheless the new kaiser persisted in keeping them, apparently on the premise that he could not rule over a German empire without possessing colonies, no matter how much of a liability they might be. This also led to trouble.

Meantime, tensions were heightened when, in the early 1900s, Great Britain began signing agreements with France and Russia over various colonial and trade issues. This was more significant than it appeared because it represented for the first time in centuries an official smoothing over of Anglo-French relations—a fact not lost on the Germans, who were all too aware of Britain's formidable sea power. Thus, day by day, year by year, the sun inched its way across the horizon of the new century silently marking the grim inevitability of a world at war.

In time the Germans tried to muscle in on the more desirable colonies of North Africa, which might have led to an early outbreak of world war. In 1905 the French attempted to turn Morocco into what amounted to a French protectorate and the kaiser was convinced by his diplomats to appear at Tangier during his cruise of the Mediterranean and assert equal rights for Germany in Morocco. This set off the dangerous First Moroccan Crisis since it was implied that if Germany did not get what she wanted, she might go to war with France. Basically, it was just saber rattling on the kaiser's part, but the situation did not simmer down without repercussions. Britain, smelling peril in Germany's territorial aspirations, next formed an entente with Russia, which was already allied with France, posing a new and even more galling threat in the suspicious Teutonic mind. In *The Scramble for Africa*, Thomas Pakenham reminds us that "Relations with Germany had cooled to ice since Britain had signed the entente with France." Now that Russia, too, was in the picture, Germany trundled out her old complaint of being "encircled" by enemies, a claim she first had employed under Frederick the Great at the beginning of the Seven Years War.

As if this were not enough, another rub was in the offing. Determined to be second to none in naval power, the new kaiser authorized a series of fleet appropriations designed to bring his German navy into parity with Great Britain. This of course caused British alarm and consternation, since supremacy at sea was the bulwark not only of her national defense but of her position of worldwide power and empire. As Churchill remembered: "All sorts of sober-minded people in England began to be profoundly disquieted. What did Germany want this great navy for? Against whom, except us, could she measure it, match it, or use it?" Thus began the greatest and costliest ship-building race in the history of the world, which was to last until the outbreak of war. It has even been argued that this was a major cause of the world war since consequent army and navy bills caused the citizens of Germany to become so heavily taxed that conquest and expansion became almost a necessity.

Still not content, the kaiser also began to foster a foreign policy designed to harass and disturb his neighbors, possibly on the novel theory that if bullied and intimidated other nations might choose to become closer to Germany, instead of distancing themselves from her. Following a military action that was a prelude to the Boer War (1899–1902) the kaiser had inflamed British public opinion by intimating that Germany might challenge England and intervene in South Africa on the side of the Boers. During the war itself, the German press and public were exceedingly hostile to the British. Next came the First Moroccan Crisis, in 1905, and following that, in 1911, came the second.

In the spring of that year Germany again tried her hand in Morocco, asserting that one of its private companies was being denied by French and

British interests the right to establish a port in the harbor of Agadir on the Atlantic coast. The French intended to negotiate, protesting that there were no German installations whatever in Agadir, but Germany forthwith announced it was sending a warship into Moroccan waters to "protect German interests." As Churchill put it, "All the alarm bells throughout Europe began to quiver." Basically, it was just more saber rattling on the part of the kaiser, and the warship finally left without firing a shot.

The barrage of German threats, warnings, and ultimatums had thoroughly energized the French to the likelihood of German aggression. France began to think on a war footing, bolstering her reserves and strengthening her regular army. Great Britain, too, was beginning to be drawn into the fracas, and issued a warning to Germany that England would side with France in the event of war. Meantime, Germany had begun to meddle in Afghanistan in an attempt to thwart the British from reinstalling a puppet caliph government.

During this time the English, and to a lesser extent the French, began to surmise that if Germany attacked France she would do so by invading northwestward through neutral Belgium and Holland, since the topography of the French frontier bordering Germany was not often conducive to invasion. After their defeat in 1871 the French had constructed a series of enormous and elaborate fortresses at places like Verdun and Belfort to bar any German advance along their common border. Belgium, however, was relatively flat and open, with few natural defenses.

Belgium maintained the theory that as a neutral, she must remain *absolutely* neutral, and even on the eve of war she refused assistance from France and England to help strengthen her defenses. The British had good reason to suspect German treachery in Belgium, owing to a conversation King Leopold had had with the kaiser more than a decade earlier. On that occasion the kaiser had asked the Belgian king politely whether, in the event of war, the German Army could use his country as a doormat into France. Just as politely, King Leopold refused, but then wasted little time telling the British about that remarkable request.

*   *   *

Not surprisingly, the invasion-through-Belgium strategy was precisely what the Germans had in mind. In 1905 the German chief of the General Staff, Count Alfred von Schlieffen, completed his scheme to win a German victory in the event war broke out with France and Russia. His plan assumed that because of the various alliances, if war came Germany and her ally Austria would be fighting on two fronts. Schlieffen determined that the prudent course of action was to attack France immediately and defeat her decisively before the Russians could fully mobilize—and only then turn east to meet the Russian threat. Schlieffen envisioned leaving a modest force along the French border to hold the French armies at bay, while the main thrust would come from the north on the German right flank to envelope any opposing forces in Belgium. In bypassing the heavily fortified French frontier, the German armies would deliberately violate Belgian—as well as Dutch—neutrality and sweep down into northern France, capturing Paris and bringing France to her knees. It was, in Schlieffen's mind, to be another Cannae—or so the scheme went.

Donald Kagan explains that "By 1912 German policy had created the *Entente* [between Britain, France, and Russia] which pursued a policy we might call containment and the Germans called *Einkreisung*, encirclement." Like the kaiser, Schlieffen was haunted by this perceived enclosure by hostile powers and declared, "We are surrounded by an enormous coalition, we are in the same position as Frederick the Great. Now we can escape from the noose." In any case, his plan remained the linchpin of German war policy, with some modification, for nearly a decade—up to the outbreak of the war.

Meanwhile, the perpetual tinderbox in the turbulent southern regions was firing up. In 1912 the Balkan states erupted in war against their centuries-old oppressor, the Turks, and managed to free themselves from the remains of the Ottoman empire. Then they turned on one another in the Second Balkan War (1913) in a squabble for territory and hegemony—the spoils of the first Balkan War. This was where the trouble lay, since both the Austrian and Russian empires felt they had a claim on the Balkan states—Austria because she had always believed the countries below her southern borders were in her sphere of influence, and Russia because so many of the Balkan peoples were fellow Slavs with whom they shared common linguistic and cultural roots. This of course raised matters to the crisis level since any outbreak of war between Austria and Russia over the Balkans would, due to alliances, necessarily bring in France on the Russian side and Germany on the Austrian, and the Schlieffen plan would undoubtedly be set in motion. Even though the crisis finally abated, tensions remained high throughout the year.

In Germany, especially among the military hierarchy, there had been much talk of general war for more than a decade. In 1891 Field Marshal Helmuth von Moltke, chief of the General Staff, died at the age of ninety-one. His replacement, Schlieffen, reigned until 1905 and then this crucial post fell to Moltke's nephew and namesake, fifty-six-year-old general Helmuth Johannes Ludwig von Moltke, an aide to the kaiser, who dabbled in mysticism and played the cello. At the same time that Bismarck, even in retirement, was warning that "The Great European war could come out of some damned foolishness in the Balkans," the younger Moltke himself was declaring, "I believe war to be unavoidable and the sooner the better." Moltke's rationale for this intemperate declaration was that by his planner's projections France and Russia by 1917 would have overtaken Germany in combined military might, and so Germany might just as well get on with it now while the getting was good. Otto Friedrich, biographer of the Moltke dynasty, has reported that Moltke "continue[d] to think that a European war must come in the end and that this will essentially be a struggle between the Germanic and the Slav races." Kaiser William believed this too.

Thus, the pistol of war was now cocked and it remained only for someone to touch its hair trigger. This came soon enough, on June 28, 1914, when a fanatical eighteen-year-old Bosnian-Serb nationalist named Gavrilo Princip shot and killed the Austrian heir to the Hapsburg throne, Archduke Francis Ferdinand, and his wife, who, against all good advice, had arranged to ride in a motorcade through the streets of Sarajevo. Worse, the parade had been set for St. Vitus' Day, anniversary of the wretched 500-year-long subjugation of the Serbians by the Ottoman Turks following the Battle of Kosovo.

The furious Austrians (whom Churchill described as Germany's "idiot ally") immediately and correctly suspected that Bosnia's militant neighbor Serbia had committed this act of "state-sponsored terrorism" in a bid to

rid the Balkans of any and all Austrian rule. After a month of foot stomp-
ing, fist shaking, and throat clearing, Austria delivered a series of demands
upon Serbia that amounted to an ultimatum. Before doing so, however, the
Austrians had sought the counsel of Germany, and received not just the go
ahead but outright pressure to declare war, even though the Germans expected that Russia would not take the matter lying down, and fully realized that this could bring the wrath of France, and England also, down upon
their spiked helmets. For his part, the kaiser declared, "Finally, the famous
encirclement of Germany has become an undeniable fact."

Among other things, the Austrians demanded that Serbia suppress all
anti-Austrian propaganda espoused by newspapers, military or civil officers,
schools, and so forth. What was worse, and even more unacceptable—and
the Austrians obviously knew this—the Austrians finally demanded they be
permitted to use whatever means they wished to put down any "subversive"
activities in Serbia. In other words, Austria would in effect be given authority over Serbia, which had only recently won a bloody fight for independence.

To the great surprise of everyone, Serbia acceded to all of the demands
but the last and suggested that it be put to international arbitration. But minds
had already been made up and Austria declared war on Serbia the day after
receiving their reply; two days later they were bombarding the city of Belgrade
from gunboats in the Danube.

The German press was of course full of news of impending war, managing in the process to convince the German people that they were about to
be attacked from all sides. Despite record-breaking heat in Germany that summer, people anxiously hurried back from seashore or mountain resorts. German athletes in training for what would have been the 1916 Olympics in Berlin
must have taken pause at the prospect of being ordered into the army. The
German socialist party began organizing peace rallies; nervous investors lined
up at banks and brokerage houses. A tense pall of uncertainty hovered over
the country, broken frequently by mass rallies of enthusiastic flag-waving,
anthem-singing, warmongering German patriots.

When Austria attacked Serbia, Nicholas II, czar of Russia and the kaiser's
cousin (they called each other "Nicky" and "Willie" in the telegrams they
traded right up until the war), ordered a partial mobilization of his army.
The Russians' interest in their fellow Slavs was such that they were deter-

mined to prevent any Austrian conquest of the Serbian nation. In those times, mobilization, particularly full mobilization—at least in the mind of Germany—was the equivalent of declaring war. The day before Austrian shells began falling, a fatally belated fear of the prospect of Russian mobilization produced a sobering effect on the kaiser. Like a bully confronted with the possibility of a real fight, he tried at the last minute to dissuade Austria from declaring war on Serbia. When she did so anyway, the kaiser nevertheless bowed to his military and political advisers and delivered Russia an ultimatum to stop mobilizing or Germany itself would mobilize and war would inevitably follow.

The Russians did no such thing, however, and despite the frantic efforts of diplomats from many countries—particularly Great Britain—Germany declared war on Russia August 1, 1914; citing the Franco-Russian alliance, two days later she declared war on France. "Kaiser Bill" had become the ultimate tool of his military establishment.

The Schlieffen Plan was immediately set into motion. This same day, Germany invaded more or less neutral Luxembourg, and that evening delivered an ultimatum to neutral Belgium that war would be declared on them by the next morning unless they permitted the German Army to pass through their country unmolested. The Belgians refused.

On the afternoon of August 3, Great Britain delivered an ultimatum of its own. The British foreign secretary demanded that Germany respect Belgian neutrality, which, to protect the security of the east coast of the English Channel and the North Sea, England had guaranteed by an 1839 treaty to uphold. This of course was not the only reason for the ultimatum; protecting tiny Belgium sounded good for PR purposes, but British foreign policy has been remarked upon time and again over the centuries for its deviousness. Foreign Secretary Sir Edward Grey probably came much closer to the true English political position when he stated: "It could not be to England's interest that France should be crushed by Germany. We should then be in a very diminished position with regard to Germany. In 1870 we made a great mistake in allowing an enormous increase of German strength; and we should not be repeating the mistake."

All England, especially London, was thrown into a mood of expectant confusion. It was the long August Banking Holiday and many people had already left for trips to the shore or the countryside. The remaining inhabitants took to the streets where they could be the first to receive any news from the continuing stream of "extra" editions being hawked by newsboys. German waiters by the tens of thousands and other expatriate Germans packed their bags and boarded ships for home. Patriots waved the Union Jack and sang "Rule Britannia" and "God Save the King." Peace marchers waved the red flag and sang "The Internationale." Soon fights broke out between them, while England waited in nervous excitement.

When the Germans did not respond and the ultimatum expired at eleven next night, England declared war, prompting Sir Grey to make this melancholy observation: "The lamps are going out all over Europe. We shall not see them lit again in our lifetime."

★ Chapter Two

And so the storm broke. True to the Schlieffen Plan, Germany had marshaled a token force to shore up the Austrian armies along the eastern frontier against Russia and, on August 4, launched the bulk of its strength westward to invade Belgium and France. This consisted of 2 million men—the largest mobilized army in history—divided into eight separate armies of about 250,000 men each, outnumbering the French strength of 1,300,000, which were divided into five armies under General Joseph Joffre.

At that time, Britain had no troops in France, no conscription at home, and scant plans to compete in any war of this magnitude. Her only land forces were her small regular professional army of 250,000, whose main business since the Napoleonic Wars was the policing of unrest in the colonial empire, in whose far-flung outposts most of them were located when war was declared. They had recently begun calling themselves the "Old Contemptibles," after a remark reportedly made by Kaiser William about Britain's "contemptible little army."

The German onslaught into Belgium seemed irresistible but soon came the snag: at the last moment, Moltke got cold feet.

According to the Schlieffen Plan, a left wing of five army corps would hold the French at the German frontier. Meanwhile a titanic right wing of thirty-five corps would cut a twenty-mile scythelike swath through Belgium and down into northern France that would envelope Joffre's army, which, presumably, would be facing eastward against the Germans along the French-German border. Moltke began to fear that the French might instead choose to attack his own weaker left wing and head straight for Berlin at the same time he was headed for Paris. Accordingly, he now began strengthening his left wing by transferring troops from his right, in the impossible attempt to be strong everywhere. In fact, the French strategy was precisely what Moltke had feared. The French, in the event of war, intended to immediately take the offensive and attack the Germans in Lorraine.

On August 4 the Germans crossed the Meuse river and attacked the fortified city of Liège, held by a small force of 40,000 Belgian troops, which Germany would smother with more than a million. Unfortunately for the Germans, Liège was basically a "bottleneck" for such huge armies to pass through. A few miles south of it lay impassable mountains and the entanglements of the vast Ardennes Forest, while a few miles to the north was a strange little tongue of land belonging to Holland, called "The Appendix." While the violation of Dutch neutrality, if necessary, had been contemplated by Schlieffen, Moltke and the German government had decided against it for political reasons (they did not want to go to war with Holland, too), with dire consequences, as we shall see. And so while the Germans began their bombardment and investiture of bottlenecked Liège, precious days, even precious hours were lost as five great German armies tried to funnel through this narrow passage into Belgium. The reason time was so crucial was that Schlieffen's plan had set an outside timetable of six weeks for the destruction of France; it was his assumption that anything longer than that would allow the Russians to complete their mobilization and weigh down on Germany from the east with unbearable force.

In the meantime, on August 14, the French launched a surprise offensive eastward at the German forces in their lost provinces of Alsace and Lorraine as two French armies assaulted the German Fifth and Sixth Armies on the French-German frontier. This was the strategy embodied in Plan XVII, the French counterpart to the Schlieffen Plan. Under Plan XVII only this offensive would defeat a German invasion. It was designed to force the Germans to transfer troops from their center, which the

French assumed would be farther north, near Luxembourg, whereupon the French would slam into that weakened link and split the German army in two, precipitating its destruction.

At first it appeared the French attack might succeed. The Germans were pushed back to the east nearly twenty miles before the French ran into a buzz saw. The Germans had only been fighting a delaying action against the Frenchmen. On August 20 they sprang their trap and attacked from the stronghold of the Morhange Mountains. It was a slaughter marked by concentrated artillery and machine-gun fire, and after a single day's fighting the broken French were driven all the way back to Nancy, whence they had started. One sixty-two-year-old French corps commander lamented in horror at the "astonishing changes in the practice of war."

These "astonishing changes" were all too apparent. After the Franco-Prussian War the French had spent enormous sums and efforts fortifying their common border with the Germans, but shortly before the war broke out another school of thought appeared in the person of Colonel Loiseau de Grandmaison, who, with other young officers, rejected the notion of a static defense and called for a strategy of attack in case of war. Joffre, who became Chief of General Staff in 1912, subscribed to these views, and thus was born the notorious Plan XVII. A British observer who had watched the French assaults said: "Whenever the French infantry advance, their whole front is at once regularly covered with shrapnel and the unfortunate men are knocked over like rabbits. No one could live through the fire that is being concentrated on them." True to his dictum to the end, Colonel Grandmaison was shot down at the head of one of his infantry attacks.

Joffre, assuming that the Germans had been sufficiently weakened by his attacks in the south, now unleashed his attack on what he wrongly perceived to be the German center in the Ardennes Forest, a great morass of ravines, hills, and peat bogs. But the Germans were ready for it, pitching into the flank of the French and crushing them. Winston Churchill, always the keen commentator, noted that "The French infantry marched to battle conspicuous on the landscape in blue breeches and red coats. Their artillery officers in black and gold were even more specially defined targets. Their cavalry gloried in ludicrous armour. The doctrine of the offensive raised to the height of a religious frenzy animated all ranks, and no rank was restricted by the foreknowledge of the modern rifle and machine guns. A cruel surprise awaited them." And indeed it had: the brave though butt-headed French suffered more than 300,000 casualties in these initial attacks—Plan XVII having been drawn up before the true effects of the modern armaments that Churchill describes above were fully understood.

Far more troublesome was that up in Belgium the Germans, even though they were now behind schedule, had broken the Liège fortress and, farther south, crossed in force to the west of the Meuse, a likelihood that French commander Joffre had earlier deemed improbable. So improbable to the French that they did not even know the Germans were there in great force; it remained for a British airman to report seeing a gray-clad German army pouring into Belgium that was so large he was unable to estimate its full strength. The reason Joffre had been skeptical of any German design to attack France through Belgium was that he had grossly underestimated the forces the Germans were able to concentrate on their right (or northern) wing. He had refused to believe that the Germans would gamble on a tardiness of Russian mobilization, and therefore have at their disposal against France far more troops than he imagined. Nor had he counted on the ferocity and effectiveness of the hundreds of thousands of spirited reserve troops soon to be fighting with the German regular army. (He should have expected it, though, since reports were readily available that the Germans had been engaged in massive new railroad constructions along the Belgian frontier near Liège. In fact, during the first three weeks of the war 3,100,000 German soldiers were transported across the Rhine in 11,000 trains running around the clock.) In any case, now thoroughly and justifiably alarmed, Joffre sent his Fifth Army north onto Belgian soil to stem the German tide. But it was too late.

Meantime, the invading Germans were quickly gaining an international reputation for barbarism: burning towns, executing civilians, raping and mutilating women (including, some said, nuns), pillaging, taking hostages, and imposing grievous war taxes. The Hague Convention of 1907 was an international pact governing the rules of war that had been signed by, among others, all the parties now in conflict. It was violated when the first German soldier set foot on Belgian soil.

During the Franco-Prussian War of 1870–71 many French civilians had sniped at the Germans and to prevent this from happening again the German field marshal in charge of military government in Belgium now threatened the Belgian populace, "Punishment for hostile acts falls, not only on the guilty, but on the innocent as well." Thus, in the city of Dinant the Germans executed 612 men, women, and children. In Tamines they rounded up nearly 400 Belgian men and machine-gunned them to death. They burned the magnificent university library at Louvain and even opened the gates to the lunatic asylum at Bailleul, causing the deaths of many bewildered inmates who wandered into zones of fire. These acts were, in effect, nothing less than terrorism, designed to inspire fear and obedience in the Belgians.

For their part, the Germans complained that the "perfidious British succeed in holding us up before the world as the guilty party," and began spreading stories in Berlin newspapers about French soldiers gouging out the eyeballs of captured Germans. In some cases their indignation was legitimate. Stories based on rumor began appearing in British newspapers that the Germans were spearing babies and cutting off their hands and mutilating young women. They were now referred to by almost everyone as "Huns," an allusion to the barbarity of Attila. One actual event some months later, however, completely galvanized British outrage and world condemnation toward the Germans: the execution of the English Red Cross nurse Edith Cavell. She was accused and convicted by a German court-martial of aiding wounded Belgian soldiers, and of helping others to escape to Holland, and was shot by firing squad.

By now the first wave of the British Expeditionary Force (BEF) had arrived under the command of General Sir John French and, though at the time it numbered only a little more than 80,000 men in four infantry divisions, on August 22 it was ordered to the region of Mons in Belgium to link up with the left flank of the French Fifth Army, which was centered on the fortress town of Namur at the confluence of the Meuse and Sambre rivers. The land into which the British army marched must have appeared to even the most unsophisticated soldier a strange and unsatisfactory place to conduct battle. This was coal mining country, with slag heaps, mining pits, brickyards, industrial smokestacks, and blast furnaces. The region was dotted with dozens of small dirty mining villages peopled with men, women, children, ducks, pigs, chickens, and cows—an unnatural conurbation with thousands of places for an enemy to hide from bullets and artillery shells. It was a far cry from the broad, open South African veldt where those few Englishmen who had actually been in combat had fought the Boers a decade and a half before. In any case, aside from the exhaustion of marching day and night in the stifling heat, the British were relieved August 14 to encamp unmolested around Mons.

Next day the full fury of the German turning movement in Belgium fell head-on upon the French at Liège, caving in the center of their line. Fearing envelopment General Charles Lanrezac, the French Fifth Army commander, decided to withdraw. He gave little advance notice to the British, who were soon to come under extremely heavy pressure near Mons and were in danger of being cut off. Now the allies were in their most precarious position so far. After Liège, Namur, which lay fewer than sixty miles from the German border, was considered to be the next key to the invasion of France, the last major fortified position in southern Belgium. Now it had fallen. In less than three weeks the Germans had ground up the French offensives on the frontier and were suddenly driving the French and British southward from Belgium into France. It might have dawned on the British commander, Sir John French, that this was the very countryside where British under the Duke of Wellington had defeated Napoleon at Waterloo a hundred years earlier but, if it did so, it does not seem to have had an encouraging effect upon him. In fact, General French was even contemplating a withdrawal of his forces to the Channel coast for possible evacuation back to England: he realized, on encountering huge enemy forces he had not anticipated, that for Germany this was an all-or-nothing gamble.

Sir John had once aspired to follow his father into the navy but later joined the army where he served as a cavalryman in the major theaters of conflict during the Victorian era: the Sudan, India, and the Boer War, where he distinguished himself leading a brigade. It was there where he became indebted to a wealthy young major, Douglas Haig, who would replace him sixteen years later as commander of the British armies. Haig loaned French

£2,400 (the present-day equivalent of $100,000) to stave off bankruptcy, which would have ruined his army career. French had a mercurial personality given to deep mood swings. He was also an incorrigible womanizer who was once disciplined for having an affair with a superior's wife.

Nevertheless, French rose rapidly in the army and was chief of the General Staff when an event convulsed Great Britain and brought it to the brink of civil war. As events were unfolding in Sarajevo, the current British government was about to vote for Irish Home Rule. This infuriated the Protestants of Ulster, (who remain infuriated to this day), from whose population many high-ranking British officers were drawn, and many of them resigned in protest, since they would be the ones called upon to put down the all-but-certain rebellion by their fellow Irish Protestants. French was among those who resigned, but with the onset of war the Irish Problem subsided and, at the age of sixty-three, "Johnny" French was named commander of the BEF and ordered to take it to France.

Despite Sir John's pessimism, the French commander, Joffre, remained sanguine about keeping the Germans out of France, hoping to lure them into a false sense of security. He believed that if the two armies he was keeping along the southern French-German frontier could hold back the Germans to the east, and his armies to the north could hold together in a strategic withdrawal back into France, the German offensive would begin to lose momentum through exhaustion and a too far strung out line of supply. When that point was reached Joffre contemplated a massive counterattack by all of his forces. It was, however, a very close thing.

For nearly two hot August weeks the weary French and British soldiers trudged southward around the clock nearly 160 miles toward Paris, fighting costly and savage rear-guard battles against the heads of the various German columns that now came pouring into France. It was indeed a strange, almost surreal experience. The skies opened up with pouring rain while the British rear guard fought delaying actions in slag heaps and spoil pits and mining towns. They retreated through Belgian and French villages while church bells rang and children sang and the inhabitants went about business as usual. At night along the marching route the skies to the north were lit with the fires of those same villages as the Germans occupied and burned them. Occasionally an automobile, often a Rolls-Royce, would snake through the throng, occupied by a British officer who had had it ferried over from England, equipped with a chauffeur serving crumpets and tea. At times, British officers were so much in the dark regarding German movements that they resorted to telephoning post offices in French villages and asking if the Germans had arrived there yet. Many soldiers were made prisoner when the Germans showed up unexpectedly. One British cavalryman found himself cut off behind enemy lines near Cambrai. A French family took him in and hid him in a cupboard, in which he remained, even while German soldiers were billeted in the house, for four years until near the end of the war.[1]

By September 5, five German armies were arrayed on line across 200 miles of France—mostly along the river Marne—from Verdun in the east to the outskirts of Paris itself, in sight of the Eiffel Tower. Afterward, an officer of the German General Staff wrote, "It was not long before the walls and hearts of Paris were trembling, and it seemed as if the conspiracy which half the world had been weaving against us for so many years was to be brought to a rapid conclusion. Then came the Battle of the Marne."

This was too true. Moltke, directing operations from a command post 200 miles behind the battle lines, was in fact inhabiting a fool's paradise. Convinced that his armies had thoroughly beaten the French, he ordered even more troops withdrawn from his crucial right wing to be transported east to fight the Russians. With these and other transfers, Moltke, in order to strengthen his left wing, had depleted the Schlieffen Plan's mandate for at least seventy-nine divisions to attack on the German right wing in Belgium by one-third. (On his deathbed, a year before the war began, Schlieffen was reported to have said: "The struggle is inevitable. . . . Remember to keep the right wing strong.") In any event, in a moment of supreme confidence, Moltke now directed his army commanders to pursue the withdrawing allies closely and relentlessly, such were his hopes of swift and decisive victory.

What Moltke didn't realize was that the French had built up an entirely new army just outside Paris.

On September 6, Joffre struck. General Alexander von Kluck, commander of the German First Army, which was holding down the right flank

---

1. The cupboard is on display at the Imperial War Museum in London.

of the German line nearest Paris, soon concluded that he had been led into a trap. Instead of conducting his army west of Paris, as ordered—between Paris and the sea—Kluck had led it east of Paris, to maintain the link between himself and the other four German armies, but, in the process, he exposed his flank to Joffre's new army now outside Paris.

"And silence, only silence, in Paris," wrote author Frederick Palmer, who was there, "the silence of the old men and the women, and of little children who had ceased to play and could not understand. No one might see what was going on unless he carried a rifle. No one might even see the wounded. Paris was spared this, isolated in the midst of war."

Joffre, utilizing his now shortened interior lines of communication, was able to transfer by railroad fresh French troops wherever strength was needed and the attack he launched began to roll up Kluck's right flank. In this so-called Miracle of the Marne, thousands of French soldiers were also rushed to the battlefield by a seemingly endless stream of Paris taxicabs. Within three days Moltke's other armies, which had been assaulting strong new French positions, recoiled from the Marne as well. It was almost a reversal of the Battle of the Frontiers a month earlier, when the French broke their armies against strong German positions. However, this time it was the Germans attacking and the French defending from sites of great strength.

Joffre issued the following order to the French forces: "As we are to begin the battle upon which depends the fate of the country, it is necessary to remind all that the time for retreat has ended. . . . A soldier who can no longer advance must guard the territory already held, no matter what the cost. He must be killed in his tracks rather than draw back."

The fighting that followed was horrendous. One soldier wrote, "A flood of anguish surges over us while the bullets whistle about our ears, and suddenly, while my brain remains very clear, and I count on the almost certain repulse of the attack, my overstrung nerves shake my body, my teeth chatter, my legs, arms, hands and fingers tremble, my will loses control over my rebellious frame and while loading the cartridges into the stock of my rifle, I jam the weapon."

While the Germans crashed haplessly against the French positions and the French counterattacked with success after success, Moltke himself, ensconced in his headquarters back in Luxembourg, realized what was happening. On September 9, only three days after Joffre struck, he wrote dejectedly to his wife: "Things go badly. We shall lose the battles East of Paris."

About the same time, the German admiral Alfred von Tirpitz wrote in a private letter: "The French are led excellently, which is not the case with us, unfortunately. Moltke has collapsed physically. Don't say a word about that!"

Thus Moltke himself had thoroughly wrecked the vaunted Schlieffen Plan—by far the most important stratagem of the war—and, to add insult to injury to it, he also ordered his two remaining armies along the German-French frontier to attack the French forces opposite them, a move that failed completely, as Schlieffen had always predicted it would. Moltke had erred in two ways. First, he depleted his crucial right wing, which was to sweep through Belgium and deliver the coup de grâce to the French Army. Second, he allowed General Kluck to misalign his army in front of Paris. The fortunes of war had changed in a matter of a few hours, and if the Germans had not been so stubborn they would have given it up then and there and gone back to Germany. But the Germans were a stubborn people.

On September 11 Moltke finally visited the front. Taking stock, he ordered a general retreat to lines linking up along the frontier with his Sixth and Seventh Armies and to the more defensible terrain outside Verdun, north to the Oise river, some 120 miles away near Noyon. There, and probably for good reason, Moltke the lesser suffered a nervous breakdown, and four days later the kaiser fired him and sent as his replacement General Erich von Falkenhayn, the German war minister. It was almost six weeks to the day since the Germans had begun their invasion and they were further away from crushing France than they were at the beginning. Furthermore, Schlieffen's presumptuous six-week time limit for victory in the West was coming back to haunt the Germans. Russian mobilization had proceeded apace and the czar's armies were now attacking in East Prussia. German defeat at the First Battle of the Marne had unraveled Moltke's expansive schemes, and he has been reported, accurately or not, to have announced to the kaiser, who had arrived at his headquarters, "Majesty, we have lost the war!" There were certainly others who thought so, and it became commonplace in some English and American circles—notably of the pacifist-industrialist Henry Ford—to declare that "the war will be over by Christmas."

Lost war or not, there now began one of the most frantic series of maneuvers in the history of warfare, which, if not precisely accurate as to strategy, was what the newspapers ultimately named the "Race to the Sea." Both the French and German northern flanks were exposed or, in military parlance, "in the air." The Allies' problem was to keep the Germans from again turning their left flank while the Germans' problem was precisely the opposite. Another way of looking at it is that each side was trying to get ahead of the other, so that they could "bend back" their enemy's flank and "roll it up," something like a window shade. This is one of the oldest and most effective tactics in organized war.

What followed was a monthlong, deadly series of crablike, sidling movements spiraling almost due north from the German-French positions on the Oise all the way up 150 miles through France and Belgium to some then unknown end point on the North Sea. As the Allied soldiers pursued the Germans back past the once neat villages through which they had so recently retreated, a pall of stench hovered over them from the rotting corpses of men and animals and smoking ruins of homes and buildings. What was accomplished might be likened to a deadly embrace between people who loathe each other: waltzing round and around and in the end nothing more than that, save thousands of lost lives.

Rudolf Binding, a German officer who later became a well-known poet, described the pathetic conditions to which the French and Belgian towns had been reduced: "Four weeks ago this country could be called rich. Plenty of cattle and pigs. Now there is no wine cellar in any of the towns that was not confiscated by the Germans. No grocery, egg, butter, flourshop that does not have to supply to the Germans only. No horse that was not taken away, no automobile, gasoline, railroad car, no house, no coal, oil, electricity that does not work for us, is not utilized by us . . ."

During the Race to the Sea the German objective was to end-run around the French and British armies and secure positions in ports along the English Channel and North Sea. These were the towns of Boulogne,

Calais, and Dunkirk in France; Nieuport, Zeebrugge, and Ostend in Belgium. Not only would this tighten the noose around France, it would provide ideal submarine and warship bases from which the Germans could attack British shipping and troop transport in the English Channel and, at least in the minds of some alarmist Englishmen—including the renowned British secretary of war, Sir Horatio Herbert Kitchener—also supply Germany with useful bases from which to launch an invasion of England itself.

In the intervening time, another glitch was bedeviling the German plan, with its inflexible timetable. Far from rolling over and playing dead as the Germans anticipated, the small army of Albert, king of the Belgians, had been fiercely resisting the German invasion of its little country. After the fall of Liège and Namur, Albert withdrew his army toward the heavy fortifications of Antwerp, thus emplacing a dangerous obstacle to the north of the territory Germany had already occupied. This had earlier forced Kluck, commander of the German First Army, to detach some 90,000 men from the crucial right wing to besiege Antwerp, thereby removing them from the fight as it developed, and was developing, against the French and British armies in France.

The Race for the Sea began September 18, six weeks and four days after the Germans had crowed that they would be occupying Paris. Marching and riding in trucks and railcars, the French and British rushed troops through France toward Belgium, while the Germans did the same on their side of the line. From Noyon on the Oise each struck repeatedly at the other's flank as momentum pulled them ever northward. There were no less than ten of these desperate and violent clashes between September 18 and October 6, but the only thing either side succeeded in doing was to prevent the other from turning its flank and keep everybody's coffin makers busy. In each of these battles it was said that the Allies, as they were now known, always arrived one day late and one corps short. In any event, this stage of the fighting did not stop until both armies reached the North Sea, where there was nowhere else to go.

Meanwhile, the newly formed British Naval Division had landed on the Belgian coast and reached Antwerp, an effort organized by naval minister Winston Churchill to save that vital city. It was, however, to no avail because the Germans brought up a number of behemoth 17-inch howitzers acquired from, and manned by, the Austrians. Mounted on railcars their 2,000-pound

shells, "the size of a full-grown hog," began to obliterate the Belgian fortifications from five or six miles away. Having no defense against this, on October 6 King Albert ordered his five Belgian divisions to evacuate Antwerp and
head westward, toward the sea. There they met two fresh divisions of British
infantry, which had just landed at Ostend and were destined for Antwerp.
There was nothing for them to do but join the Belgian retreat. Antwerp fell
on October 9, but its determined, drawn-out resistance had given the main
part of the British Expeditionary Force time to move in good order from the
outskirts of Paris all the way up to Belgian Flanders. Rupert Brooke, the most
famous young English poet of his day and a brand-new lieutenant with the
British Naval Division at Antwerp, was inspired to write his famously patriotic verse:

> *If I should die, think only this of me:*
> *That there's some corner of a foreign field*
> *That is for ever England . . .*

Six months later Brooke was dead, vanquished, not by a bullet but by
a mosquito, whose bite turned septic and gave him blood poisoning while
on a ship bound for the abortive campaign in Gallipoli, where he most likely
would have been killed anyway.

But before we let Brooke pass entirely from the scene, an examination of his psyche and motivation for supporting the war sheds light on
why so many young men of the British aristocracy and upper classes raised
in the tranquillity of Edwardian and Georgian England suddenly and willingly offered themselves up to the stink and death of the trenches. In one
of his letters after the retreat from Antwerp, Brooke wrote: "It hurts me,
this war. Because I was fond of Germany. There are such good things in
her, and I'd always hoped she'd get away from Prussia and the oligarchy
in time. If it had been a mere war between us and them I would have hated
fighting. But I'm glad to be doing it for Belgium. That's what breaks the
heart to see and hear of."

Brooke, who was a socialist and an atheist, positions that had become
somewhat fashionable among many upper-class intellectuals of his day, goes
on to describe the suffering and destruction wrought by the Germans on

the city of Antwerp and its citizens: hundreds of thousands of refugees, things on fire or blown to bits, old men weeping, frightened women and children. He states: "It's queer to think one has been a witness to one of the greatest crimes of history. Has a nation ever been treated like that?"

The answer, of course, is that all through history a great many nations and peoples had been treated like that, except that Brooke had not been there personally to witness it. His compassion at the fate of the Belgians had quite remarkably turned him away from the skepticism of socialism-atheism into an altruistic young Englishman, willing to fight and die for what many believed was the noblest cause since the Crusades. His views on the subject were not at all uncommon among other young English intellectuals and members of the wealthier classes who were soon to be fighting and dying in unparalleled numbers on the plains of Flanders and in France.

Compare this with the beliefs of another young patriot on the opposing side. The day Germany declared war, twenty-five-year-old Adolf Hitler, a struggling artist and minor political activist, was among a huge throng gathered in the Munich town square to celebrate. A subsequent enlargement of a photograph of this scene shows a grinning, passionate-eyed Hitler, "overpowered by stormy enthusiasm," as he recalled afterward. "I fell down on my knees and thanked Heaven from an overflowing heart for granting me the good fortune of being permitted to live at this time," he wrote in *Mein Kampf*. A few days later, while the patriotic strains of "Die Wacht am Rhine" and "Deutschland uber alles" still rang from multitudes of young German voices clambering to get into the fighting, Hitler, although he was an Austrian by birth, somehow wangled his way into the German Army as a private in a Bavarian infantry regiment. He was not unlike the millions of raw recruits, many of them mere schoolboys, who chaotically clogged the enlisting stations in those first few days of the war and were enrolled in the German Army as reservists. Unlike Rupert Brooke, who saw as his duty being a champion of the abused Belgians, Hitler wrote to his landlord and landlady, from whom he had been renting a seedy room in a Munich tenement house, that he was in fact looking forward to the war and hoped to "get to England." As Hitler biographer Ian Kershaw points out, "The First World War made Hitler possible."

*   *   *

To this point, the fighting on the Western Front had been mostly fluid. Cavalry was being used liberally to screen movements, reconnoiter, and even attack. Men dug in where possible to shelter themselves from fire, but there was nothing like the elaborate network of trenches and barbed-wire obstacles that were soon to become symbols of the war in the west.

The new chief of the German General Staff, Falkenhayn, now decided to organize a new Fourth Army with Grand Duke Albert of Württemberg, consisting of four corps of reservists, Adolf Hitler among them. Many of these young men were school-aged and had only six weeks of basic training before being pitched into battle. Now that the Belgians, French, and British were linked up in the far north with their left wing resting on the North Sea at Nieuport, no further flanking movements were possible and Falkenhayn knew that a direct frontal attack was the only recourse if a breakthrough in Flanders was to be achieved. To perform this crucial task, he sent his Fourth Army north, as well as his Sixth Army, under a formidable general, Crown Prince Rupprecht of Bavaria, a bon vivant and distant cousin to the English king, George V.

Before all the arrangements for a large-scale attack could be made, sporadic but savage fighting characterized the early weeks of October all along a line south of Ypres in France and extending through the Belgian lowlands up to Nieuport. It was marked by one conspicuous factor: both sides grossly miscalculated the strength of the other. The British army, having clawed its way north along with the French during the exhaustive clashes in the Race for the Sea, entered the city of Ypres on October 11, hoping to turn the flank of the Germans. They were completely unaware of the strength of the advancing enemy, not realizing that the vast German reserve divisions were being brought against them. Afterward, official British figures put the Allied strength in Flanders in mid-October—British, Belgian, and French—at 263 battalions against some 426 for the Germans, approximately 280,000 soldiers versus 500,000, respectively. These were dispersed on a battlefront roughly forty miles long, from Armentières in the south up to Nieuport on the sea in the north.

The Germans saw things quite differently. Their official report on the battle repeatedly refers to "the enemy's numerical superiority, and the strength of his positions." They claimed that "over every bush, hedge and fragment of wall floated a thin film of smoke betraying a machine gun rattling out bullets." When the British read this later they were incredulous. As one British staff officer put it, "To those who were there and saw our thin and straggling line and the hastily constructed and lightly wired defenses—mere isolated posts and broken lengths of shallow holes with occasional thin belts of wire and none of the communications trenches of a later date—they provoke only amazement." Further, the officer pointed out that at the time there were only two machine guns alloted to each battalion, "and of these many had been damaged [in the earlier two months' fighting] and had not yet been replaced." In fact, what the inexperienced German troops were mistaking for machine guns was actually the rapid shooting of small clusters of British soldiers of the professional army who had been carefully trained to deliver deadly accurate individual rifle fire at a rate of fifteen rounds (and often more) per minute.

Meanwhile, the British were gearing up for a long war, despite any business about it being "over by Christmas," or, as the kaiser had put it, "before the leaves fall." From the outbreak, Lord Kitchener realized that the mere 250,000 men of his regular army could contribute little in a conflict that involved millions. He therefore made a broad appeal for volunteers, and to the astonishment of the world by the time the Battle of the Marne was winding down nearly 500,000 men had enlisted in the British armed services—and this would soon swell to 2,000,000 and, later, millions more. These became the "New Army," or "Kitchener's Army."

They came from all walks of life and often joined as a group from their profession or school or town or city. There were Pals battalions, Chums battalions, Brokers battalions, Bankers battalions, Miners battalions, and so forth. (This would have devastating effects on those towns and institutions when, in future battles, their casualties became grotesque.) One striking feature of this new army was that it was to be officered on the line in large measure by the British upper crust, young men of education and standing who acquitted themselves magnificently in the bloody years to come, as evidenced by the stupendous casualty rates (nearly 100 percent) among their ranks.[2] Though all these new volunteers had yet to be equipped and

2. In organizing such a vast army, the authorities next had to decide who would lead it. They concluded that the line officers should be selected from Britain's Public

trained, and thus were useless to the immediate need for at least six months to a year, they soon became a formidable fighting force for a country as small as England.

By now the German people were becoming perplexed by such news as they could glean from the military-controlled press. At first the papers printed stories of great victories at such places as Liège, Namur, Brussels, Mons, and Antwerp and of course the stories of the German armies sweeping across France to the very gates of Paris. But soon the casualty lists began coming in and the news was darker, of stalemate—albeit temporary. Worse still, so confident in swift victory had the Germans been that they had not even instituted plans for rationing food and other items to the civilian population or allocating measures for industry. Still, on both sides the people remained optimistic.

For the Germans there were still recollections of the glorious conquests of Frederick the Great and Moltke the Elder in the later Prussian Wars where victory was won by outmaneuvering the enemy; likewise, both the English and the French recalled the maneuvering of armies on a grand scale and the decisive victories that flowed from this, at least during the early Napoleonic Wars. In modern times European events such as the Seven Years War and the Thirty Years War were considered things of the past. Wars, as all these nations understood them in the century just ended, were usually short-lived affairs, fought by professional armies and highlighted by battles lasting sometimes only hours or even days, but rarely for months and certainly not years.

This was not so to those on the army general staffs of both sides who had studied carefully the lessons of the American Civil War. General Ulysses S. Grant's policy of relentless attrition had replaced the old practice in which a side that has been thrown back usually skulked off to fight another day. It was in this way that industrial nations would now fight their wars, with a superiority of weapons and manpower that would, sooner or later, grind an enemy into submission.

(i.e., private) Schools, where, presumably, the best, brightest, and wealthiest sons were enrolled, as well as from its premier universities, Oxford and Cambridge. Eligibility to volunteer began at the age of eighteen.

Chapter Three ✪

Flanders is the ancient name for the mostly flat countryside that stretches from the North Sea coast in Belgium south to the French coast along the English Channel. Its name in Flemish means, literally, "flooded land," and it is no bigger than the size of greater Los Angeles. It lies on the same latitude as Quebec and the average temperature is 49 degrees. It rains there practically every other day. Over the centuries the Belgians had drained it by an elaborate system of locks, dams, canals, and ditches and had channeled most of the overflow into the river Yser, which rises in central Flanders and flows northwesterly toward the sea. Its pastoral scenes and portraits of lively village life and its inhabitants remain immortalized by its many painters, including such well-known artists as Rubens, Brueghel, van Eyck, and van Dyck.

Belgian farmers over the years raised root crops of beets, turnips, and potatoes as well as flax, cotton, tobacco, grain, and fodder. They kept cattle, sheep, and pigs, chickens, geese, and ducks. Years earlier, in the outlying areas, wealthy merchants and farmers erected elegant castlelike châteaux, around which villages and farms sprang up, each with its ornate church; they planted trees, maintained roads, and not too infrequently fought off invaders.[1] It is

---

1. During the previous thousand years Flanders had been subjected to the depredations of the Spanish Duke of Alva until the English (under Oliver Cromwell) and the French

an ideal place for poppies to grow. For the most part, though, the water table remains fewer than two feet beneath the rich clay and sandy soil, an ominous factor that would be of considerable concern in the times to come. A Belgian author described the climate thusly: "Water is everywhere; in the air: on the ground: under the ground. It is the land of dampness, the kingdom of water. It rains three days out of four. The north-west winds which, breaking off the tops of the stunted trees, making them bend as if with age, carry heavy clouds of cold rain formed in the open sea. As soon as the rain ceases to fall, thick white mists rise from the ground giving a ghost-like appearance to men and things alike."

The central town in Belgian Flanders is Ypres, which, by the fourteenth century, had become the center of the cloth trade in Europe. It was then inhabited by more than 40,000 souls and widely known for its magnificent stone structure called the Cloth Hall, finished in 1260, in which cloth of all description was bought and sold. Over time, Ypres had declined in trading importance and lost more than half of its population, but at the outset of the war it was still a quaint medieval European city with its imposing St. Martins Cathedral. Its large cobblestone town square regularly served as an open-air marketplace for farm produce and other goods. On clear days, from the tops of the towers of cathedrals and the Cloth Hall one could see the North Sea. By all accounts, in 1914 Ypres was a serene and lovely place. The thick fortress walls of the city, designed in the seventeenth century by the renowned French military architect Sébastien Vauban, had by then been breached for a railroad, which brought tourists to admire the medieval ornamental spires and neat, clean buildings and shops. Then, in the autumn of that year, the Germans came.

Ypres sits at the foot of a series of ridges, an eight-mile-long arc of high ground to the east that semi-encircles it like a huge amphitheater. The highest ridges are no more than 160 feet tall but afford a complete and commanding view of the entire plain of Flanders, as well as of Ypres itself. (It may be remembered that 160 feet is roughly the height of a sixteen-

---

ousted him, then occupied the region themselves. Then the Dutch came in 1715 and later the Austrians. In the early nineteenth century Napoleon himself arrived, but was defeated there in 1815 at the Battle of Waterloo.

story building.) On or near these ridges, from south to north, were located the several dozen villages and terrain features that would forever figure prominently in the history of warfare: the villages of Messines, Wytschaete, Ploegsteert, Hollebeke, St. Eloi, Hooge, St. Julian, Zandvoorde, Lange-marck, Zonnebeck; the features of Nuns' Wood, Gheluvelt, Zillebeck, Hill 60, Pilckem Ridge, Polygon Wood, and—the most bloodcurdling name of all—Passchendaele.

During the autumn of 1914, as a result of the almost ceaseless fighting on these slopes and in these same woods, the old British professional army—the "Old Contemptibles,"—was virtually annihilated, and soon afterward the volunteer civilian "New Army,"—"Kitchener's Army"—would endure a bloodbath of unprecedented proportions. Toward the end of the war, years later, the newly conscripted British Army replacements also would leave untold numbers in the rotted, fetid landscape. It was in this small confine of Belgium from 1914 to 1918 that more than a million soldiers were shot, bayo-neted, bludgeoned, bombed, grenaded, gassed, incinerated by flamethrowers, drowned in shell craters, smothered by caved-in trenches, obliterated by underground mines, or, more often than not, blown to pieces by artillery shells. It became one of the most vast graveyards on earth.

In the early autumn of 1914 no one, on either side, would have pos-sibly imagined this.

On October 10 General Sir John French was feeling sanguine, now that the Germans had been thrown back on the Marne. He told the French commander, sixty-two-year-old General Joseph Jaques Joffre, that it was his intention to attack the German army in Belgium and drive it from Brus-sels and for that matter from everywhere else in the country. Joffre was much pleased and ordered the generals of his own divisions in Belgium to cooperate with General French's British force. Joffre had earlier chafed when French told him he intended to move the bulk of his expeditionary force northward from the north of Paris into Belgium and northern France, closer to his supply lines at the Channel ports, because Joffre also suspected, correctly, that in the back of French's mind was the thought that by doing this he would also be in a better position to evacuate his army back to

England should the military situation go sour. Now it appeared to the rotund old Frenchman that the British had gotten their second wind.

In any case, in mid-October a British main force moved into Ypres—part of the 7th Division of the half-strength corps of General Sir Henry Rawlinson. They were led by a kilted regiment of Gordon Highlanders, bagpipes and all. Typically, it was raining.

The small advance force of about 8,000 Germans that had entered the city October 3 had wisely withdrawn in the face of the oncoming British and French, and the city was still intact and viable; the shops and the markets in the main square were still open, and for the time being it was business as usual. The relief of the indignant citizens was palpable, however, since the Germans had looted and pillaged everything of value they could carry: jewelry, money, watches, silver, and clothing. Before they left, the Germans wrote on the blackboard of the Catholic church: "The Germans fear God, but apart from Him they fear nothing in the world." Be that as it may, they were gone when the British arrived.

What neither the British, the Belgians, nor the French understood, however, was that the full force of a new German army of youthful reservists, a quarter of a million strong, wild with enthusiasm but trained for only six weeks, was massing behind the ridges to the east and preparing to unleash its fury upon them.

By now the Allied armies in Flanders consisted of the remnants of the Belgian army, which, after evacuating Antwerp, had moved to the North Sea coast at Nieuport and linked with the French who had taken positions south of there to Ypres. From Ypres, the British line linked with the French to the north and extended southward into France, connecting with the main French armies. The British, therefore, were basically like a link in a chain between the French and Belgian forces. Until now the military situation had been chaotic and, according to Captain Ian Hay, who was there: "Confusion reigned supreme. Belgium and the north of France were one huge jumbled battlefield. Friend and foe were inextricably mingled and the direction of the goal was uncertain. If you rode into a village, you might find it occupied by a Highland regiment or a squadron of Uhlans [German cavalry]. There was no front, no rear, so direction counted for nothing. The country swarmed with troops which had been left 'in the air,' owing to their

own too rapid advance. [Such must have been the case of the British cavalryman who lived out the war in his cupboard.] Snipers shot both sides im-
partially. It was all most upsetting."

Meanwhile, back in England, not only were the people in the dark
about what was going on across the channel, but the government itself was
confused. From the beginning, Lord Kitchener and the War Office had
draped a cloak of secrecy over operations, banning reporters and correspondents from the battle areas. A number of these, however, went over
on their own hook and of them several were thrown in jail. By early October Sir John French began to realize this was a mistake, and told the secretary of state that journalists, "of good type, under control, would be less
harmful than irregular correspondents." But no action was taken at the time
on this more than reasonable advice.

As for the government, events were moving so rapidly that it was hard
to get a clear picture of the strategic situation, let alone the tactical one; all
that was certain was that many more troops were urgently needed and so
each day shiploads of British soldiers, as they arrived from the far-flung
reaches of the empire, were being unloaded at French ports, including the
140,000 sepoys of the Indian Corps.

By now the British had invented terms for the German soldiers: Huns,
Jerries, Fritz, or, after the French, the Bosche. As for themselves, the En-
glishmen were known as Tommies, from the poetic character Tommy
Atkins, the quintessential soldier of the British empire created by Kipling:

> It's Tommy this and Tommy that,
> And Tommy how's your soul;
> But it's Thin Red Line of Eroes
> When the drums begin to roll.

Most of the British troops detraining near Ypres at that point belonged
to the First Army Corps under command of General Sir Douglas Haig, who
would fifteen months later replace French as commander in chief and become the most controversial figure of the war. Haig, who had just turned
fifty-four, was a cavalryman who had served with distinction in the Boer
War under his present boss, Sir John French. Born in 1861 into the wealthy

family of scotch whisky distillers, Haig was educated at Oxford, where he played an excellent game of polo, and then on to the Royal Military College at Sandhurst where he graduated with honors. As one of his instructors predicted, "Before he is finished, he will be top of the Army." Now a handsome, granite-chinned man, and well comported with graying hair and mustache, Haig was the epitome of the professional British army officer: taciturn—some said inarticulate—and aloof—some said arrogant—and shy of women—some said misogynistic. He did not marry until he was forty-three, proposing to his wife, Dorothy, one of the Queen's maids of honor, only two days after he'd met her on a golf course near Windsor Castle. Responding to eyebrow-raising over their short courtship, Haig, who had fought in the Sudan, Indian, and South African wars and was by then a major general, retorted, "Why not? I have often made up my mind on more important matters than that of my own marriage in much less time."

In any case, Haig met with Sir John French on October 16 at St. Omer, France, the new British headquarters, while his remaining units were still entraining in France for their deployment in Flanders. Now that the Germans had been thrown back at the Marne, General French was supremely confident of a quick victory over the Germans, whom he estimated had only a single corps in front of him. On October 19 French ordered Haig to attack the Germans forthwith and drive them from Bruges and Ghent and then, with the enemy on the run, to move either north or south as the situation dictated.

Haig wasn't so sure. His own intelligence was reporting large numbers of the enemy massing before him. Ever since the battle for the Aisne back in the summer, Haig had mistrusted intelligence reports coming from French's headquarters and so had fine-tuned his own intelligence section in I Corps. It was logical to Haig that intelligence gathered on the spot was more valuable, at least tactically, than intelligence received from Army Headquarters forty or fifty miles away at St. Omer. The man Haig selected to run this operation was John Charteris, who as a captain in India had served as Haig's military secretary. By all accounts, Charteris was urbane and could be utterly charming; he held sway in the military mess with funny stories and anecdotes. His was later to become one of Haig's most controversial staff appointments, for while Charteris was bright, witty, hard-working, and thorough, he was also so devoted to Haig that it has been charged—and not without reason—that he disliked telling Haig anything Haig did not want to hear. In the military intelligence business, the consequences of this can be grave.

Nevertheless, by ferreting information from the Belgians and by reexamining reports from General French's own intelligence headquarters Charteris concluded they were facing not the single depleted German corps, which French believed, but as many as *three* German corps and, though he did not know it at the time, they were actually facing more than *five*. The First Battle of Ypres was about to begin and, far from Sir John French's grandiose scheme of driving the Germans back to Germany, the British Army was about to engage in the fight of its life.

For about two weeks previous there had been desultory but savage fighting all along the line from Nieuport on the coast to the Belgian-French border and beyond, farther south. At this point, however, the term the "line," as it became to be known, should be clarified, and no better explanation is to be found than that by the military historian Gordon Corrigan: "The 'Line' at this stage of the war might more properly be described as 'the forward edge of the battle area.' The complex array of professionally constructed trench lines to be seen later in the war, with saps and bays; traverses and bunkers; support, reserve and communications trenches did not exist, far less were there any fire steps, walkways and concrete shelters. Men dug where they could, improved existing drainage ditches, built sandbag breastworks where the height of the water table made digging and standing in a trench impossible, or simply lay on open ground with banks and hedges for cover. The line was not continuous and there were gaps everywhere. At this stage the British had no grenades or trench mortars [but the Germans did] and the Cavalry had been hastily issued with bayonets and given some rudimentary instruction in their use. There was no [barbed] wire except what the troopers took from farm fences and even digging implements were in short supply. British artillery, both in terms of guns per mile of front and of shells per gun per day, was considerably less than that of the Germans." It was under these conditions that General Sir John French hoped his war-winning offensive at Ypres would be launched.

"On 20 October the battle broke out along the whole line, on a front of about sixty miles." So says the official German report on the action, and it goes on to speak of the "numerically superior," allied forces facing the German Army. The conclusion was ridiculous, even if they believed it. By this time reinforcements arriving daily across the English Channel had brought the original British Expeditionary Force up to about 250,000 men (about 100,000 of whom were in Belgian Flanders, ferried to the front in London omnibuses replete with colorful advertisements for alcholic beverages, cigarettes, tonics, and the like). The Belgian Army had by now been reduced to about 70,000 and the French Army in Flanders consisted of two corps of infantry, totaling about 100,000, including two divisions of Moroccans from French North Africa, Muslims wearing fezzes and dressed in pantaloons, and one corps of French cavalry. Thus the Allies could muster a combined force of about 270,000 to contend with half a million Germans.[2]

The day before the big battle opened, General French put into motion the first phase of the British assault to roll up the German right flank—an eastward sweep by Rawlinson's 7th Division to capture and secure the town of Menin and consolidate the cavalry's occupation of the ridges that overlooked Ypres.

It quickly turned toward a disaster. British cavalry and infantry on the ridges began to see huge columns of smoke and flame where there were towns and villages on the plains to the east. Then came the swarms of pitiful refugees, weeping women, children, old men carrying what they could, many with horse carts or dog carts, all headed toward Ypres. And behind them were the dark gray–clad masses of the German Army, tens of thousands of them: infantry, horsemen, wagons, artillery, spread out on the distant plain like so many toy soldiers. Worse, reports were pouring in to Rawlinson's headquarters that, as one observer put it, "something very nasty was skulking at the far end of the Menin Road."

2. One might compare these figures with those of America's greatest battle: at Gettysburg fifty years earlier, General Robert E. Lee had about 75,000 Confederates against 95,000 Federals.

The two French divisions to the north, on the British left, were being pushed back with deliberation and the Belgians, even farther north and anchored on the sea, had attacked but were coming under heavy pressure from German units then unknown to Allied intelligence. More ominous, Rawlinson's corps reported taking very heavy casualties from German artillery and its advance was halted. This news, coupled with reports of heavy fighting on his southern flank all the way down to La Bassée, might have struck in General French a note of caution, but again it did not. Instead, in one of his mercurial "up" moods, he remained exquisitely confident and clung to his theory that north of Ypres there was probably no more than a single understrength German corps. In fact, they were facing Falkenhayn's entire Fourth Army, which Sir John French had not known existed but was soon to find out. And so in this spirit of ebullience, French ordered Haig's newly arrived I Corps into the fight. It was just in the nick of time, because next morning, October 20, the German storm was unleashed along the entire northern sector of the Western Front.

Ironically, Sir John French had opened his big offensive to drive the Germans from Belgium at precisely the same time as von Falkenhayn launched the German Army in his own offensive to capture Dunkirk and Calais and other French ports on the English Channel. This would have made cross-Channel supply and reinforcement of the British forces in northern France and Belgium difficult, if not impossible, and further tightened the noose to strangle France. The clash, with Ypres as the centerpiece, was horrific. For several days Sir John still clung to the belief that he was attacking, while in fact his troops were barely able to hold their own ground and in many cases failed to do so. What had happened, in addition to the gross miscalculation of German strength by British Headquarters, was that by an amazing combination of bad luck and stupidity, a British officer had got himself captured by a German patrol and on his person they found he was carrying a detailed set of orders for General French's attack, showing objectives, locations of units, dispositions, timetables—in short, everything the Germans needed to nullify French's offensive.

There should have been more concern at Allied headquarters, especially after it was known that the officer with the attack orders was missing. That, coupled with disturbing reports from Belgian citizens and aviators of the Royal Flying Corps that great masses of Germans were detraining in Brussels and Courtrai, which was just east of the Ypres ridges, should have given General French pause. But it did not.

October 20 was a miserable day: mist, rain, cold. After wisely deciding to hold one of his two infantry divisions in reserve, Haig marched his second division, along with a division of cavalry, out two and a half miles east of Ypres into the shadows of the Passchendaele Ridge, and waited through a nasty night to launch his attack in the morning. On the other side of the line, according to the German history of the battle: "All the more therefore were the hopes of Germany centered in the Fourth Army, which was fighting farther northwards, for in its hands lay the fate of the campaign in Western Europe at this period." This newly organized Fourth Army was composed in the main of the cream of German youth from the high schools and universities. Their employment in the German offensive at the First Battle of Ypres was roundly condemned, both during and after the war, for reasons that soon became apparent.

Haig's own ordeal began on the morning of October 21. His orders were to drive the Germans from Thourout, well northeast of Ypres, but it was immediately obvious that he was facing a good deal more than "an understrength corps." One of his problems was that the Germans outnumbered him five to one in artillery pieces and this quickly began to take its toll. Worse, after having captured the operations order, the Germans were able to register their guns on the places where they knew the British planned to attack. Their superiority became all the more deadly.

Under the circumstances—outmanned, outgunned, and outwitted by the captured plans—it would seem that the British army was doomed to defeat. But there was one thing the Germans had not counted on: the men under Haig were not just ordinary troops; they were British professional soldiers who had been steeled to endure the most severe hardships and tragedy and still persevere. And this they would do in the following days with the utmost audacity, until there were, in fact, very few of them left.

So much went on in so many places and with so many thousands of people during the next week that it might be useful at this point to follow the progress of a single soldier as he weaves his way through the tangled, savage, and disjointed fighting that characterized the first battle of Ypres. Twenty-seven-year-old Lieutenant William "Willie" Fraser was among the kilted soldiers of the Gordon Highlanders regiment who had first marched into Ypres on October 14 to the tune of bagpipes. He kept a diary, in which he described Ypres as "quite a pretty little city surrounded by a wall and a moat."

Like most officers of the "old army" Willie Fraser came from an upper-class background and had graduated from the Royal Military College at Sandhurst. He had served with the battalion in India before the war and then, along with his brother Simon, also a lieutenant, was thrown into the maw of Sir John French's offensive near the village of Zandvoorde on the plateau a couple of miles from Ypres. Here he experienced shell fire for the first time, which he described with typical British understatement as "a most unpleasant experience." For several days, while other regiments on his flanks were being heavily engaged, except for the constant shell fire, Fraser's battalion did not see much action.

Then the Germans began shelling them with large Krupp guns: "Big guns they are, and the shell has a most awe-inspiring scream, . . . the shells sound like an express train going through the air . . . I wonder what the name of this battle will be?" The brigade began to take casualties. "It was a ripping October morning and an old cock pheasant came out of our little wood and stalked about, not caring a rap for the firing which started again with the daylight. A machine gun was putting a lot of bullets round the haystack behind which the limbers were, and corpl. Andrews was wounded in the leg and one horse wounded too." Willie Fraser went on to list a number of his regiment's officers and men who were killed, and described their funerals, but all in all it had been rather quiet. Then, on October 22, the Germans attacked again.

On a front of nearly twenty miles tens of thousands of men came to grips and did their best to murder each other in the cold, dank, misty hills around Ypres. In many places the fighting was hand-to-hand. That morning divisions of the German Fourth Army consisting in large part of students, attacked the British line, such as it was. (Contrary to the official German report on the action, it was certainly not "a well-planned maze of trenches behind barbed-wire entanglements." At best the British fought from hastily scraped out holes in the ground and there was no wire to speak of, save that scrounged off local farms.)

In a fit of Wagnerian frenzy, the German students came on arm-in-arm or waving their rifles in the air, singing, and with their spiked *pickelhaube* helmets festooned with flowers. By the thousands they were shot down. Even though they outnumbered the British at times six to one that morning, they faced the most professional and elite regiments in the British Army, if not the world: the Black Watch, Coldstream Guards, Scots Guards, Camerons, Grenadier Guards, Irish Guards, Staffords, Gordon Highlanders, Green Howards, Royal Scots Fusiliers, Welsh Fusiliers, and others almost too numerous to mention, including the Hussars and Dragoons of the cavalry corps. When it was all over, the British Official History estimated that at least half of these youthful Teutonic warriors—100,000 of them—had been shot down. The Germans named the battle "The Massacre of the Innocents."

Nevertheless, it was clear both to Haig and Rawlinson, the corps commanders, that the Germans were far stronger than they and that, at best, the British Army was only holding its own. Worse, the French cavalry division protecting the British left gave way under a new German onslaught, and though many French soldiers continued fighting it was feared that this might fatally expose the Allied flank.

Back at his headquarters at St. Omer, Sir John French's mood swung from euphoria to despair as reports began pouring in and the magnitude of the German forces he faced became obvious. The French commander Joseph Joffre arrived at Sir John's headquarters that afternoon to say that he had ordered up another French corps to Ypres to throw into the battle. But so low had Sir John's spirits sunk that he began talking to Joffre about building a huge reinforced camp around the French port of Boulogne into which the entire British Expeditionary Force could retire if defeated. Then, if necessary, British warships could ferry the army back across the channel to England.

General Joffre was shocked; he informed Sir John that no such thing could be thought of; that the Germans must be stopped in their tracks there and then. After Joffre left, Sir John's mood seemed to swing again toward optimism and he wired Secretary of War Kitchener that while "here and there we were slightly driven back . . . the enemy are vigorously playing their last card." This of course was ridiculous. The British were being driven off the ridges that commanded the plain of Ypres and reports from the Royal Flying Corps continued to indicate large masses of Germans moving toward the fight. Haig's two beleaguered divisions were facing a full five German divisions and the onslaught was poised to continue.

At midafternoon of that day, however, Haig saw the handwriting on the wall and called off his "attack," despite General French's orders to continue it. He ordered his men to dig in where they were. That night a German soldier, awaiting his orders to attack next morning, wrote in his diary of all the "horrible things" he and his youthful comrades had witnessed in their first day of battle: fields of dead cattle, smoking ruins of villages, and "corpses, corpses, and more corpses." Nevertheless, he took care to add, "These things harden us up for what is to come. We certainly did not want this war! We are only defending ourselves and our Germany against a world of enemies who have banded together against us."

Meantime the British public was finally getting a taste of the war and at least a vague notion of its dimensions. Still under the threat of arrest, many reporters had nevertheless gravitated to the fighting. Among these was Phillip Gibbs of the *Daily Chronicle,* a thirty-seven-year-old self-educated Londoner who had been a war correspondent a few years earlier in the First Balkan War. As Haig was ordering his exhausted and shot-up troops to dig in, Gibbs sent a dispatch to his newspaper: "Within 24 hours of crossing the frontier between France and Belgium I have been under fierce fire in the greatest battle of modern times, which is now being fought on our long battle front extending through both these countries."

Writing by candlelight when he could find some respite, Gibbs told how astonishing it was "to find how soldiers quite near the front are in utter ignorance of the course of a great battle. Many of the officers and men with whom we talked could not tell us where the Allied Forces were, or where the enemy was in position." He went on to describe how the soldiers mistakenly believed that the Germans had been driven back "many kilometers between Nieuport and Dixmude." Then he turned to the war itself. "From each little town smoke was rising in separate columns, which met at the top in a great pall of smoke, as a heavy black cloud cresting above the light on the horizon line. At every moment this blackness was brightened by puffs of electric blue, extraordinarily vivid, as shells burst in the air. From the mass of houses in each town came jabs of flame, following the explosions which sounded with terrific, thudding shocks." When he got to Dixmude, Gibbs, who had attached himself to an ambulance section as a way to get close to the fighting, found it "a fair-sized town, with many beautiful buildings, and fine old houses in the Flemish style. When I saw it for the first time it was a place of death and horror."

Fortunately for the Allies, during the fight of October 22, not only the British but the French and Belgians as well began to receive reinforcements, including Indian troops for the British from the First Lahore Division. Athough the battle was still raging all along the line, General Ferdinand Foch, commander of the French Northern Army Group, envisioned a general Allied counterattack along the entire front. It was his fear that the now apparent strength of the Germans would allow them to concentrate on selected points of a static, allied line and achieve a breakthrough. Foch requested that the British join in his attack and Sir John French agreed, ordering it for the next morning with barely seven hours' notice. This was plainly absurd, given the magnitude of the undertaking.

Meantime, on orders from the Belgian king himself, the floodgates at the mouth of the Yser were opened and the sluice gates at Nieuport were dynamited, letting the North Sea rush in to flood all the land from the sea southward to Dixmude, about fifteen miles north of Ypres. Like Holland, that part of Belgium is below sea level and the land reclaimed only by dikes. This stupendous act, which took about a week to become fully effective, created an impassable water barrier, which the Germans could not cross and behind which, to the west, the Belgian Army could take refuge.

It was a desperate thing to do; for miles around, the floods inundated homes and fields and woods, which were subjected to the devastating effects of salt water. One German history, written during the war, crowed that the maneuver simply freed the 75,000 German troops on the other side of the flooded area to move south to join in the fighting around Ypres. Further, the German historian actually became indignant: "By his order the King of the Belgians destroyed for years the natural wealth of a considerable part of his fertile country, for the sea-water must have ruined all vegetation down to its very roots." Be that as it may, by his bold act—a kind of reverse of "sewing the fields of the conquered enemy with salt"—King Albert's decision had wisely shortened the effective Allied line by twenty miles and provided an efficient mask of the far northern flank in Flanders.

★ Chapter Four

Most unfortunately, during the fighting of the past several days, critical terrain features east of Ypres had to be abandoned by the British; these included the cavalry positions on the Passchendaele Ridge, at Hollebeke, Broodseinde, Becelaere, Houthem, Warneton—villages on the all-important ridge lines that overlooked the plains of Ypres. Now, with their artillery and machine guns upon these commanding heights, the Germans had almost complete observation and enfilade of the British positions opposite and predictably commenced a steady and deliberate bombardment of them. For the British soldiers in their hastily scraped out holes and ditches, this was sheer and constant terror, and a new attack ordered by General Sir John French, despite General Haig's protest for a delay, was designed in part to rectify the situation by recapturing the lost high ground to the north.

Like the opening day of the battle on October 19, however, it was again the Germans who seized the initiative with attacks of their own and the British, outnumbered two to one, three to one, six to one, ten to one in places, could do little but try to hang on to what they had. On October 23, frenzied fighting again raged all along the line; the British beat back a serious German penetration near Langemarck with dreadful casualties but left the ground strewn with German corpses. That night the French agreed to take over the north part of the British sector, freeing Haig's I Corps to support General Rawlinson's beleaguered single-division IV Corps, which was under heavy German assault.

Next morning, the twenty-fourth, near a forest called Polygon Wood, under the slopes of Passchendaele Ridge, the Germans attacked with a mighty force that nearly brought disaster. A battalion of the Wiltshire regiment was suddenly surprised and virtually wiped out by three battalions of Germans. With no British reserves behind them, the Germans suddenly had a clear way into Ypres itself. It was midmorning when news that the Wiltshire battalion no longer existed came rushing back to the headquarters of Major General Sir Thompson Capper, commanding the 7th Division. Capper urgently sent back for help to Haig's 2nd Division, which had been resting after the French relieved them the night before. Not only that, he mustered everybody on his own staff that he could find to throw into the gap: clerks, servants, staff officers, runners, orderlies, communications men, horse tenders, drivers, and, according to one report, even a cook, armed only with his ladle.

The fight that followed was a vicious hand-to-hand affair, with bayonets, gun butts, knives, rifles, pistols, clubs, fists, as thousands of men commenced murdering one another in the tall sun-dappled forest of pines and firs. At some points the bodies lay so thick on the ground that it was difficult for runners to pick past them to get word of the situation back to headquarters. By midafternoon, the Germans had been ejected from Polygon Wood and the line somewhat restored, but beside this heroic effort by the British soldiers, it was the Germans themselves who were most to blame for not exploiting the breach and pushing through not only to Ypres but to their ultimate strategic goal, the French ports of Dunkirk and Calais on the English Channel. After they destroyed the Wiltshire battalion in Polygon Wood, the German commander had not known quite what to do next. He had taken his objective and his first notion was to hang on to it. But the fact was, for more than two hours the Germans had a golden opportunity to drive a wedge that would have split the British army, won the Battle of Ypres, and, had they managed to take the French coast, quite possibly won the war.

In any event, with the failure to rupture the British line in any substantial way, according to a German history, "For the time being any further thought of breakthrough was out of the question." The historian goes on to describe how German troops "met the enemy full of keen fighting spirit, and had stormed his positions singing 'Deutschland uber alles' regardless of casualties, and had been one and all ready to die for their country; but they suffered heavily against a war-experienced and numerically superior opponent entrenched in strongly fortified positions."

Exaggerated as that was, the British were well up for a little respite. Some found it in Polygon Wood, as the fighting there quieted down temporarily after the Germans were expelled. In the center of the Wood was the site of the Belgian Cavalry School at Ypres and carved out between the trees was a sort of steeplechase course, complete with all kinds of obstacles for horses to jump over. One observer remembered, "The sight of these fences was too much for some of our young officers, and in spite of the fact that there was a good deal of shelling going on and quite a number of shells were dropping into Polygon itself, a dozen or so of our young bloods were soon careering round the school and over the fences until they were sternly ordered by the Brigadier to stop." Others found time to supplement their army rations by shooting some of the pheasants and rabbits that still inhabited the Wood, despite all the inhospitable activity that had, and was, occurring there.

Meanwhile there was a serious problem with the British artillery that threatened to ruin the whole campaign. There had developed a dramatic shortage of shells, since no one before the war had ever dreamed of fighting of this magnitude. Sir John French reported to Secretary of War Kitchener that he was about to run out of ammunition very soon and desperately needed resupply. Lord Kitchener, who knew the munitions factories were currently incapable of producing anything near what Sir John needed, instructed the British commander to "practise economy." Each artillery piece was then restricted to firing only nine shells per day and, as one officer remembered sourly, "To fire a shell you almost had to put the reasons for it in writing." In the months to come the ammunition crisis would become so dangerous that when the story broke in the press it was instrumental in toppling the British government.

While the Germans pondered their next move, there was a four-day lull in the fighting—if you can call taking thousands of casualties a day a "lull."

During this period one of Sir John French's euphoric moods left him so cocksure that the Germans were on their last legs he informed Kitchener in a series of telegrams: "Battle practically won . . . situation growing more favorable every hour . . . enemy incapable of making any strong and sustained attack . . . need only press the enemy to ensure complete success and victory . . ." And so forth.

But nobody seemed to have told the Germans any of this, and even if they did the Germans were having none of it. In fact, by October 29 a whole new German army of six divisions had arrived and was placed under the command of General Max von Fabeck. Included among this formidable force was the half-trained regiment of Bavarian volunteers, to which Adolf Hitler belonged. Not only that, but the kaiser himself had arrived on the scene, determined to become a personal inspiration to his troops. As soon as the Allied armies were crushed and Ypres conquered, he planned to parade triumphantly through the streets of the city.

The German storm was unleashed October 29 from the southeast toward the northwest, up the Menin Road near Gheluvelt in the north to Ploegsteert Wood in the south. It fell on the exhausted and bloodied 7th Division, which Sir John French had just placed under Haig's command, and to their right, on General Sir Edmund Allenby's dismounted cavalry. General von Fabeck, the German commander of the attack, issued an order of the day stating, "We must and will conquer; settle for ever with the centuries-long struggle, end the war, and strike the decisive blow against our most detested enemy [England]. We will finish with the British, Indians, Canadians, Moroccans and other trash, feeble adversaries, who surrender in great numbers if they are attacked with vigor."

With this inspiration ringing in their ears, von Fabeck's Germans tore through the misty morning with such fury that they simply overwhelmed much of the British advanced position. Ironically, the British already knew where and when the attack was coming, thanks to the stupidity of a German corps commander who sent out uncoded orders over wireless radio. Haig's chief of intelligence, John Charteris, was jubilant: "I suppose he thinks we do not know any German! . . . God bless him! I'll give him a drink if ever I see him when the war is over."

Yet knowing about an attack and being able to stop it are different things. Casualties since the battle opened had reduced the 7th Division by about 40 percent when the Germans fell upon it, and also a force of dismounted cavalry, driving them out of the village of Zandvoorde. Among those defending near the village was a battalion of the Gordon Highlanders, Lieutenant Willie Fraser's regiment. Let us resume his story, five days after we last left off.

As the German attack got under way, Fraser began to lose friends. "Rony Menzies [Willie's cousin] is killed or captured," he wrote to his mother, "the evidence so far as I can find points to the latter—so if his mother writes to you, would you tell her I think he is captured."

"We were told to expect an attack by a whole German army corps early next morning [owing no doubt to the interception of the German wireless message], so we spent the night digging for all we were worth. The next morning was very foggy, one could not see more than 100 yards at first, though it got clearer as the sun got up. We could hear the Germans advancing—they come on quite slowly, line after line, saying '*houra, houra*' [hurrah] all the time and soon fire opened all down the line."

Fraser, who was in charge of a machine-gun section, described the action to his older brother George, who was a naval officer serving with the fleet: "I went off with one gun to see if I could be of any use. When I got there I found that they had broken through, and were in possession of a small wood in rear of our trenches. And this the Grenadiers were making desperate efforts to retake, aided by one company of my regiment. The Germans were in great force and we had no reinforcements up to make an effective counterattack. That wood cost us some of the best lives in the regiment, among them [Captain] Ortho Brooke, who was at St. John's with you and one of the finest fellows that ever drew breath. The Grenadiers started that day with only about 300 men left out of 1100 and there they lost nearly all the remaining officers and a good many of the men."

Fraser's battalion was forced to withdraw but made the Germans pay dearly for every inch of ground. "One of the platoons had managed to enfilade the Germans as they advanced in their thick lines, and were there about an hour and a half, before they were forced to retire, during which time they accounted for about 500."

Later that day, Willie Fraser's brother Simon had been bandaging a fellow officer who had been hit and had just given him a drink of water when a German shell exploded. The injured officer, Lieutenant Peter Duguid, later wrote to Willie and Simon's father, Lord Saulton: "Though I ran to him at once there was nothing I could do. I am sure he did not suffer. I had to go to the hospital but Captain Huggins told me his body was brought in that night."

Willie wrote to his older brother George: "It was about seven o'clock when they brought in Simon's body, I knew he was killed. I told you how he was killed in my last letter, so I won't go over it again. Poor old Sim. He went in good company that day, George. Well, I buried him next morning, the attack had started so there was no one there but me. Some of my gun team dug the grave, and I read the burial service, or part of it, and the Pipe-Major played The Lament. We had no cross with his name on to put up and no time to put it up if we had it. But I know the place."

Next day, October 30, there was none of the usual preliminary bombardment by German artillery. Then at dawn a sudden wind blew away the fog to reveal a dense mass of von Fabeck's Germans coming along both sides of the Menin Road toward the village of Gheluvelt, which was defended in forward positions by elements of Haig's 1st Division: the Black Watch, Coldstream Guards, the Camerons, Scots Guards, the Welsh and the South Wales Borderers. These were among the old regiments of the army whose antecedents had fought in most of the British campaigns on the continent and elsewhere up to the Napoleonic Wars, and then they fought him, too, at the Battle of Waterloo, just down the road. They had fought the Americans in the Revolution and in the War of 1812. They had fought at the Khyber Pass in Afghanistan and in South Africa during the Zulu and Boer Wars and in Egypt and Khartoum and the Sudan under Kitchener and a dozen other places where Britannia ruled, or wished to. But they had never fought anything such as this.

*   *   *

Complicating matters for the British was the fact that von Fabeck's artillery numbered nearly 800 guns while Haig's command had fewer than 350, and even these did little good to support the infantry, since their nine-round-per-gun-per-day limit was to be directed primarily at German artillery batteries. At first, the assault seemed irresistible. The fighting was again hand-to-hand in many places, desperate men shooting and gouging and strangling and clubbing and stabbing one another in a swirling fog punctuated by brilliant flashes of exploding shells. The British line gave in a few places, but piecemeal reinforcements and counterattack forces somehow won much of it back by nightfall, October 30.

Nevertheless, to the south the crucial village of Zandvoorde, a key Allied stronghold on the Gheluvelt Plateau, near where Willie Fraser had been fighting, was finally lost to the Germans who simply overwhelmed a battalion of Royal Welsh Fusiliers and several squadrons of cavalry that had been holding it. The Welsh Fusiliers were virtually wiped out; only eighty men were left from its original strength of 1,100. The cavalry were also wiped out, almost to the last man. Among their number, fighting as infantry, was twenty-seven-year-old Charles Sackville Pelham Worsley, who was General Haig's brother-in-law. Lord Worsley commanded a machine-gun section with the Royal Horse Guards, one of three elite cavalry regiments that in peaceful times serve exclusively the British Crown.[1]

Worsley was due to be relieved just as the Germans bore down on his positions but stayed behind with his machine-gun section to help after another section's gun had jammed. They were all killed: no one's body was ever found except for Worsley's, which was recognized by a German officer of aristocratic lineage and given a proper burial. Though the German officer was himself killed a few days later, Worsley's young widow managed through delicate diplomatic connections—including the American embassy in Berlin—to obtain a precise map of his gravesite, and after the war his body was reinterred in a British cemetery near Ypres.

Three days earlier another highly ranked member of the British aristocracy was killed a few miles from where Lord Worsley would die. He

---

1. They are to this day prominent in their shining breastplates and plumed helmets escorting the royalty around London during parades and ceremonies.

was twenty-three-year-old Prince Maurice of Battenburg, grandson of Queen Victoria and a cousin of both Kaiser William and the czar of Russia. He died of shell fire while serving with the King's Royal Rifle Corps, leading a charge near the village of Zonnebeck, and is buried in the same cemetery at Ypres as Lord Worsley.[2]

The Germans quickly moved their artillery into Zandvoorde, from which they were now able to fire upon the British from the south as well as from the east, a disagreeable development. After burying his brother, Lieutenant Willie Fraser took up his duties with his machine-gun section to try to drive the Germans from Zandvoorde, but he was halted by a murderous fire. Fraser's battalion had had no food or water all day and was being heavily shelled. The casualties were appalling. Out of 26 officers and 812 men the previous week, the fighting strength of the battalion had been reduced to a single officer and 205 men. Willie Fraser was not among them. His shoulder had been shattered by shrapnel, there was fighting and killing all around, and the Germans captured him. Having studied German in Frankfurt in 1909, he was astonished to hear a German sergeant yell out an order to shoot him. Willie yelled to a German officer, and when the officer spoke Willie recognized his accent and asked if he was from Frankfurt. When the officer replied that he was, Willie asked him in German, "Don't you wish you were there now?" The two men exchanged forced grins and the officer ordered his men not to harm Fraser. A note added to the diary says: "Shortly afterwards in the general melee the Germans withdrew" from their foremost positions to the west of Zandvoorde, and Willie managed to get lost and drop into a ditch where he lay in some agony, covered with mud and unrecognizable, until he saw some British troops return and advance against the same Germans, moving through a wood.

"Then an English and a Scottish soldier came running along either side of Willie's ditch. Willie tried to lever himself up and the English soldier yelled, 'There's one of the bastards,' and aimed a ferocious kick at Willie's mud-

2. It is an interesting sidelight that the British royal intermarital connection with the Germans was so strong, and public suspicion so deep, that the Battenburg family soon changed its name to Mountbatten and the king himself ultimately transferred his family's royal lineage from the German House of Saxe-Coburg-Gotha to the House of Windsor.

covered figure. The boot landed on the wounded shoulder and Willie—a man who rarely swore—let out a stream of the strongest language he ever remembered using. The Scottish soldier stopped, his ear attentive to his native tongue, 'That's no a Jerry bastard,' he announced, 'it's one of our officers!'"

Despite the loss of Zandvoorde, back at his headquarters in France at St. Omer, a jubilant Sir John French wired Kitchener that if they pressed on next day, "It will lead to a decisive result." What Sir John did not appreciate, however, was that the full brunt of von Fabeck's army—five infantry divisions, 75,000 men—of which historian David Lomas tells us French was "blithely unaware," intended to hurl itself upon him at dawn.

Haig, however, was closer to the action with his headquarters at the "White Château," near a place on the Menin Road they called the Halte. It was the farthest place east from Ypres where the trams stopped before turning around for another trip. It would not be long before the spot became world infamous as "Hellfire Corner." Haig was not nearly so convinced as Sir John that the Germans were beaten. In fact, events of the day had persuaded him of just the opposite and, instead of planning to attack as French had directed, Haig again ordered his command to dig in and consolidate. Haig's intelligence chief, Charteris, wrote: "By nightfall we began to hope that the worst was over. In fact, it was just beginning." Haig's directive for the next day included this: "Orders as to the resumption of the offensive will be issued when the situation is clearer than it is at present."

It was a good thing, too, because the renewed German attack of October 31 burst in full fury upon the reduced British battalions defending Gheluvelt along the Menin Road. The morning opened with a furious artillery bombardment by German heavy guns. Then, as the kaiser himself watched through binoculars from the eastern ridge, the German divisions of Army Group Fabeck began assembling for their attack. There were two major objectives: first, to smash through at the Gheluvelt Plateau directly to the east of Ypres and, second, to capture the Messines Ridge to the south, which was another important commanding height.

Somewhere among this mass of gray-uniformed Teutons attacking Gheluvelt was Private Adolf Hitler. Describing the action later, he wrote that his regiment was nearly annihilated that day, being reduced from 3,600 to 611 men. (This according to his biographer Ian Kershaw; other reports put it that the regiment *lost* 611 out of its 3,600 men.) Its commander also died in the bargain. Hitler reflected later that this baptism of fire destroyed his earlier idealism and enthusiasm for war. The sights he saw at Ypres, he said, convinced him that "life is a constant horrible struggle," a theme he harped on later in *Mein Kampf*. Hitler's precise role in the fight is unclear, but he must have done something well or at least done nothing wrong, because a few days afterward he was promoted to corporal, a rank he was not to rise above during the four remaining years of the war.

A German official historian describes the character of the fighting as having "Almost the savagery of the Middle Ages in it," perhaps an understatement. All along the line the battle seethed back and forth, with the Germans capturing strong points and villages, only to be ejected by determined British counterattacks. The British war machine was now being strained to its utmost.

Nevertheless, the German High Command remained "profoundly disappointed" by the lack of a breakthrough the day before. Even though the British had been pushed back at various points, their line still held. Now, on October 31, a Sunday, the German attempt to break through and capture Ypres got full-swing under way. Just one more push would do it, so the German thinking went.

The weakened British battalions defending Gheluvelt were shoved (or, in some cases, literally blown) out of their trenches and, shortly before noon, the village and its château were captured, and the road to Ypres and to victory was again within German grasp. Now there happened one of those grand episodes of war in which ordinary men elevate themselves to the stuff of heroes. There were barely 1,000 of Haig's soldiers to fight off 10,000 Germans. The remnants of the Scots Guards and the South Wales Borderers were holding on by the skin of their teeth near the stables of the Gheluvelt Château with the expectation of being overwhelmed any moment. To make matters worse, a ration of defective rifle ammunition had been issued to them the day before, and now many men were finding that their rifle bolts were jammed. Brigadier General Charles FitzClarence, who commanded the Guards brigade, rode into the fray after hearing that Gheluvelt was lost. Sizing up the situation, he immediately galloped to the headquarters of division commander, Major General Samuel Lomax, and requested the use of the army's final reserve, the half-strength 2nd Battalion of the Worcestershires, which had been lagered nearby in Polygon Wood. FitzClarence ordered Major Edward B. Hankey, the battalion commander, to rush his men to Gheluvelt, expel the Germans, and reestablish the line.

With only seven officers and fewer than 500 men, Hankey knew the odds were against him. He issued the men a ration of stew and rum, told them to leave behind all equipment except rifles, ammunition, and bayonets, and then marched them out toward Gheluvelt, after leaving one company to block the Menin Road into Ypres. At first they were partially protected by woods and a streambed, but then there appeared before them nearly a thousand yards of open ground, which would have to be crossed to get at the Gheluvelt Château. Hankey did not hesitate. He told the men to advance "at the double," and led them running for dear life across the open stubble fields, which had already been registered by German guns. A hundred of them were cut down by shrapnel before they reached the château, but their luck and courage held out for most of them.

About 1,200 Germans were milling about the château grounds; some were looting inside, some shooting at the Welsh and the South Wales Borderers who still clung tenaciously to a flank; others were eating rations or just standing around savoring their imminent victory. Among these were elements of the regiment of (still, as yet) Private Hitler. All were thoroughly shocked when Hankey's men, now down to about 250, burst out of the woods and onto the lawn, shooting and bayoneting the Germans as they came. In any case, the Germans dropped their arms, their loot, and their food and ran away, and the British line was restored. Greeting the commander of the beleaguered South Wales Borderers, Hankey said, "My God, fancy meeting you here." The commander, Colonel Leach, replied, "Thank God you've come."

For his part, of the Worcesters' bold attack at the Gheluvelt Château, General Sir John French was to say after the crisis had passed, "England and the Empire were saved from a great disaster."

*   *   *

Word of the retaking of Gheluvelt had not filtered back down to Haig's headquarters but news of another event did, which provoked yet another crisis. A day earlier, Haig had visited the headquarters of his 1st Division commander, General Lomax, and found that he and his staff were crowded into a tiny cottage. Haig suggested that they move into the Hooge Château, where Haig had his headquarters, along with the headquarters of the 2nd Division. Haig himself would move into the "White Château," nearer Ypres. When word came that Gheluvelt had fallen, Haig rode out to see for himself what could be done. The roads were crammed with a profusion of wounded men, artillery pieces, supply trucks, ambulances, wagons, and horses.

From all he could see, Haig concluded that a withdrawal might be necessary and instructed his two division commanders, Generals Lomax and Munro, to begin planning for a defense of Ypres itself. These two retired to the Hooge Château where, shortly after 1 P.M., a German heavy shell exploded, mortally wounding Lomax, injuring Munro, and killing every staff officer in the room except one. Thus, at the most critical hour, Haig's two most important subordinate headquarters had ceased to exist.

As if this wasn't enough, Sir John French, anxious to get a closer look at the situation, arrived at the scene in a motorcar. "They have broken us in," Haig told him. The news of the loss of Gheluvelt deeply distressed Sir John and he rushed off to try to find General Foch to ask for the French Army's help. Moments later, word of recapture reached Haig's headquarters and Haig's aide-de-camp rushed after Sir John to give him this piece of good news, but if it had any effect on him he did not show it. When Sir John ran into Foch later in the afternoon, quite by accident, Sir John was full of gloom and doom: the British army was in retreat and defeat was in the air. He told Foch that unless the French came to his assistance, "There is nothing left for me to do but go up and be killed with I Corps." Foch was not only a tactful man, but a confident one as well. Whatever he thought privately of Sir John's histrionics, he told him, "You must not think of dying, but of winning." He then promised to send Sir John a full division of the French Army and emphasized that retreat was simply unthinkable: "The men must dig in where ever they find themselves and hold on to the ground they now occupy."

In the meanwhile, another nasty and brutal fight had been going on all day southwest of Gheluvelt—the battle for the critical heights of the Messines Ridge. It had begun before dawn with a great German bombardment of the villages of Messines and Wytschaete, followed by an attack by the southern wing of Army Group Fabeck. Defending Messines were several detachments of British cavalry, soon reinforced by the London Scottish regiment. This was a "territorial" regiment and not a regular professional army unit; it was something akin to a National Guard or Home Defense outfit—"weekend warriors." These were volunteers mainly from a very social group of Scots business professionals who delighted in throwing grand balls, dinners, and receptions and marshaling their own rugby and soccer teams. They had yet to see fighting in a war and were the first territorial regiment to be sent into combat.

The Scottish were thrown into the breach atop Messines Ridge and ordered to support the tattered cavalry regiments there. They arrived in Wytschaete shortly after dawn and during the day made a series of short, desperate rushes across open terrain to get to the crest of the ridge near the village of Messines. They were shelled horribly along the way and by the end of the day had been reduced from 750 to 400. Among the casualties was the future movie star Ronald Colman, who was shot in the leg early in the fight. That night, Halloween, beneath a full harvest moon, they were attacked again by German soldiers who came on in waves with bands playing and bugles trumpeting. The Scottish held their ground for a while, staving off assault after assault, at times fighting hand-to-hand. Their problems were complicated because they had been issued older and inferior rifles dating to the Boer War, whose bolt mechanisms proved faulty, and so they were forced to load each shot individually. It was maddening.

With communications disrupted as usual, the Scots did not know that during the early morning hours an order had been given for them to fall back. In the light of fires started in buildings and haystacks by artillery shells, they saw Germans massing on three sides of them, including their rear. Providentially, the smoke from the fires had drifted into some of their trenches and allowed the Scottish to escape—at least most of them. They ran through the smoke in little groups or even one by one, until they reached friendly lines. It was obviously a harrowing experience for men who only weeks earlier had been working as lawyers, bankers, stock brokers, and the like. One "Old Contemptibles" trooper who watched the bedraggled and cut-up Scotsmen retire observed, somewhat patronizingly, that "They should never have been sent there. They were a Territorial regiment, never heard a shot fired before." But the fact was that very soon most of these territorial regiments would be arriving and hurled into the fray. Until Kitchener's "New Army" was trained, and with the depleted condition of the "old" army, the Territorials were about all that would stand between the British empire and ruin.

For the next four days the fighting for the Messines Ridge was chaotic. The ridge was captured by the Germans, retaken by the British, taken by the Germans again, and retaken again. In describing the fighting around Wytschaete, a German historian complained about "The treacherous methods of the Indians [which] greatly exasperated our men: crouching in the hedges, and with machine guns concealed up trees, the defeated Asiatics allowed our troops to pass them by, and then got up and stabbed them in the back with their knives." This paints a fairly dramatic picture until one considers that the Indian troops had been withdrawn from that particular sector before the battle began.

At one point Hitler's company was part of the German attack near Wytschaete. In *Mein Kampf* he described in somewhat purple prose how the spirit had moved him: "From two hundred throats the first hurrah rose to meet the first messenger of death. Then a crackling and a roaring, a singing and a howling began, and with feverish eyes each one of us was drawn forward, faster and faster, until suddenly past turnip fields and hedges the fight began, the fight of man against man. And from the distance the strains of a song reached our ears, coming closer and closer and closer, leaping from company to company, and just as Death plunged a busy hand into our ranks the song reached us too and we passed it along: *Deutschland, Deutschland uber Alles, Uber alles in der Welt.*"

During the fighting Hitler's commanding officer was wounded and lay in the open near a burning church. Exposing himself to dangerous fire, Hitler crawled out to rescue him, and for this he was awarded the Iron Cross, Second Class. He was wounded in the arm and said to have been treated in the crypt of the church, where William the Conqueror's mother-in-law was buried. On the third of November, just as the battle was wind-ing down, Hitler was promoted to corporal. He began to feel, as he stated later, that some sort of divine providence was watching over him, and tell-ing him what to do—a sensation he never got over.

At the end of it all the Messines Ridge remained in German hands and would in years to come prove a very bloody thorn in the side of the British army in the Ypres Salient.

For the British at this stage of the battle the situation was frightful. They had been fighting almost continuously for two weeks and Haig's com-manders did not think they could stand another onslaught. The British Official History describes "Infantry brigades reduced below the establish-ment of battalions, and cavalry regiments below that of squadrons, with only some thirty medium heavy guns—some of which were obsolete—and with the imminent danger of lack of gun ammunition, the future looked gloomy and doubtful. The sin of unpreparedness for war on the British nation was indeed being visited on its children, the men and officers of the British Expeditionary Force." It was too true; those children, born with cherubs hovering over their cradles, now knew as much about killing and dying as they knew about living, and many, many more would die before it was over.

Haig desperately needed to relieve his 1st and 7th Divisions, who had been in the line since the battle started. The 1st Division, whose normal complement was 18,000 men, was now down to about 3,500. To replace the 7th, Sir John sent Haig a division from II Corps, which had been fighting at the far end of the British line near La Bassée, and when it crawled into the trenches it numbered no more than the decimated 7th. But at least these men were somewhat rested, since Falkenhayn had already pulled large numbers of German soldiers out of the southern sector in France to throw them into the cauldron at Ypres.

General Foch was also receiving reinforcements from his own com-mander, General Joseph Joffre, and once again became optimistic that an attack could defeat the German army. He convinced Sir John of this, and the British commander wired his boss Kitchener that he and Foch believed the Germans were actually pulling troops *out of* Ypres and sending them east to fight the Russians. This of course was nonsense, based on faulty intelligence. Falkenhayn was in fact assembling six fresh divisions in one great gambit to wreck the British Army and capture the English Channel ports. These included the elite Prussian Guard, considered the fiercest professional soldiers in the German Army, as well as two divisions Falkenhayn was able to free from the part of the front north of Ypres, which the Belgians had flooded.

Falkenhayn's logic ran this way: the German Army must attack somewhere in the Salient every day to keep up the pressure; so far this tactic had caved the British line in places but had not yet broken it; he could see the handwriting on the wall if they did not break it—stalemate. He knew from prisoner interrogations that the British were much extended; one great "push" could do it, might do it, had to do it. Falkenhayn set the big attack for November 10, but ordered continuous fighting until then up and down the line so as to give the Allies no chance to recover or strengthen their positions. Suffice it to say that at any given moment between November 2 and November 9 along the thirty or so miles of front that constituted the extended Ypres Salient, there were at least one or more attacks or counterattacks in progress, made all the worse for both sides when the freezing rain and fog of winter set in.

Meantime, Haig was growing anxious over the lack of cooperation. In an attack on November 6 between the junction of the French and British line at St. Eloi, the Germans stormed the village and drove to within two miles of Ypres itself. Haig restored the British part of the line but the French did little to retake theirs. Haig was livid and telegraphed to Sir John that if the French did not restore their sector, "I recommend my force to be withdrawn on a N.S. [north-south] line through Ypres." This was drastic talk, and Haig probably knew it was an empty threat, but it goes to show the strained relations between the two allies. They would not get much better in the years to come. Haig went on to complain that the French staff rarely visited their own lines and relied mostly on secondhand information, adding that, "We all feel that the French are not doing their fair share in attacking the enemy."

* * *

Falkenhayn's big "push" was to commence along the whole line from Nieuport on the North Sea down to La Bassée, sixty miles to the south in France. Both his Fourth and Sixth Armies would be involved—half a million men attacking at all points to keep the Allies from moving reserves from one sector to another. The intended German breakthrough point, however, was to be in the Salient just north of the "elbow" of the Ypres-Comines Canal, using the six new divisions. This was one of the myriad lock-controlled waterways criss-crossing Europe and England, which, before the invention of railways, were built in the early nineteenth century to transport goods. Not only had Falkenhayn assembled a formidable body of troops but he had stripped his other armies wherever possible of their available heavy artillery and ammunition. The German commander was putting all he had on this roll of the dice.

It opened on the morning of November 10, but not as planned. Fog and rain were so dense in the Salient that artillery observation was impossible from air or ground, and so that part of the attack was delayed a day. Nevertheless, the entire German Fourth Army assaulted on a line from Zonnebeck in the middle of the Salient to Nieuport, on the North Sea. Hollering out the names of the Teutonic gods of war, the Germans managed to wrest from the French little else but the towns of Dixmude and Bixschoote, which were destroyed in the process. And now, on November 11, a date that, ironically, would become famous in another way—as Armistice Day and, later, in the United States as Veterans' Day—Falkenhayn let his other boot drop. It was not unexpected.

Fog and rain continued in the Salient but the Germans nevertheless blew their bugles and whistles about 9 A.M. The soldiers of the 4th Bavarian Division scrambled out of their positions, formed up, dressed ranks, and launched themselves at the British line. They marched northwest, parallel to the Menin Road, where the newly arrived men of II Corps, with which Haig had replaced his tattered 2nd Division, waited for them. At last supplies of barbed wire had finally begun reaching the British and during the past few days they had been fortifying their lines with it. When the Germans were in gunshot range, the British cut them down with rifle fire and artillery. The Germans ran away.

Soon the vaunted Prussian Guard had its turn, 14,000 of them. They managed to penetrate where the British and French held the line near the

Menin Road between Polygon Wood and another forest called Nonne-boschen Wood (Nuns' Wood). But the British counterattacked and chased the Germans back to the original Allied line. Farther north, six battalions of the German Guards burst through near Polygon Wood, on a line manned by what was left of the Black Watch and Scots Guards, and nearly reached the rear areas where the guns were sited. Then the British artillery got into the act and shrapnel, shot point-blank, began to cut up the Germans hideously. In Polygon Wood itself the 1st Kings Regiment were bracing themselves for another assault; through the fog and battle smoke they could see the gray German uniforms in a long line out in front of them. Suddenly a wind came along and blew the haze away and what they saw before them shocked even the most battle-hardened soldier: the mass of Germans were all dead, piled in a line of heaps, cut down by British shrapnel.

Another battalion of the Prussian Guard had gone into Nonneboschen Wood, but they were without officers. Four companies of British, including a hastily assembled company of the Royal Engineers, attacked them and those who did not flee were killed or captured. As dusk fell so did a hard rain. Brigadier General FitzClarence, who had organized the rallying force during the crisis of October 31 and retaken the Gheluvelt Château, went forward in the dark to reconnoiter a position near Polygon Wood, where he hoped to counterattack. As he walked into the gloom he was fatally wounded by a rifle shot, and after that the First Battle of Ypres basically came to a close.

There was, of course, heavy fighting here and there as both the Germans and the Allies tried to improve their trench positions, but Falkenhayn had decided he had had enough. On November 17 he ordered a halt to the offensive and began detaching units needed in the East to fight on the Russian Front, where the Russians were putting up a greater fight than expected. The French army then took over the line from Zonnebeck down to Ploegsteert Wood in the southern end of the Salient. The British Expeditionary Force now stretched in a continuous fifteen-mile-long front that ran from about six miles south of Ypres to La Bassée in France.

What had happened to Falkenhayn's vaunted offensive? The information available points to a factor that Falkenhayn perhaps had not considered: his men, quite simply, were "fought out." Some battalions did not even get out of their trenches; others made halfhearted assaults before falling back. The youthful reserve units, which had been expected to support the attacking troops of the first line, were particularly hesitant, after their earlier decimations, and that possibly made all the difference in the outcome. It is one thing to send men into battle who are rested and have been trained and are motivated as to precisely what they are expected to accomplish. It is quite another to send in men who have been fighting continuously for weeks on end, men who have seen so many of their friends killed or wounded and been themselves exposed to the constant terror of artillery fire. It was even worse for the Germans, who sent in half-trained children.

Later in the war the British developed a system of laying out entire battlefields in detailed scale models the size of football fields where units going into battle would be taken during the weeks before an attack, their confidence enhanced by thorough indoctrination. The Germans had none of this at Ypres. In some cases the men had been fought to a frazzle for weeks and then were ordered to do it again. Later both sides would learn much about battlefield psychology; in fact, they were learning it now, as a sort of on-the-job training, but for the Germans it was too late. Falkenhayn and his commanders had believed, with justification, that if a breakthrough was to be accomplished, they had to do it then and there, before the British had the opportunity to fortify positions and reinforce themselves. But toward the end, the German foot soldiers simply did not have their hearts in it. Men constantly exposed to fire come to believe they will eventually die from it. Given rest and time to recuperate, their attitudes change; they regain confidence and morale. But the Germans who attacked at Ypres on November 11 had been through hell and their nerves were shot. They had been attacking, which is more strenuous than defending, and also many of their troops were green youths, unlike most of the British, who were professional soldiers. Falkenhayn's plans were upset by all this, but even more so by the valiant British soldiers who had gritted their teeth and gone at it hammer-and-tongs one last time.

Chapter Five ★

What had possessed the British and the other Allies to fight and die for such ground and put themselves in a decidedly inferior position in the Salient? The only explanation is the queer psychology of the battlefield; it is one thing to the men in the front lines, quite another to somebody looking at a map far back out of harm's way. On the one hand, the French—and General Joffre in particular, who had said the soldiers "must be killed in their tracks rather than draw back"—had developed the mind-set that not a single inch of ground should be given up to the Germans without a fight, even if that meant putting the Allies on disadvantageous terrain, such as the bulge in the Ypres Salient. For their part, the British had spilled much precious blood for their little Salient; the ground was still literally soaked with it. Basically this strategy was a political decision; the men, the officers of the line, and even their superiors at brigade and division staff positions saw the danger—even stupidity—in it. But it was too bitter a pill to swallow for Sir John French and the politicians and people back home to contemplate the earlier threat by Haig to pull back, however seriously or not he might have meant it at the time. It was completely against their grit to give up all the hard-fought ground in the Salient and straighten out the line so that it ran through Ypres itself. The result, of course, was the ominous bulge that had to be constantly manned and held by flesh and blood, overlooked now on three sides by the frowning guns of the Germans on the high ground. Quite naturally, the Germans set out forthwith to make the Allies pay dearly for their tenacity.

And so the Salient in front of Ypres assumed a more enduring shape, shrunken by the ferocious German assaults of the past month to a crescent roughly eight miles north-south and six miles deep to the west, inside which lay the Allied army; worse, the Germans now occupied the critical high ground. From their positions on the distant ridges they had a clear view of everything that moved on the plains below, and their artillery observers could call in fire from German guns positioned and protected three or four miles away behind the ridges.

Now with a sense of the inevitable, both sides began to dig in in earnest. Under the supervision of the Royal Engineers, the hastily dug out trenches were deepened—or built up—to six to eight feet whenever possible and widened to four or five feet, zigzagged so as to prevent any large stretch to be enfiladed in an attack. Trenches had been used as defensive fortifications since the time of spears and bows and arrows, most effectively near the end of the American Civil War when the Union army besieged the Confederates around Petersburg, Virginia. But the development of high-explosive artillery and static warfare dictated an entirely new type of trench, one in which men could live with at least some comfort and safety for long periods of time. Thus, the evolution of the trench reached it apogee in the First World War and has not been equaled since nor, with the invention of tanks and high-performance aircraft—let alone nuclear weapons—is it likely to be. Barbed wire was strung, sandbags stacked, fire steps carved out, and duckboards laid in the bottom. Sides were shorn up with timber and dugouts carved into the sides, which provided the only places of relative safety for the men who manned them. As protection against shrapnel they also began to build overhead shelters of heavy timbers, corrugated iron, and earth. That at least was the idea.

The problem was that in many places this simply could not be done where the water table was too high. In those frequent instances the only solution was to scrape out the trench to two or so feet, then build up a parapet of sandbags in front and *parados* of sandbags in the rear to furnish some sort of trenchlike protection. The difficulty here was that enemy artillery frequently blew the sandbags apart and in all too many cases even rifle bullets could penetrate them. Thus, a man could be standing or crouching behind a mass of sandbags and still have his head blown apart by an enemy bullet. Back at headquarters the maps might show it as a trench, but this was most unsatisfactory—as well as disconcerting—from the standpoint of soldiers who had to man such flimsy things.

Decaying corpses were frequently unearthed and in some cases incorporated into the trench system itself. Both sides had begun to organize some sort of methodical way of burying the dead. Because units were frequently moved from one section of the front to another, it was difficult for regiments or divisions to have a cemetery of their own in any particular place. But rudimentary cemeteries had to be established, and they were. In the British lines, bodies of British soldiers were removed to these, while if old French or German corpses from earlier fighting were discovered, they were usually buried in unmarked mass graves or wherever it was convenient, such as shell holes, just to get them out of the way.

From both a sanitary and morale standpoint, the sheer number of dead posed a large and unpleasant problem for all concerned. One officer wrote home after he was assigned to improve his trench systems: "There are many rough crosses marking graves, but it is impossible to dig anywhere without coming on bodies. In one trench they reported to me that they had come across a body, I had it taken out and reburied a little further on. We came across what had been a grave of a large number. The R.E. [engineer] staff officer had just then come back. We had to get done at all costs and as quickly as possible, to the correct depth to give the living men shelter and we could not divert the sandbags' position as they were already in place. The only thing to be done was to dig right on regardless of what we went through. The grave was some months old and it was a most horrible operation, especially when the flares were turned on and you saw the awful sights you were digging and picking to pieces. It was too much for some of the men and they had to be relieved. The stench was something awful. We got back here about 2 A.M. The men had rum and hot tea."

*   *   *

In many cases the groundwater level was so high that no matter what they did the trenches flooded; the underlying soil in the Flanders Plain was a thick blue clay, which did not drain well at all. Support trenches were dug somewhere within a thousand yards behind the fire trenches and connected to them where possible by communications trenches, and reserve trenches were built within a thousand yards behind all that. So-called sap trenches were dug forward of the fire trenches out into what became the no-man's-land, that area between the opposing armies, so each side could get as close as possible to the other, to hear, to see, to sneak at night. It has been calculated that the actual length of the various trench systems of both sides, if measured foot by foot from the North Sea to the Alps, would be long enough to encircle the earth. Before long there was such a maze of trenches that troops often became lost in them. The engineers began to identify trenches by numbers and letters, but eventually signs, similar to street signs, were put up by the men, most of them familiar names such as Woffard Lane, High Street, Picadilly, Fleet Street, and so on. From these trenches and their support areas the two sides now began a consistent artillery shelling, machine-gunning, and sniping of each other.

One of the ruses the British developed during this period related to the vast numbers of German waiters working in England before the war who had repatriated themselves and joined the German army. British soldiers would have someone shout out over no-man's-land, "Hey, waiter!" Invariably a head or two would appear above the German trenches, whereupon a British sniper was waiting to blow it to bits. This didn't work for very long, but in any case the Salient, as now formed, became a place of dark horror, which would get only darker and more horrible as the years passed by.

The butcher's bill for the First Battle of Ypres was higher than for any battle that either nation had ever fought in its history. The British lost more than 60,000 men; the story was the same in virtually every Allied line unit that had been fighting there: at *best*, those battalions, which had arrived full strength at 1,100 men (and most hadn't because they had been fighting since August), were now reduced to a few officers and two or three hundred men. At worst, many battalions simply ceased to exist. The British professional army, the Old Contemptibles, had effectively been obliterated as a fighting force.

It was far worse for the Germans. By initiating most of the big attacks, they had lost more than 165,000 men, according to their own casualty accounting system, which was notoriously inaccurate because the Germans counted only seriously wounded men as casualties. A great many of these losses were suffered by the student volunteer battalions that had been ruthlessly sacrificed by the High Command. The German term for it became Der Kindermord bei Ypern—the Massacre of the Innocents. These rough figures represented a combined casualty rate in this small part of Flanders of about 8,000 men a day since the battle opened a month earlier. Not only that but thousands of farm animals, abandoned by their owners when the fighting began, were now lying dead—many of them in no-man's-land—alongside the human bodies and the carcasses of artillery- and packhorses, where neither side could get out to bury them.

In that sense only it was lucky that winter was coming on. But now the men had to endure the ordeals of winter in northern Europe: rain, snow, sleet, almost every day, which turned the landscape into a sea of mud and ice. The trenches were flooded, sometimes waist deep, and the mud in them became almost like a living thing, sucking down men's boots, their clothes, even the men themselves. Feeble attempts were made to pump out the trenches but the equipment to do this was scarce and frequently broke down. Those who could afford it sent home for rubberized waders or hip boots. The army, not contemplating such conditions as these, was slow to issue those items as standard to the troops. Soon a particularly unpleasant ailment began to appear: "trench foot," in which feet long immersed in water begin to swell and then, literally, to rot. Meals had to be brought up mostly in periods of dark or fog since merely *getting* to the frontline trenches was very dangerous business, what with constant German artillery, machine gun, and rifle fire.

The American poet Alan Seeger had enlisted in the French Foreign Legion at the beginning of the war. As the Battle of Ypres was winding down he told his diary: "Fifth day of our second period in the trenches. Five days and nights of pure misery. The increasing cold will make this kind of existence insupportable with its accompaniments of vermin and dysentery. The real courage of the soldier is not facing the [bullets] but the fatigue and discomfort and misery." Seeger was killed in 1916, age twenty-eight.

Meantime, another problem had begun to present itself to both sides. Some sort of trench protocol had to be developed, since it quickly became obvious that men could not endure the stress of the trenches for any length of time. After the first battles it was generally conceded that two days—forty-eight hours—was about the most the men could withstand, and so, for a typical battalion, the rotation that was established went something as follows. Two days in the frontline trenches, two days in the support trenches not far behind, two days in the reserve trenches farther back, four or six days "in billets," and then the whole process started over again. With some variation this was the pattern until the end of the war; thus, out of a full division of 18,000, only 2,000 men would be in the frontline trenches at a given time.

If there was no attack in progress, the routine of the trenches took on a life of its own. As an eye-opener in the morning a two-tablespoon rum ration was issued in most British battalions, poured to each man from a rum jar into an iron ladle or spoon. The men cooked bacon, biscuits, and ate bread and jam and drank tea for breakfast. Every day, shortly before dawn, there was a ritual known as the "Stand-to," derived from an order reaching back to medieval times: "Stand-to-Arms." Since most attacks were launched at daybreak, during the Stand-to every man in the trenches was required to slog through the mud and mount the firestep with his weapon—bayonet fixed—and peer out into the gloom toward the German trenches a hundred or so yards away. After an hour, if it seemed that the Germans were minding their own business, the order was given to "Stand Down," and everybody set about his employment of the day. For the men, this involved "working parties" repairing and improving the trenches, "burying parties" for the dead, and "carrying parties" going to the rear for ammunition, rations, and other supplies. Snipers set about their grim business. For the officers, there were all sorts of reports to write concerning the events of the previous night and duties supervising the men or interviewing replacements.

Those not otherwise occupied sat around sewing up their clothes, smoking pipes or cigarettes, picking lice off of themselves, or just staring up at the sky, which was the only thing they could see of the outside world: to stick one's head above the trench in daylight was to invite almost certain death. A flock of birds overhead always raised great interest, as would unusual cloud formations and especially an airplane. A less welcome sight were heavy-caliber enemy artillery shells passing over, which could actually be seen in flight and cast brief flickering shadows on the trenches. Some men even wrote home asking for penny packets of flower seeds to plant in their trenches come spring. All this was done in the context of regular shelling by the German guns, which, if a barrage landed just right, often blew the trench in, burying its occupants alive. This was a particularly horrifying experience; when others rushed to the rescue with shovels, it was, according to one combatant, "like being dug up out of your own grave."

Somehow, because there was really no choice, most of the men got used to it. An officer with a line company wrote his wife: "My orderly has just returned from Brigade Headquarters in the Château and tells me one shell burst at the front door. Horrid sounds they make, you hear the whistle and hiss for some 40 seconds, coming nearer and nearer and wonder when it will stop. Then a nerve-shattering window-breaking explosion. One gets into a sort of Kismet mood. It's no use cowering down unless there is good cover; if a shell does burst in the right place (upon you) you don't know anything about it, as a rule. In the trenches there is a certain amount of cover, and if one is buried, there is always a chance of being dug out safely."

Another bizarre factor was the very proximity of the trench systems. In the Salient, they were anywhere from 10 yards to 200 yards apart—the average was probably fewer than a hundred—and the men of both armies could frequently hear their enemies laughing or cursing and often smell their cooking across no-man's-land. Compared with the impersonality of artillery shelling and sniper's bullets, this lent a strange intimacy to the war.

Just before dusk every day there was another hourlong "Stand-to," then the evening meal, which for the British regularly consisted of Bully Beef (canned corned beef) or a canned stew of meat and vegetables known as Maconochie, named after the company that made it. (For the Germans, there was sausage and sauerkraut.) After dark there was more work to do. Wiring parties climbed over the top of the parapet and busied themselves laying barbed wire or repairing wire that had been damaged by enemy artillery. Others crawled forward into no-man's-land to listening posts, checking for enemy activity. Infrequently—although as the war progressed they would become commonplace—trench raids were conducted, a patrol of men crawling through the squalid horrors of no-man's-land up to the enemy trenches in hopes of capturing a prisoner or killing a few Germans. All this night activity was punctuated by German flares, which lit up the sky with an eerie greenish glow, forcing those in no-man's-land to stop their activity and drop to earth motionless as the ghostly light flickered above them. When all the work was done and the men were back in the trenches, the British began firing their own flares, called Very Lights, after their inventor, to see what the Germans were up to.

Over in the German lines things were about the same, except that the Germans had determined to dig fortifications that were far more elaborate than those of the Allies. Falkenhayn realized that no further offensive was possible for the time being since it had finally become necessary to transfer large numbers of his troops to the Russian Front, and he instructed his commanders to have the men build the strongest possible defenses. This they did with typical German efficiency. On the higher ridges they dug down sometimes thirty feet deep, safe from all shell fire, and constructed intricate complexes of bunkers, some complete with electric lights, running water, kitchens, flooring, and furnished with chairs, tables, beds, and boudoirs looted from Belgian homes.

By contrast, the British trenches were only temporary, shabby things—purposefully so. The feeling at headquarters was that the spirit of the trench must not be defensive, to not dig in and live in luxury but always to think of the offensive that would drive the Germans back to Germany. The Germans suspected as much and in consequence a whole new defensive scheme was put into place—the concept of "defense-in-depth"— which was to be a hallmark of evolving German tactics, as well as strategy, in the years to come. It consisted of placing fewer troops in the front lines but having very strong reserve positions, which would immediately counterattack and repel the exhausted Allied soldiers if and when they reached the German trenches.

This ran contrary to the initial German strategy of "one line, and a strong one," but Germany was now having to contend with sending troops to the Russian Front and could not contemplate big offensives for the time being, though the army—mistakenly, as it turned out—believed the Allies were strong enough to attack them at any moment.

An American correspondent, Frederick Palmer, wrote of the trenches around Ypres: "The Germans were busy as beavers dam building. They had a lot of work to do before they got their defences right. We heard them driving stakes and spading; we heard their voices and occasionally the energetic, shouted, guttural commands of their officers. All through the night I never heard a British officer speak above a conversational tone. The orders were definitive enough, but given with a certain companionable kindliness."

The British Army desperately needed men, but the Liberal Party war government was maddeningly parsimonious about sending them over. Upon taking a few days' leave in London, General Sir Horace Smith-Dorrien, commander of II Corps, was appalled to find that the people had such little idea of the extent of the savage fighting that was going on just forty miles or so across the channel, nor of the peril of an army now decimated. "Their minds seem set," he complained, "on what appeared to me to be a ridiculous fear of an invasion of England."

As well, the terrific casualties during the First Battle of Ypres and realization that the war was not going to be won quickly caused dramatic changes in the way the military authorities looked at their recruiting program. The height requirement for a British soldier at the beginning of the war was 5'8"; as the First Battle of Ypres opened it was lowered to 5'5" and by the time that battle ended it was again reduced, to 5'3"; not long afterward it was lowered to 5' flat and more than 50,000 men of this meager height served in what came to be known as "Bantams" battalions. By the end of the war the British were taking men up to fifty years old into the army.

The day after Falkenhayn formally called off his great Ypres offensive, Haig was promoted to full general. When he, too, took a little well-earned time away from the front to visit London, he met with Kitchener to try to persuade him to begin sending over more of the so-called territorial battalions. In this he was not successful. Even in a conversation with his friend the king, Haig was told that the territorial forces were needed in England in case the Germans tried to cross the channel. Haig was astounded. "I remarked," he wrote, "that the surest way to prevent the enemy from attempting to invade Great Britain was to engage and press him on the Continent."

Soon it began to sink in with people that it was going to be a long war. Kitchener, of course, had recognized this months earlier when he had made the call for his volunteer army—still months away from being ready. Letters from the front—though heavily censored—were reaching homes all over England, France, and Germany; and, of course, there was no denying the frightful casualty lists. The soldiers could see better than anyone how the situation was shaping up. When it was learned that the Germans were withdrawing men from the Western Front to fight the Russians, Kitchener, to bolster spirits, announced publicly that the Allies were now facing no more than "an army of old men and boys." The men in the trenches knew the truth, though, and that wasn't it.

After the initial shock of these first clashes, pacifist groups cranked up for action. In Germany a small group of intellectuals issued a "Manifesto to Europeans," calling for an end to the conflict, with no territorial gains for Germany. Among those signing it was Albert Einstein. This was in response to an earlier German manifesto that was defiant to the end, and which had invoked the hallowed names of German *Kultur*—Martin Luther, Goethe, Kant, Beethoven, and Wagner—declaring, "We shall wage this fight to the very end as a civilized nation." This document was sent out around the world, signed by ninety-three of Germany's leading scientific and cultural leaders, including X-ray inventor Wilhelm Röntgen, the celebrated scientist Max Planck, and the theatrical trailblazer Max Reinhardt.

In England the International Women's Suffrage Alliance had issued its own manifesto calling for an end to "international differences to avert deluging half the civilized world in blood." Socialist groups began protesting as well: "Unite with the proletariat of the world who will rise up against the war." The Bolsheviks in Russia chimed in with the same message. In the United States several thousand women dressed in black mourning marched down New York's Fifth Avenue, calling for peace to the tune of a dirge. The industrialist Henry Ford chartered an entire steamship in which he installed a great delegation of pacifists to visit Oslo, Stockholm, The Hague, and other capitals, protesting the war. None of it came to anything, though, and from across no-man's-land millions of men remained in their slimy ditches, waiting for the opportunity to kill one another.

There were great changes in the wind, too, for the civilian populaces of the warring powers. In England chauffeurs, gardeners, butlers, and other servants had joined the army, and so women of the privileged classes found themselves learning to drive their own cars, plant their own flowers, and answer their own doors. Servant girls and women went off to the munitions factories while others went into the "Land Army," taking up the work of male farmworkers who had gone off to war. Thus the upper classes often had to learn to make their own beds and cook their own dinners. There was a sense among everyone that the old social systems were vanishing. Eminent historian Lyn Macdonald noted in her book *1914: The Days of Hope,* "Debrett's *Peerage* [a sort of blue book identifying British notable families] did not appear as it usually did in early spring; so many sons of the aristocracy were dead, so many baronets, and lords, and knights, so many heirs to great lands and titles had been killed, that it took the editors many months to revise the entries of almost every blue-blooded family in the United Kingdom. When it finally did appear, the 1915 edition made very sorry reading."

Unemployment in Great Britain was suddenly not a problem, though the question remained of how it was going to be paid for. The Germans partially solved this dilemma by deporting and enslaving nearly 700,000 Belgian men to take the place, on farms or in armaments factories, of the Germans who had gone to war. And there were sadder things. The dimensions and implications of the unfolding holocaust were just now beginning to dawn on the people at their various home fronts. It was not going to "be over by Christmas," by a long stretch, and the appalling casualty lists clearly showed what lay in the future. One of the most chilling descriptions of the consequence of modern war was penned by Helen Zenna Smith, a popular British journalist and playwright. Here she dramatizes in graphic bitterness a scene in which a British army nurse somewhere in Flanders imaginarily escorts her own blithe mother and her mother's friend into the world in which she now lives:

"Oh come with me, Mother and Mrs. Evans-Mawnington. Let me show you the exhibits straight from the battlefield. This will be something original to tell your committees, while they knit their endless miles of khaki scarves—something to spout from the platform at your recruiting meeting. Come with me. Stand just there.

Here we have the convoy gliding into the station now, slowly, so slowly. In a minute it will disgorge its sorry cargo. My ambulance doors are open, waiting to receive. See, the train has stopped. Through the occasionally drawn blinds you will observe the trays slotted into the sides of the train. Look closely, Mother and Mrs. Evans-Mawnington, and you shall see what you shall see. Those trays each contain something that was once a whole man . . . the heroes who have done their bit for King and country . . . the heroes who marched blithely through the streets of London Town singing 'Tipperary,' while you cheered and waved your flags hysterically. They are not singing now, you will observe. Shut your ears, Mother and Mrs. Evans-Mawnington, lest their groans and heart-rending cries linger as long in your memory as in the memory of the daughter you sent out to help win the War.

See the stretcher-bearers lifting the trays one by one, slotting them deftly into my ambulance. Out of the way quickly, Mother and Mrs. Evans-Mawnington—lift your silken skirts aside . . . a man is spewing blood, the moving has upset him, finished him—He will die on the way to hospital if he doesn't die before the ambulance is loaded. I know. . . . All this is old history to me. Sorry this has happened. It isn't pretty to see a hero spewing up his life's blood in public, is it? Much more romantic to see him in the picture papers being awarded the V.C., even if he is minus a limb or two. A most unfortunate occurrence!"

Scenes such as this conjured, but with the absolute ring of truth, were of course not limited to England. In a German military hospital a volunteer nurse named Tilla Durieux remembered: "The first time I attended an operation I nearly fainted when I was given a sawn-off leg to put in the corner. It took all my strength to pull myself together, but I can still feel the weight of that leg in my hands today."

*   *   *

Despite the many demoralizing accounts from those returning from the front, the general populations of all the countries at war (except perhaps Belgium, since 90 percent of its land was under the iron fist of the Germans) somehow managed to remain confident about the outcome. In England it became fashionable to dress up children in little khaki army field-service uniforms as well as the traditional sailor suits. Not only that, but the Boy Scouts, founded only a few years earlier, began to assume an active role in ferreting out spies and assuming other duties of Home Defense. This led to a number of embarrassing episodes for the Boy Scouts, who tended to see German spies behind every bush. Fancy London department stores such as Harrods and Fortnum & Mason began to offer a vast array of items that might be useful in the trenches: flashlights, periscopes, hammocks, waterproof gear, and food gift packages that friends or relatives could mail to the soldiers.

The general feeling, bolstered by the British press, was that the Germans had been held, France had been saved, and most everyone believed Kitchener's vast New Armies, which would take the field in a matter of months, would crush the Huns and drive them back across their borders. An attitude of fierce resolve was building throughout England. British fury against Germany was further enflamed when, a month after the First Battle of Ypres had ended, a fleet of German warships dashed across the channel and bombarded towns on the east coast of Britain. The attacks killed or wounded several hundred people, including children, and was, as historian Martin Gilbert points out, "the first occasion on which civilians had been killed in Britain by enemy action since 1690."

In Germany, too, most hopes remained high. Despite some earlier success on their part, the Russians had finally been handed a terrific defeat at the Battle of Tannenberg, where 30,000 Russians were said to have been killed and their commander committed suicide. As well, just as the Battle of Ypres was winding down, German spirits were uplifted by news that Turkey (antagonized over British incursions in the Middle East, which they saw as their "sphere of influence") entered the war on the German side, dumping one more empire into the cauldron.

Back in England, Lord Kitchener, who had crossed the channel to analyze the stalemate on the Western Front, concluded that, until his New Armies could take the field in 1916, the German lines constituted one giant "fortress" that could not be cracked, and it would be necessary to conduct "operations elsewhere." This soon led to the disastrous adventure by the British army at Gallipoli. Meanwhile, the French were asking for more British troops. Kitchener replied that, by summer, "you will have one million trained English soldiers in France," but he refused to send any more until then, except as replacements. This only deepened traditional French suspicions of the English. The "operations elsewhere" invariably centered on the use of the great British fleet, and included proposals to attack Germany through the Baltic Sea, to attack Turkey, and even a cross-channel invasion of the German-held portions of the north Belgian coastline. Winston Churchill, who now ran the British Admiralty, feared that the Germans would be able to launch devastating submarine attacks from these Belgian ports, which, ultimately, they did.

The French were dismayed by these notions, since the Germans were occupying a large part of their country and most of Belgium, too. Their only thought was to drive them out as soon as possible. The ubiquitous Colonel Charles Repington, war correspondent for *The London Times,* claimed that General Foch himself defined the irrational French mistrust of British intentions. By Repington's account, Foch invited him into his headquarters for a hush-hush meeting where: "He took up a map of Northern Europe, spread it out, and asked me solemnly how much European territory we [the British] should expect for ourselves at the end of the war."

Both German and British attacks in Flanders continued throughout November and into December, and though many men were killed on both sides there was nothing like the intensity of the battles of October and early November.

Meantime, the Germans were becoming apprehensive over the accuracy of the British shell fire on their rear areas. They blamed it on spies and Belgian citizens using homing pigeons and other signaling devices, but they singled out the grand old architectural towers of churches, châteaux, and other structures in and around Ypres, which they said were housing British artillery observers. Thus they systematically began to bombard these spires and, as an official German historian so piously put it, "So the blame must not be laid on us for the gradual destruction of the magnificent buildings of Ypres, which gave such a fine view of the surrounding countryside."

To accomplish their task the Germans employed a weapon that the British had not yet seen—the huge 17-inch howitzers, which had earlier caused almost unfathomable damage at Antwerp. Father Camille Delaere recorded in his diary that German shells had ruined the hospital Notre Dame. "Arthur Demos was mortally wounded. He died a few moments after receiving extreme unction." The priest was probably in the best position of anyone to chronicle the destruction of Ypres. He rushed from one place to another during the shelling, giving help wherever he could, even while his fellow citizens began a mass exodus of the city. "A cow in a barn and a horse in its stable were killed at the farm of Nestor Boudry. Oscan Seghers was killed, also a woman. Many, many wounded. Many soldiers hit." The next day he reported, "The bombardment of the town starts up about 9 o'clock and never stops. There were many fresh victims. Joseph Notebaert, a good family man, had his hand cut off, his two elder children killed, the three others wounded."

Father Delaere went out again with his "devoted vicar" to assist the nuns of the hospital in removing patients back to the town of Poperinge, away from the shelling. "The evening was quite terrifying. The incendiary shells mixed with shrapnel shells started fires all over the centre of the town, and many of our loveliest buildings were destroyed . . . black sky, intense heat, flames like red clouds thrown up by a storm—sublime among the horror—the flames leaping, the beams of the houses crashing down." There was no fire brigade to put out the fires and no water for them if they had been there, and so the city blazed and exploded and crumbled. The German shelling was relentless: "The force of the shells on the Place Van den Peereboom in front of the cathedral was so tremendous that the tramway rails were cut clean off and blown some distance away. An enormous hole appeared in the street, so big you could hardly say where it ended. It covered at least fifty square meters."

*   *   *

A word should be said about developing airpower. Both sides used observation balloons to observe enemy lines and to direct artillery fire. By the
last year of the war there could be at any given time 300 of these sausage-
shaped giants hovering above the trenches on the Western Front, nearly
one for every mile and a quarter between Switzerland and the North Sea.
From their baskets, the observers had a unique view of the battlefield; on
a clear day they could see fifteen miles or more and, unlike observers in
airplanes, there was little vibration, so they could use their binoculars and
telescopes, too.

They would be inflated with highly flammable hydrogen and allowed
to rise some 3,000 to 5,000 feet, tethered to the earth by a cable with a telephone wire in it, through which the observer could phone down valuable
information. The observer or observers were suspended in a basket beneath
the balloon, later equipped with parachutes, for it soon became a favorite
sport of the opposing sides to send airplanes up to shoot down balloons as
they appeared. There were other perils, too: a balloon was susceptible to being
hit by lightning, its cables severed by shrapnel, or the balloon itself hit by
enemy artillery. Strong winds often snapped cables, and since the prevailing
winds blew off the sea toward the German lines Allied balloonists were frequently blown into enemy territory and taken prisoner.

Increasingly, airplanes played the greater role. At the outset of the war
it was generally believed that engine-driven aircraft would be used primarily for reconnaissance, as they had been so useful in gathering information
on troop movements in the confused early days of fighting. However, it was
quickly learned that they were extremely useful in artillery spotting as well.
During the first few months, the pilot would make his observations about a
target, or where his own artillery was landing, and then have to set down on
the ground and either telephone the battery with positions or corrections
or, if he was close by, personally go to the battery. Other methods included
having the pilot drop smoke flares upon the positions that the artillery was
to bombard. A crude wireless telegraphy was developed, however, allowing
the aircraft a direct link with the ground; the plane was usually attached to a
particular battery and from that vantage point the pilot or his observer could
tap out in Morse code immediate corrections to the bursts exploding beneath him.

As the war opened, the number of airplanes on both sides was piti-fully small, just a handful—after all, the airplane itself was barely ten years old—but by war's end there would be more than 22,000 in the British army alone, capable of reaching unheard-of speeds of more than 100 mph and altitudes of 20,000 feet or more, and dropping large payloads of bombs, even as far as Berlin itself. The Germans had about as many and the French more. Even in those early days the opposing sides recognized that airplanes were formidable weapons. At first the only armaments they carried into the air were rifles and pistols and an occasional grenadelike bomb that could be dropped from the plane onto a target. Later, machine guns were mounted in the cockpit to be fired by what was then known as an "observer." In 1915 the German Anthony Fokker developed a device that synchronized the propeller with a machine gun, which allowed a pilot to fire straight through the spinning prop at his enemy—an enormous leap. The Allies quickly du-plicated the technology and this marked the beginning of serious aerial combat.

In Flanders meantime, the weather turned so bad that, mercifully, on many days during the remainder of 1914, even limited attacks became impos-sible. Now Christmas was approaching, the time when many pundits had predicted that the war was supposed to have been over. Many a soldier huddled in his trench on either side of the lines wished it would be, but knew it wouldn't. At Christmastime the soldiers began receiving all kinds of gifts from their various countries. The kaiser sent his men boxes of ci-gars, the Queen sent each Tommy gift packages of pipe tobacco, cigarettes, or chocolate. There were multitudes of other gifts, too, some from private corporations, most from the families of the men themselves. There were so many of these packages that a British officer complained that they were disrupting his operations and even getting his men killed as they tried to bring them up to the front lines.

Then, on December 25, 1914, one of the most remarkable episodes in the history of warfare unfolded in Flanders. Not long after the daylight Stand-to, most of the German firing dropped away. Then the sounds of Christmas music began to waft across no-man's-land: German music, some of it accompanied by bands, and the sounds of Germans singing "Silent Night," "O Tannenbaum," "Adeste Fideles," and other Christmas carols. The British, peering warily over their parapets, were astonished and amazed, but soon they, too, began returning Christmas serenades.

They were further astounded to see Germans climbing up on the top of their trenches, unarmed, and waving, some holding up little Christmas trees. Soon they saw a few of them begin walking toward the British lines, grinning and laughing. It was a cold but sunny Christmas morning, and a strange air of goodwill seemed to overtake these men who had been killing each other all through those long bloody months. Now they were clambering into no-man's-land by the thousands and wishing one another well on the most sacred holiday of their year. They gathered in groups and before long began to exchange presents. The men gave whatever they had: "watches, rings, cigarette cases and tubes of ointment." The Germans also had beer and schnapps and gave away some of their cigars. The British gave away cigarettes and plum puddings. Names and addresses were exchanged, as were uniform buttons and cap badges. They took pictures of each other. They communicated as best they could, and in at least one section of no-man's-land a soccer ball was produced and a lively game broke out between the men of the opposing armies. Line officers used the occasion to bury some of the bodies of men and carcasses of animals in front of their trenches, which they had not been able to do as of yet.

An officer of the Scots Guards said of the Germans, "They protested that they had no feeling of enmity at all towards us, but that everything lay with their authorities, and that being soldiers, they had to obey. I believe they were speaking the truth when they said this, and that they never wished to fire a shot again." The officer even mailed a postcard given to him by a German who had an English girlfriend in Suffolk before the war, although "she probably would not be a bit keen to see him again."

As the day wore on, all sorts of fraternal activities ensued. The Germans invited some of the Tommies into their trenches, and sat them down to Christmas dinner, complete with beer, wine, sausage, sauerkraut, and Christmas trees. At one point a rabbit dashed out of the remains of a cabbage patch and both Germans and Englishmen chased and finally pounced on it. Another ran out and they got it, too, each taking back one rabbit

BEF IN FLANDERS, *Situation, 20th October 1914*

Legend:
- ***XXI*** Allied Unit
- **2ⁿᵈ** German Unit
- Frontline
- Major River
- Minor River
- Canal
- Int'l Border
- Province Border
- Attacks

North Sea

Zeebrugge

Ostend

BRUGES

BELGIUM

Steene

3rd Res Korps

Ghistelles

Nieuport

3rd Div

2nd Div

St Georges

St Pierre

Cappelle

Couckelaere

Thourout

1st Div

Pervyse

22nd Res Korps

WEST FLANDERS

Dunkerque Canal

Ghyvelde

Furnes

4th Div

Oostkerke

St Jacques Cappelle

Dixmude

Zarren

Clercken

23rd Res Korps

Fourth

Dunkirk

Colme Canal

Fr 87th Terr

Merckem

Honthuist Forest

Staden

Vijfwegen

Bergues

Killem

Yser

Fr 89th Terr

Bixschoote

Poelcappelle

26th Res Korps

Roulers

Rumbeke

DE MITRY

Langemarck

Army

Elverdinghe

St Julien

Zonnebeke

Passchendaele

Poperinghe

Vlamertinghe

Br I

St Jean

Polygon Wood

27th Korps

Ypres

Hooge

Zillebeke

Dickebusch

Gheluvelt

St Eloi

Yser-Comines Canal

Zandervoorde

Menin

Cassel

Kemmel

Messines Ridge

CAVALRY CORPS

Weryicq

Halluin

Mt Kemmel

Comines

FRANCE

Douve

Messines

Ploegsteert Woods

1st, 4th, & 5th Kav Korps

Hazebrouck

Bailleul

Ploegsteert

TOURCOING

19th Korps

Nieppe Forest

Houplines

ROUBAIX

Aire

Merville

Armentieres

Br III

2nd Kav Korps

Neuf Fossé Canal

St Venant

Chapelle-d'Armentieres

LILLE

Laventie

Lys

13th Korps

Lillers

Fromelles

Aubers

CONNEAU

Army

Neuve Chapelle

Sixth

Clarence

Br II

7th Korps

Seclin

N

Bethune

La Bassée Canal

La Bassée

PAS DE CALAIS

Givenchy

Cuinchy

Fr XXI

0   5 Miles

Pernes

Carvin

14th Korps

0   8 Kilometers

Courtesy of Eureka Cartography & Globes

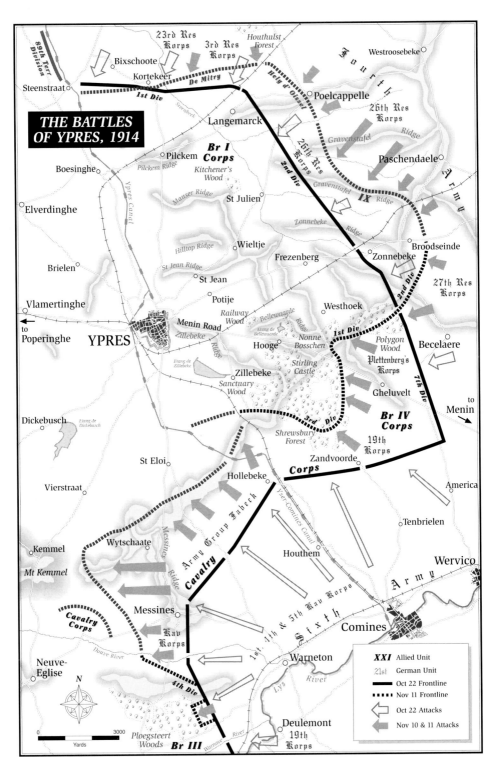

THE BATTLES
OF YPRES, 1914

89th Terr
Division

Steenstraat
Bixschoote
Kortekeer
23rd Res Korps
3rd Res Korps
De Mitry
1st Div
Houthulst Forest
Helg d'Oisel
Westroosebeke
Fourth

Poelcappelle
26th Res Korps

Langemarck
Pilckem
Pilckem Ridge
Br I Corps
Kitchener's Wood
Mauser Ridge
St Julien
26th Res Korps
2nd Div
Gravenstafel Ridge
Paschendaele
Army
IX

Boesinghe
Elverdinghe
Ypres Canal
Zonnebeke Ridge
Army

Brielen
Hilltop Ridge
Wieltje
Frezenberg
St Jean Ridge
St Jean
2nd Div
Zonnebeke
Broodseinde
27th Res Korps

Vlamertinghe
to Poperinghe
YPRES
Menin Road
Zillebeke Ridge
Potije
Railway Wood
Bellewaarde
Etang de Bellewaarde
Bellewaarde Ridge
Hooge
Nonne Bosschen
Westhoek
1st Div
Polygon Wood
Plettenberg's Korps
7th Div
Becelaere
to Menin

Dickebusch
Etang de Dickebusch
Etang de Zillebeke
Zillebeke
Sanctuary Wood
Stirling Castle
3rd Div
Shrewsbury Forest
Gheluvelt
Br IV Corps
19th Korps

St Eloi
Zandvoorde
Corps
America

Vierstraat
Hollebeke
Yser-Comines Canal
Houthem
Tenbrielen

Kemmel
Mt Kemmel
Wytschaate
Messines Ridge
Army Group Fabeck
Cavalry
Wervico
Army

Messines
Cavalry Corps
Douve River
Kav Korps
1st, 4th & 5th Kav Korps
Sixth
Comines

Neuve-Eglise
N
4th Div
Warneton
Lys River

Deulemont
19th Korps

Ploegsteert Woods
Br III
Warnave River

0   3000
Yards

XXI Allied Unit
21st German Unit
━━━ Oct 22 Frontline
••••• Nov 11 Frontline
⬜ Oct 22 Attacks
⬛ Nov 10 & 11 Attacks

Courtesy of Eureka Cartography & Globes

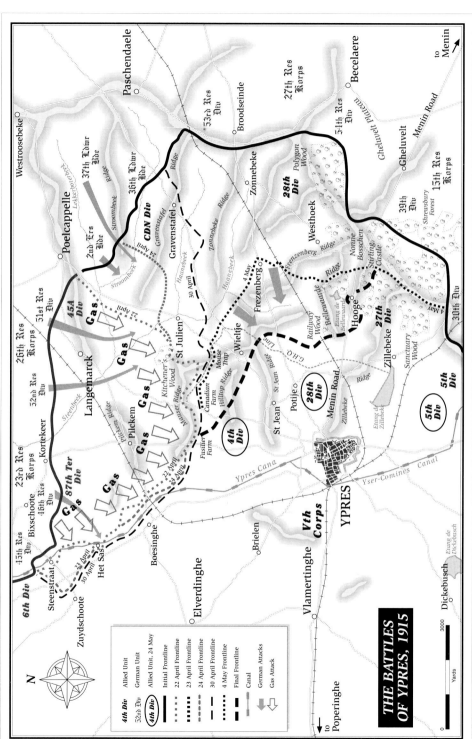

THE BATTLES
OF YPRES, 1915

Courtesy of Eureka Cartography & Globes

German infantry marching through Flanders Fields in 1914.

London omnibuses were sent over to Flanders to ferry troops to the front. *Courtesy of Imperial War Museum*

A fanatical-eyed Adolf Hitler (*circled*) in the Munich plaza on the day war was declared. He later wrote: "I fell down on my knees and thanked Heaven for granting me the good fortune of being permitted to live at this time!" *Courtesy of Imperial War Museum*

In October 1914, to stem the German tide, Albert, king of the Belgians, blew up the floodgates and dikes of the Yser River, flooding an enormous section of Flanders with seawater, making it impassable. *Courtesy of Imperial War Museum*

The main square in Poperinge in 1914: the British supply base and rest center eight miles behind Ypres. Many buildings were damaged during the war. It was here that the Talbot House, a refuge for British soldiers, was formed.

Ypres just before the war, with the Cloth Hall and St. Martin's cathedral in the background.

The magnificent Cloth Hall at Ypres, dating from the thirteenth century, in 1914, before the Germans came.

A view of Ypres in the last year of the war. *Courtesy of Corbis*

A German flamethrower attack in 1915. The British were still reeling from the first German poison gas attack at Ypres a few months earlier, when the Germans unleashed liquid fire for the first time.

After the first German poison gas attack at Ypres in 1915, British soldiers were hastily issued goggles and a gauze mask for protection.

Poison gas blinded many soldiers. Here a line of British moves forward to a dressing station, each with his hand on the man in front for guidance.
Courtesy of Corbis

The poet-lieutenant Edmund Blunden, who fought at Passchendaele, and later wrote about it. *Courtesy of Imperial War Museum*

Canadian private Will R. Bird who remarked when hearing that his regiment was going to the Ypres Salient in 1917: "I mentioned Ypres and he cursed the place. Rumors of what waited ahead of us had disturbed everyone." *Courtesy of CEF Books*

Canadian private Donald Fraser wearing a "jerkin" of sheepskin, issued to protect against the cold Flanders winter. He said of the Ypres Salient: "The traffic in human flesh in this region is scandalous. The Germans themselves have a dread of this front." *Courtesy of CEF Books*

Captain John McRae penned the immortal World War I poem "In Flanders Fields" over the grave of a dead comrade in the Ypres Salient. He would not survive the war. *Courtesy of CEF Books*

The famous British recruiting poster featuring Lord Kitchener, the Hero of the Sudan. *Courtesy of Imperial War Museum*

"That astronomical annoyance, the star shell, which momentarily enables you to scrutinize the kind of mud you are in." One of the many "Ole Bill" cartoons by Lieutenant Bruce Bairnsfather.

One of the most ingenious contrivances fabricated during the war to deceive the enemy was the "phony tree trunk." This device, made of steel and with fake leaves, was put into position at night after the real tree had been sawed down. When a man climbed into its hollow insides it made an excellent observation post on the front lines. *Courtesy of World War I Document Archive*

A miner wearing a "protomask" attempts to rescue a comrade who has been injured in an underground explosion. *Courtesy of Imperial War Museum*

Sir John Denton Pinkstone French, the British army commander in chief at the beginning of the war. He was later replaced by Haig, who has been accused of masterminding French's removal. *Courtesy of Corbis*

General Sir William Robertson, chief of the Imperial General Staff. He was Haig's ally in London against the machinations of Prime Minister David Lloyd George. *Courtesy of Corbis*

General Erich von Falkenhayn commanded the German armies during the first year of the war. He failed to break the British lines at Ypres, which forced the war into a trench stalemate. *Courtesy of Corbis*

Erich Ludendorff was considered the brains of the new German command. He pushed for the resumption of unlimited submarine warfare, which ultimately brought America into the conflict. *Courtesy of Corbis*

British artillery fire was so intense during the Third Battle of Ypres that dogs were used to bring up rations, messages, water, and ammunition. Many dogs died.

A horse broken down in the Ypres mud. Official records state that nearly half a million horses and mules were killed during the war. *Courtesy of Imperial War Museum*

Here is what the men lived in much of the time. *Courtesy of Imperial War Museum*

A grim King George V visits the grave of his nephew, young Prince Maurice of Battenberg, who was killed in the autumn of 1914 during the First Battle of Ypres. Later the family changed its name to Mountbatten to disassociate itself from anything German. *Courtesy of Imperial War Museum*

William "Willie" Fraser, who was in the war from the start, being wounded several times and rising to the rank of colonel. His brother was killed at the First Battle of Ypres and Fraser buried him himself amid the gunfire.
Courtesy of General Sir David Fraser

The Hooge Chateau in 1914 before the battle began.

The wreck of the Hooge Chateau in 1915. The previous year at the height of the First Battle of Ypres, it had been used as headquarters for two British divisions. A shell burst in, killing one army commander and badly injuring another. By the end of the war nothing was left of it but a low pile of bricks and dust. *Courtesy of Imperial War Museum*

Men clearing ground for more graves at the Hooge Cemetery.

Women and children were the backbone of British labor during the war. Here they inspect a warehouse containing more than half a million artillery shells. Many were killed in accidental explosions and their hair almost always turned yellow from the noxious ingredients of gunpowder.

As First Lord of the Admiralty, Winston Churchill pushed for the disastrous operation at Gallipoli. Afterward, he was forced to resign and rejoined his old regiment at Ypres as a major. Here he is shown wearing a French helmet given as a gift. *Courtesy of Imperial War Museum*

Sir Douglas Haig conversing with Prime Minister David Lloyd George. In the middle is Joffre and the man to the left was a newspaper reporter named Thomas, whose accounts of the war were scoffed at by most of the soldiers. *Courtesy of Imperial War Museum*

apiece. The singing continued: "Good King Wencelas," "The Boys of Bonnie Blue Scotland," "It's a Long Way to Tipperary," and ended with both sides singing "Auld Lang Syne." For thousands of men on both sides, filthy, haggard, and brutalized, it was a truly moving experience. The Scots Guards officer noted: "It was absolutely astounding, and if I had seen it on a cinematograph film I should have sworn that it was faked!"

By no means was this vast fraternization universal; it was common in those parts of the line held by Saxons, Bavarians, Silesians, Hannoverians, Pomeranians, Württembergers, and the like; but where the warlike Prussians held the trenches there was little or no celebration, and shooting was the order of the day. And, as historian Denis Winter points out, the contacts, at least on the part of the British, were characterized by suspicion: "The English respected a brave and resourceful enemy, but there was no love or liking." For his part, Adolf Hitler was appalled at the behavior: "There should be no question of something like that during the war," he wrote.

Be that as it may, word of the unofficial truce began to filter back to higher headquarters, and around nightfall runners were sent rushing to the trenches of both sides with orders calling for an immediate halt to such chumminess and threatening stern measures against any officer who permitted it to continue. It is a wonder what would have happened if, all at once, everyone had disobeyed them. In any case they didn't, and next morning the killing began again as usual.

Not long before midnight, December 31, all along the line the Germans unleashed a terrific volley of rifle fire. The British quickly understood that it was not aimed at them, but was meant to celebrate the New Year. They soon returned the favor, not that there was anything much to celebrate. It had been six weeks since the last great battles for Ypres had come to a growling close and the Germans, now reduced in numbers—both by transfers to the east and casualties—were more or less secure behind their trenches, protected by their large quantities of machine guns, each of which could equal the fire of an entire rifle platoon. (Ironically enough, both the machine gun and barbed wire—the two weapons most responsible for the stalemate on the Western Front—were American inventions, which the Americans would ultimately have to confront when they entered the war.)[1]

The British were now settling down to the harsh business of trench life and of finding ways to either annoy the Germans, keep them pinned down, or, possibly, crack their lines. It was quickly apparent that the British needed some kind of artillery weapon for up close and immediate use in the trenches, since dependence on artillery batteries far in the rear was unreliable—telephone lines were all too frequently cut by German artillery and runners were all too often shot down. A Cambridge history professor actually submitted a design for an ancient Roman-style catapult, but when the contraption was built it did not work well. Finally, Haig's First Army workshops began fabricating a crude version of a trench mortar. It was simply a metal tube—often sewer pipe—welded at one end, into which charges and an explosive projectile were dropped. If successful, the projectile would be hurled into the air and presumably explode on the German lines. As it turned out, it was almost as dangerous to the men firing it as it was to the Germans. By the end of the year, though, the frontline troops would have in their arsenal a formidable weapon in the form of the Stokes mortar. Invented by Sir Wilfrid Stokes, it was a simple and effective weapon with a built-in primer and adjustable screw-type elevation that could lob a twenty-pound projectile up to a thousand yards, with shells color-coded to indicate the distances they would travel. It was capable of firing twenty rounds a minute; by the end of the war there would be a hundred of these for every mile of British-held trench. The Germans already had their own trench mortar, a thing known as the Minenwerfer (mine thrower). It lobbed a drumlike projectile (which the British called a "flying pig") ten

---

1. The Germans adapted the American munitions designer Hiram Maxim's machine gun and at the outset of the war had more than five times the numbers that the British and French had. This was later rectified. The British used the Vickers machine gun, similar to the Maxim. Both were water cooled and fired at a rate of 500–600 rounds per minute. The French employed an adaptation of the Hotchkiss machine gun, air cooled, but with a similar rate of fire. One problem with the water-cooled guns was that there was sometimes not enough available water and on occasion the gunners had to urinate into the water jacket to keep the weapon from overheating.

times larger than the British version, which made a peculiar and widely dreaded *woof, woof, woof* noise as it tumbled slowly through the air and blew a crater in the ground bigger than an elephant. There was practically no protection against it if it landed in your trench; you just took your chances.

The Germans had hand grenades, too, which the British called "potato mashers." They consisted of an explosive charge contained in a metal casing attached to a wooden stick and timed to burst with a four-second fuse. And it looked like a potato masher. To counter this, the British began putting together "jam tin" grenades: jury-rigged devices in which timed explosives were put into used food containers equipped with a fuse and tossed forty or so yards at the enemy (and which too often blew up in the thrower's face). By the end of 1915 the British would have in their hands the manufactured Mills grenade, shaped like a pineapple, but much smaller, and by the end of the war tens of millions of these had been used to blast Germans from their positions.

Sniping quickly evolved into a deadly specialty. Both sides used loopholes, shields made of plated steel with a hole drilled through it, so the sniper in his trench could peep out at prospective targets. At first, some British soldiers employed the extremely powerful rifles used by safari guides to kill elephants and rhinoceroses. If the bullet from one of these even hit the metal plate of the German sniper's loophole it would shove it into his face, maiming him, but the enormous recoil of those rifles sometimes separated the shoulder of the shooter, or caused other injuries. German snipers had the advantage of mounting their rifles with sophisticated optical telescopes, which Germany was famous for manufacturing. The Germans also cunningly organized their snipers into separate two-man units—one the spotter, the other the shooter—and kept them in the same sector for weeks on end, even when other troops were being rotated. This gave the Germans the advantage of having a sniper who knew every bump, indentation, and blade of grass in his zone of fire. Often snipers camouflaged themselves and crept out into no-man's-land to do their hard business closer to the enemy. To avoid snipers, both armies began using periscopes to see what the other side was up to, but if a sniper's bullet hit the lens of the periscope it often sent glass shards into the eye of the man looking through it.

All this had become the reality of the Western Front, in Flanders and elsewhere, as the war moved inexorably through the winter and toward the spring of 1915. On a happier note, during the winter a young infantry lieutenant named Bruce Bairnsfather had an inspiration. A longtime amateur artist before the war, Bairnsfather conjured up a cartoon character known as Old Bill, which came to delight the entire British army with its wry depiction of life in the trenches. It was picked up by a popular magazine and circulated up and down the line all during the war. Old Bill or "Old Walrus Face," as he came to be known, was as hapless a soldier as ever lived and became as beloved as Bill Mauldin's Willie and Joe were to American GIs in World War II. Everyone from privates to generals could empathize with Bill as he endured shell fire, sniping, army food, work parties, and the like. It was a small entertainment, amid the grotesqueries of the war, but it made the men smile and took their minds off ghastly things for a moment or two.

Chapter Six ★

Everyone knew it had to start up again in earnest once springtime arrived and the ground thawed out. The Allies were unwavering in their determination to attack the Germans, and with fairly good reason. They were losing thousands of men each and every day merely through "wastage," the name coined by British Headquarters to describe all the killings, woundings, maimings, accidents, injuries, and illnesses that were the by-products of static trench warfare along a 450-mile front. (The Germans, of course, experienced this same gruesome phenomenon, but were helpless to relieve it by any attempted breakthrough since they had their hands full on the Russian Front.)

For the British Expeditionary Force, however, the situation at least was not as bad as it had been. Help, for one thing, was on the way. Though the Old Army, which had taken the field the past August, had been virtually destroyed, there were now some 350,000 British soldiers in France and Flanders. This was the result of the continuing arrivals of those remaining Old Army battalions that had been stationed in the far-flung corners of the empire, reinforced by drafts from some of the territorial battalions in Great Britain. Not only that, but the dominions and colonies themselves were sending strong forces. Even as the First Battle of Ypres was winding down, in addition to the large corps from India that was already in the field an entire Canadian corps was sailing for the Western Front, and others were soon to be on the way from South Africa, Australia, and New Zealand (though these last two would be diverted to participate in the disastrous attack at Gallipoli, fruit of Kitchener's "operations elsewhere" policy).

Yet in these early months all was not well with the caliber of many replacement troops being sent over from England. When the call had gone out for recruits, many former soldiers and ex-militiamen signed up, a number of them for the pay but with no real idea of the horror and stresses they would encounter on the Western Front. Knowing how desperately troops were needed, the enlistment centers often forwarded these men out to the front as "drafts," without proper training or examination. The results, during the early months of 1915, were disappointing. A veteran company commander in a regular-army regiment—the Royal Irish Rifles— wrote, "On the whole, I like all my men, and I think they like me, but I want to get quit of all my old rum-swillers who should never have been enlisted. I have one man who hasn't a tooth in is head. I confess that with my Company I sincerely hope I shall see little of [the war]. So many of them are far too old and stiff to move quickly; they can't run, much less make a charge. We all loud and strong curse the War Office, the recruiting officers and the Commanding Officers for sending out drafts of such miserable things."

Meantime, in early March, just south of Ypres, the British attacked at Neuve Chapelle with no result other than gaining "a slice of ground about the size of a moderate farm," and nearly 12,000 casualties. But at least they learned something; namely, that the artillery ammunition shortage was severely hampering any potential effort to expel the Germans from French and Belgian soil.

With the arrival of the Canadian Corps, beginning in February and stretching through March, 1915, the BEF now took over from the French the entire length of line in the northern part of the Salient and, to the profound regret of many, would remain responsible for holding it for the duration of the war. Because of the shortages of artillery shells, no large-scale operations were contemplated for the time being, but British Headquarters busied itself planning so-called limited attacks to wrest a particular piece of ground or a terrain feature from which the Germans were annoying them. One of these, perhaps the most notorious, was known simply as Hill 60.

Canada first presented itself on the battlefields of Flanders when a battalion of Princess Patricia's Canadian Light Infantry, 1,098 strong, took over a section of trenches on a snowy February 24, 1915, five days after they had landed on the continent. The "Princess Pats" were a brand-new regiment formed as the war began by a millionaire from Montreal named Hamilton Gault, who paid for it from his own pocket. The regiment took its name from the daughter of Canada's Governor-General, the Duke of Connaught, a son of Queen Victoria. Its ranks were composed of many former British servicemen who had immigrated to North America and it was led by high-ranking officers of the Crown who had been serving on the duke's staff in Canada.

Among the Princess Pats who arrived at Ypres was a forty-eight-year-old infantry captain named Agar Adamson who had fought in the Boer War but, despite his age, he was certainly no "miserable thing," as the officer of the Royal Irish Rifles had lamented about his own aging troops. In fact, Adamson produced an extraordinary diary and collection of letters to his wife, which, like that of Willie Fraser of the Gordon Highlanders, allows us to follow the contiguous exploits of yet another single soldier as he makes his way through the maze of four years' fighting in the Ypres Salient.

Captain Adamson himself was quite an interesting character. He came from a well-to-do though not wealthy Canadian family, but was educated at Cambridge, where he excelled at horsemanship and athletics, if not necessarily his studies. Returning from the Boer War at the age of thirty-three he married a beautiful and very rich young debutante, Mabel Cawthra, and it is to her that his remarkably erudite war letters are addressed. He always headed them "My dear Mabel," and signed off with "Ever thine." By the time Adamson reached Ypres he was middle-aged, stout, almost blind in one eye from a sporting accident, and wore a monocle, hardly the typical figure of an infantry line officer. But he was competent, of good humor, with a twinkle in his good eye and a wry smile, and his men liked and respected him; at his age he must surely have been a father figure.

Several weeks after their arrival, the Princess Pats went into battle in "some very bad" trenches near St. Eloi, thirty yards opposite the soldiers of the ferocious Prussian Guard—they who eschewed the Christmas Truce. At the time, the battlefield was considered more or less "inactive," and it was here that Captain Adamson got his first taste of World War I: "Dear Mabel, It is beyond my powers to describe what has happened in the last 4 days, but I know if I read what I am going to write, I doubt if I would be able to believe it was not written by a liar or the ravings of a lunatic."

He tells of his arrival in the trenches and the relief of those who had been manning them. "We went in with 28 men after crawling in the mud for about a mile. The trench consisted of sandbags about 5 feet high and no trench whatever. I counted about 25 bodies, French, German and English, including one officer of the Leicester regiment. This trench has been going for about three months." He tells of being unable to bury the dead because of gunfire; as well, his men could not improve the trench by digging it out because the French had interred the corpses of their men (who had been killed within the trench) in the floor of the trench system itself. He remarked on the smell, and added, " I suppose one can accustom oneself to anything."

He went on: " In my trench I lost 6 killed and 21 wounded (this out of the detachment of 28). Poor Colquhoun who went out alone in the dark to place his snipers, never came back. The Kings Royal Rifle Corps report having found him in the German sap in front of the trenches with 6 bullets in his head."

Major Gault, who had founded and financed the regiment, was shot badly in the wrist. Another officer had three fingers shot off and a major named Ward was shot through the head and later died.

At one point a squad of Royal Engineers arrived with orders to dig under Adamson's trench through to the German trench, only ten yards away. These men were new, not only to the engineers but to the army. "They got frightened at the rifle fire and when they came to a dead Frenchman refused to dig further. I had our men remove him and they started again and came back to me to say they had hit another dead man. They were shaking and crying, so I sent them back to the support trenches ¾ of a mile in the rear as they were having a bad effect on my men. We could hear the Germans talking and sapping in front of us. A constant rifle fire was kept up at our breastwork."

For the next two days there was almost continuous shooting, machine-gunning, grenade throwing, and, from the German trenches, mortar fire. Replacements were sent to Captain Adamson as his casualties mounted. At one point the battalion commander suggested doubling Adamson's strength, "but when he saw the conditions of the trench, he saw it could not hold with the slightest pinching, 28 men." By his last morning in the trench, Adamson found himself, "with 2 dead men, 1 (telephone) operator, 17 men (and) one badly wounded man, his leg shot to pieces." They were due to be relieved, but the problem was, now, how to get out of the trench without everyone being killed. Between all of them they had only one working rifle; mud and malfunctions had rendered the rest inoperative, and their telephone line had been cut by German artillery. All they could do was lie huddled in the trench. It was finally decided that just after dark they would crawl out through a drainage ditch, about 100 yards away. When Adamson gave the signal, he and his men threw away their greatcoats (the coat when waterlogged weighed ninety pounds) and began crawling to the drainage ditch, which, to their disgust, they found filled with foul water and "full of dead bodies, including horses," some of which had been there for three months. Somehow, even with the Germans firing on them, most made it through.

Later Adamson recorded, "I got the men some tea and Rum. None of us ever expected to get out, our only salvation was that the Germans had no idea how weak we were. All the men on both days behaved splendidly and particularly those with me for the last spell; with the exception of the bomb thrower, who was a Royal Engineer and in a dreadful state of nerves, poor fellow. I suppose he could not help it, but one man like that under said conditions is a danger, when men are trying to save their [own] nerves." Thus was a soldier's baptism of fire, during a "quiet" time in the Ypres Salient.

Hill 60, which the British were so determined to occupy, was not really a hill at all but a mound of dirt 60 meters tall that had been created many years earlier from the spoilage of digging out the cut for the Ypres-Comines railway. Over time, trees, grasses, and flowers had sprouted on the hill and it had become known locally as Cote des Amants, a sort of lover's lane. Two similar but lower mounds of dirt were nearby, known as the Caterpillar, which lay behind the German lines, and the Dump, which lay behind the British. During the late autumn battles French troops had lost these less than impressive heights. And now the Germans were enjoying them as excellent artillery observation posts to register a devastating fire on the British positions and on Ypres itself. Hill 60, in fact, was the highest point on the Messines Ridge. Thus it was decreed by High Headquarters that Hill 60 must be retaken. On the face of it, it seemed a reasonable proposition, if such bloodthirsty endeavors can ever be described as "reasonable."

Before the British attack on Hill 60 could get under way, some curious and excruciatingly difficult preparations had to be undertaken. These were the beginnings of what would soon become perhaps the most stupendous physical enterprise in the history of warfare: massive underground tunneling to explode great mines under the enemy's positions. Mines, with their sudden devastating shock effects, had been utilized for years; during the waning days of the American Civil War, for instance, when the Union army was besieging the Confederates in their trenches around Petersburg, Virginia, General U. S. Grant had authorized the establishment of a tunneling operation composed of miners from the Pennsylvania coal fields to dig under the Confederate fortifications and place explosives there.[1]

Now, fifty years after that, a unique figure appeared on the scene. He was Major J. (Jack) Norton Griffiths, a forty-two-year-old millionaire adventurer and member of Parliament. Griffiths owned an engineering firm that had constructed many of the underground networks of small, narrow tunnels carrying water pipes, sewer lines, telephone cables, and electrical wires under English cities. Jack Griffiths's operations were markedly

1. Unfortunately for Grant, when the mine blew up there were not enough reserve troops to breach the gap and the troops (many of them black soldiers) who assaulted the stunned Confederates found themselves being shot down in droves inside the enormous crater created by the explosion.

different from the massive commercial mining enterprises that dotted the countrysides of Great Britain and other parts of the empire in which large tunnels were required to extract iron, coal, and precious metal ores from the ground. To drill beneath the streets of cities for such things as pipes and cables, all that was required was an orifice as small as 2 feet by 3 feet instead of great excavations tall enough for men to stand up and move around in and cart out tramcars of ores. And instead of pickaxes or drilling machines, Griffiths employed a small army of men who were called "clay kickers."

It worked this way: the clay kicker crawled into the small tunnel and lay back on a device known as "the cross." This was a piece of wood shaped like a cross and tilted at about a 45-degree angle so that the kicker was upright but tilted backward and facing the soil to be "kicked." Upon his feet he strapped on steel spades known as "grafting devices," and then commenced to dig out the clay with his feet, the cross being moved forward when necessary. The lumps of clay were removed by a man lying next to him and passed back to other men who took them out of the tunnel in sandbags or in some cases handcarts. It was dirty, dangerous, strenuous, and very unpleasant work, but with rotations around the clock clay kickers could tunnel a steady ten feet to fifteen feet per day toward the enemy lines.

Griffiths had become aware that the soil beneath the Ypres battlefields was composed mostly of clay—and thus ideal for his type of tunneling—and immediately proposed to the army that he assemble a detachment of clay kickers and employ them in mining operations on the front. Unfortunately, nobody in the army understood what "clay kicking" was and at first his proposal was met with skepticism; perhaps more so when he got down on the floor of various staff headquarters and demonstrated the technique to an astonished group of senior officers.

Soon, however, the Germans began successfully exploding their own mines against the British front farther south in France, which caused severe consternation at headquarters. Griffiths made his case to Secretary of War Kitchener himself, declaring that it was too much to ask men who were being shot at from the ground and shelled from the air to endure the ominous possibility that at any moment they could be blown to smithereens from beneath the earth. The men in the trenches had become so nervous, in fact, that they began to construct rudimentary underground "listening devices" to try to detect German mining. One of these consisted of filling a large oil drum with water; in the icy Flanders winter, men in the trenches would take turns sticking their ear into the freezing water to see if they heard any activity within the earth.

Griffiths finally won his point in January, 1915, by marching into the office of Secretary of War Kitchener and giving his "clay kicking" demonstration on the floor. To Griffiths's understandable shock, the reaction of "The Earl of Kartoum" was reported to have been, "Get me 10,000 of these men." In early February, miners from Great Britain, in the army or out, were formed up in tunneling companies; before the war was over there would be 60,000 of them in the Mining Corps working, molelike, in the ground.

In any case, it had been decided that exploding mines beneath the German positions on Hill 60 at Ypres would facilitate its recapture and the clay kickers were set to the task. It was a tormenting experience, especially for men who only a few scant weeks earlier had been peaceful civilians. First of all, the mining equipment issued to them by the army was outrageously outdated—some of it had been in storage since the Crimean War ended, more than fifty years earlier! Worse, they had been given little if any of the training of regular recruits, not even rifle practice, and were thus woefully unprepared for what they found at the front. One unit of the clay kickers being led up to the firing line under the cover of darkness had their guide killed and, in the confusion, they fled back to their starting point. When they were finally rounded up and reached their trench, fifty yards from Hill 60, they found themselves exposed to constant rifle and shell fire; not only that, but no sooner had they started to dig than they began to encounter the inevitable decaying corpses, which broke apart when they tried to remove them and had to be put piecemeal into sandbags and heaved out of the trench.

Nevertheless, working around the clock in eight-hour shifts, the clay kickers began to make steady progress. A main shaft was dug down sixteen feet and then a tunnel started out under no-man's-land toward Hill 60. Working by candlelight, the men soon began to experience serious oxygen shortages. A bellows system was rigged up, pumping in fresh air by hose, but still they suffered the effects of oxygen depletion: headaches, dizziness, nausea, blackouts. A few of the men were known to have had their hair turn white. At one point they began to hear the disturbing sounds of Germans counter-mining toward them and one day actually broke through into a German tun-nel. When an officer went down to investigate and shone a flashlight into the hole, he was greeted by a pistol blast, which tore through his jacket but luckily did not injure him. This was apparently the first incident of what would come to be known as "The War Underground." Before it was over, hundreds of men would be shooting, knifing, grenading, and strangling one another in the very bowels of the earth.

By April 17, a pleasant spring evening, the operation was complete. In the several "clay kicked" tunnels beneath Hill 60 the British had placed thousands of pounds of explosives. At exactly 7 P.M. a plunger on an elec-tric detonator was pushed and an enormous eruption went off: dirt, lum-ber, sandbags, rifles, ration boxes, Germans, and parts of Germans were sent hurling more than 100 yards into the air. At least one curious Tommy was killed by flying debris when he stood up in his trench to see the show.

Even before the roar of the mine had died away, a tremendous British artillery fusillade began to explode on Hill 60. Then, British soldiers with bayonets fixed began to leave their trenches to the tune of bugles and cross into no-man's-land. Most of the Germans on Hill 60 had simply been blown to bits or buried alive by the explosion, and of the stunned hundred or so who survived, most were bayoneted by soldiers of the Royal West Kent regiment. The British occupied the hill and had lost only seven men, including the luckless observer killed by flying debris, versus a thousand or more Germans. But soon the melancholy and all too familiar complaint of "someone had blundered" began to find its way into conversations and correspondence.

As the British Official History points out, by taking Hill 60 the plan-ners had, in effect, created a new and dangerous bulge, or salient, in the al-ready dangerous Ypres Salient, thereby exposing those soldiers manning it to fire on three sides, in particular from the Caterpillar. The Germans, of course, wasted no time deducing this unfortunate fact and commenced a steady and deadly shell fire upon Hill 60 as well as launching a series of fran-tic counterattacks to regain the lost ground. So desperate and bitter was the fighting that four Victoria Crosses (the British equivalent of the Congressional Medal of Honor) were awarded, all the more remarkable since the turf in question involved little more than a couple of acres. And by this time the hill was barely a topographical feature anymore; the Official History points out: "The surface of Hill 60 was a medley of confluent mine and shell craters, strewn with broken timber and wire: and in this rubbish heap it was impossible to dig without disturbing the body of some British or German soldier." Nonetheless, the British held out against the incessant shelling and German counterattacks of increasing fury—sometimes five assaults a day.

While all this was going on at Hill 60 half a dozen miles south of Ypres, the balmy afternoon of April 22 had been oddly quiet for the Canadians and French colonial troops manning the trenches north of the Sailent. They were, in fact, awaiting orders for a major Allied attack against the Germans, which would hopefully drive them from Flanders. What the British High Command did not know was that the Germans had finally decided to launch a major attack of their own all along the Ypres Salient, in hopes of breaking the stalemate or at least improving their trench positions and kicking the British out of Ypres.

In part the German rationale for a major attack was to test a controversial and startling new weapon they had developed, about which we will hear much more. And, in part, it had to do with the arrival of the Canadian soldiers, which German General von Fabeck on the eve of his great final attack at First Battle of Ypres saw fit to lump in with the "Indians, Moroccans and other trash, feeble adversaries who surrender in great numbers if attacked with vigor." It is ironic that when those uncharitable words were uttered in November, the Canadians had not yet even arrived in Europe! In any event, the Germans were gambling that the new and untried Allied troops would be easy to crack.

Suddenly, at about 5 P.M., a furious German artillery barrage crashed down on the French positions to the northeast of Ypres, which were manned by a colonial division of Algerians, dressed in pantaloons and fezzes, and a territorial division of French Africans. At the same time, those Canadians who dared to peep over their parapets noticed a strange and menacing-

looking cloud, several miles long, rise up from the German lines and begin rolling across no-man's-land.

It was a heavy, low cloud, as far as the eye could see; they described it
variously as "greyish-yellow," or "greenish-yellow," and also as "two clouds
. . . which appeared to merge into each other." As the thing roiled toward
them, the Canadians were baffled. Some thought it was some kind of smoke;
others concluded a new type of gunpowder was being used by the German artillery. It was not long before the cloud reached the French lines to
the north, which were joined to the Canadians' immediate left. As the dense
cloud enveloped the French, nothing could be seen of them. Suddenly, the
Canadians heard the French fire begin to slacken, then stop altogether. Not
long afterward, the French artillery also ceased to fire. Those Canadians
nearest the French began to experience burning in their eyes, and coughing, and then inability to breathe; in effect, strangling.

Men in the reserve trenches in the rear were shocked to see thousands of the Algerian and African troops streaming past, eyes rolled up
white, stumbling, staggering, falling, clutching their throats. Those few who
could speak at all were gasping *"gaz! gaz! gaz!"* On their heels were seen
thousands of Germans crossing no-man's-land behind the gas cloud. Even
though they were receiving no fire to their immediate front, the Germans
were coming on tentatively, staying well behind the cloud. Meantime, the
dimension of what was happening stunned those witnessing the pathetic
condition of the French soldiers who had managed to escape. As a Canadian artilleryman, Major Andrew McNaughton, described it: "They literally were coughing their lungs out; glue was coming out of their mouths.
It was a very disturbing, very disturbing sight."

And that wasn't the worst of it; many of the Frenchmen already lay dead
or dying in their trenches because the gas, being heavier than air, naturally settled
there and suffocated them on the spot. Many of those who escaped thought that
if they just got to fresh air, they would be all right, but that wasn't the case at
all. They staggered into dressing stations vomiting and turning blue from
suffocation. There the doctors and orderlies waited upon them helplessly, since
they had no idea how to treat gas injuries. The gassed men could only gape at
the medics pitifully, most unable to speak, staring with terror-filled eyes,
coughing greenish-yellow froth and blood. Some of the men died quickly,

others took days, their faces and extremities turning from a bluish color to a dark green and finally to black as they drowned in their own fluids. In an effort to find out the cause of their deaths, the doctors performed autopsies on some of the men. What they found was chilling: lungs literally bursting, spongy, and filled with albumin and the vessels of their brains badly swollen.

It did not take the Canadians long to figure out what was causing these horrifying things. Shortly after the attack a Canadian Sanitary Corps officer with a background in chemistry noticed that the brass uniform buttons worn by men who had been exposed to the gas near the French line had begun to tarnish green, a sure sign of chlorine. It was quickly concluded that as at least a temporary measure, men experiencing a gas attack should urinate on their handkerchiefs and hold them over their mouth and nose. The theory was that the ammonia in urine would to some extent neutralize chlorine gas.

There was no real excuse by the high commands for having allowed the men to be gassed in the first place: both the French and the British had ample warnings that the Germans were planning a gas attack, and an imminent one, at that.

A month earlier German prisoners had mentioned to their French interrogators that their army was preparing some kind of poison-gas attack, but that they knew not much else about it. The information was published in an intelligence summary, but little was done. Then, on April 13, a week before the attack, a German deserter wandered into the lines and willingly provided detailed information on preparations for the gas attack—even handing over to the Allies a respirator, which had been issued to the special German troops who were responsible for releasing the gas. This information was also published. The commander of the French 11th Division, General Ferry, into whose hands the German deserter had fallen, warned both his superiors and the British, suggesting that they shell the German lines to explode the gas. Instead, he was reprimanded for having stepped out of channels to alarm the Allies and told to put such "nonsense" out of his mind.[2] Not only

2. After the gas attack General Ferry was relieved of command because, according to the historian Jack Ward, "he had been correct." In 1932 Ferry published a magazine article about the gas attack, thoughtlessly revealing the name of the German deserter, who, after the war, had repatriated to Germany under the guise of having been captured. The German was promptly arrested and sentenced to ten years' imprisonment; when, in the following year, the Nazis came into power, he was not heard from again.

that, but a German high-priority requisition for "twenty thousand respirators" for "asphyxiating gas" was intercepted. Furthermore, a Belgian spy reported that gas was going to be used. Still no one acted. Then, a few days before the first gas attack at Ypres, during the bitter fighting for Hill 60, British soldiers reported experiencing some sort of "lachrymatorious-like symptoms." Evidently during all the artillery shelling upon the hill, one or more of the gas cylinders had been broken. Still, nothing was done.

Perhaps this was negligence; perhaps it was simply because no one knew what to do about it. In fact no one in the Allied armies had the faintest idea what a gas attack would be like—what it would look like, what its effects would be, how to prevent it or defend against it. In any event, with all the shelling and shooting going on up and down the lines, it is possible that the Allies simply swept the matter under the rug, hoping the rumors were unfounded. Nevertheless, a dreadful new weapon had been introduced to the world, which, in the months and years ahead, would become an abominable feature in practically all battles of the war.

And now the Second Battle of Ypres had begun, with a spontaneous, bloody momentum all its own.

The Germans had begun contemplating poison-gas warfare some months earlier at the suggestion of Dr. Fritz Haber, a chemist who had been elevated from the NCO ranks to captain and put in charge of chemical operations. Germany had employed tear gas, sneezing gases, and other irritants in France, but to little or no effect. Chlorine, however, was a different matter: it was a deadly gas that caused the lungs to quit absorbing oxygen. What was more, because of its huge chemical and dye industry Germany manufactured more than 85 percent of the world's chlorine. Haber was still working on a process to fill artillery shells with chlorine, but it was decided to release the compressed gas at Ypres from large cylinders. Crown Prince Rupprecht of the Sixth Army wanted no part in that sort of warfare, but Duke Albert of Württemberg, commander of the Fourth Army, which had been so dramatically repulsed during the First Battle of Ypres, had no such compunctions. To that end some 6,000 of the cylinders were brought to the Salient.

The problem with releasing gas from cylinders was that the wind had to be just right, lest the gas blow back into the Germans' own trenches. And since the prevailing wind in the Salient blew off the ocean, west to east, this became doubly dangerous. At first the cylinders were located to the south of Ypres, along the lines that included Hill 60, but after frustrating weeks of waiting for a favorable wind, 5,300 of them were finally moved to the north of the city, in a line from Poelcappelle to Steenstraat, where the Salient curved west and the German line faced south. There they waited again for the right wind to blow; it was an exasperating interlude, since the battalions designated for the attack would have to go through all the preparations—mental and physical—of gearing up for the assault, only to have it called off at the last moment because of the wind.

Late in the afternoon of April 22 the wind finally blew in the prescribed manner and the gas was released. If it had blown just so that morning, it is likely that the Germans, with many more hours of daylight to conduct their attack, would have swept through Ypres and driven the British from the Salient, if not to the sea. As it was, they came close to doing it anyway. When the French colonials fled, they had left a four-mile-wide gap in the line, through which nearly 50,000 Germans penetrated two miles into Allied territory. By twilight there was virtually nothing to have stopped them from capturing Ypres and all the army artillery and vast supply and support dumps and stores, as well as sweeping left to capture the Canadian and British divisions holding the line to the south. Nothing except three things: First, once the Germans had pierced the Allied lines, they stopped to regroup. Since they suddenly faced no opposition at all, no one had contemplated what to do next. At that point, and with night coming on, the Germans decided to dig in. Second, the attack had been ordered more or less as an experiment to see if the gas worked; because no one had dreamed of its enormous success, there were no reserves in place to keep the battle going. It was, as several German high commanders later admitted, one of the gravest mistakes of the war. Third was the Canadians, whom General von Fabeck had earlier seen fit to describe as "trash, feeble adversaries." He would soon be eating his words. Even with all the confusion that attended the breaking of the French line and the partial gassing of the Canadians adjoining it, the officers did not panic and neither did the men, in their first real battle. Hugely outnumbered, the Canadian troops in support and in reserve and those in rest, too, were rushed up to plug the gap the Germans had made. This they did magnificently.

Among the units that had recently been relieved in the trenches and were enjoying a bit of "rest" behind the lines (this included being shelled out of a warehouse where they were billeted) was the Tenth Battalion Canadian Light Infantry. These were composed mostly of westerners, men from the wild and woolly provinces of Calgary, Winnipeg, and Alberta. They were commanded by thirty-five-year-old Colonel Russell Boyle, an Alberta rancher, politician, and veteran of the Boer War. When the Germans attacked, the Tenth Battalion was one of many that were rushed to the front.

With Colonel Boyle leading the way on his horse, they marched toward the fight about 7 P.M. on a road that was being heavily shelled. However, the mood of the battalion was one of gaiety; they were anxious to prove themselves in their first big fight. Along the way they passed hundreds of pitiful civilians lugging their few belongings, who were driven from their homes in the little towns and villages overrun by the German onslaught. As they got nearer the battle area the lingering gas was very strong, though not incapacitating. When it finally reached brigade headquarters, the battalion, which had assumed it would be defending against the Germans, was instead told to counterattack them at a place called Kitchener's Wood. By then it was nearly 11 P.M. and the attack was scheduled to take place in half an hour. A chaplain who had come along to make himself useful proclaimed to the men: "It's a great day for Canada!"

The Tenth Battalion formed up alongside a fellow battalion, the kilted Canadian Highlanders, and the order was given to move forward in silence. It went well until they came upon a thick hedge and a German flare suddenly burst above them; then all hell broke loose. Fire from multiple machine guns raked across the Canadians' front ranks, mowing down men by the dozens. One man remembered the bullets sounding "like a hailstorm on a zinc roof." Another man was astonished that "somehow a few of us were missed, while others were cut in half by the stream of lead." At that point there were two choices, fall back or push on; the Canadians pushed on.

First they stormed a German trench at the edge of Kitchener's Wood and murdered its occupants with gun butts and bayonets, and then on into the forest itself. There, according to Tenth Battalion historian Daniel Dancocks, "More hand-to-hand combat ensued. Dozens of separate, individual battles took place among the bullet splintered oak trees which hid a number of sandbagged machine-gun posts." By now, the battalion had lost most of its officers, including all four company commanders.

It was past twelve and the night was black except for the constantly flickering muzzle flashes that stabbed out from seemingly everywhere. The two battalions kept fighting their way forward, clearing the wood of Germans. When they finally got to the other side, the question became, What to do next? There were still a lot of Germans in front of them and their flanks were dangerously exposed. It was decided that since they could not hold the wood, they would return to the first trench they encountered, on the south side, and hold it. At sunup, a nose count revealed that the Tenth Battalion had lost 613 men out of the 816 that they had started with the night before, including their commander, Colonel Boyle, who was mortally wounded. The officer who would replace him, a Major Ormond, wrote: "The colonel got five bullets from a machine gun in his left groin— made a wonderful pattern in a radius of two and a half inches."

All that day the Tenth Battalion underwent what in everybody's opinion was a hideous ordeal. The Germans began to shell them in the morning and the shelling never stopped. Men were being blown up in fives and sixes. Worse were the jammed rifles. To a soldier, one of the worst things possible is having a weapon that can't be relied upon. The Canadian Army, at the insistence of the crackpot Canadian war minister, was armed with the Ross Rifle, Mark III, instead of the standard British Lee-Enfield. Because of tooling differences, it would not accept British ammunition, even though it was the same caliber, and would consistently jam. One officer reported that it took four men to keep one rifle working in his section of the trench. The problem was endemic to the entire Canadian Army and it is a wonder that they accomplished anything at all. Meantime, the day after the German attack, Duke Albert of Württemberg, commanding the Fourth Army, had decided that the Allied position in the Salient had become untenable, owing to the crushed French positions and the German advance. Thus he fully expected the British and French to withdraw and, almost as an afterthought, concluded that his next move should be against Poperinge, the sprawling Allied supply base and rest center about eight miles west of Ypres. To accomplish this, he had marshaled thirty-four battalions and a five-to-one superiority in artillery against just twelve Canadian battalions. Next day, Saturday, April 24, the technical specialists released another cloud of gas, directed at the Canadian lines. The Germans launched their attack to get into the British rear.

What the duke did not know was that, far from intending to abandon the Salient, the British were frantically calling up troops for a counterattack to drive the Germans back. Thus, when the Germans launched their assault, they were met with fierce resistance and no significant breakthrough was accomplished. However, the Canadian lines were forced back; the towns of St. Julian and Gravenstafel were lost, as was Pilckem Ridge, Steenstraat, and the Frezenberg Ridge, all of which would figure prominently during the fighting in the years to come.

By urinating in their handkerchiefs and clapping them over their noses and mouths as a defense against the gas, the men of the Tenth Battalion grimly hung on to a second position near the Gravenstafel Ridge, after being ordered to retire from their trench near Kitchener's Wood. But the shelling, grenading, and rifle- and machine-gun fire continued to take their toll. By now the battalion was down to five officers and 151 men, including the arrival of two rear-echelon officers, a major and a captain, who volunteered to go forward into the fight in the capacity of lieutenants.

On Sunday, April 25, it was wisely determined by Brigade Headquarters that the Tenth Battalion's position was again perilous, exposed to fire from two sides and artillery shelling from Passchendaele and the newly captured St. Julian. A runner was sent ordering a retirement but he was shot down. As the Germans mercilessly whittled at the fragment of men that were left, and clawed their way toward surrounding them, the men in the trenches could see all too well what was about to happen to them. As a last gasp the surviving commander sent out a young lieutenant to inform Brigade Headquarters of their plight. He managed to sneak back in the dark, bringing an order for them to withdraw. "Without this order," the officer then in command later wrote, " I would have maintained my position and been annihilated."

★ Chapter Seven

When the invoices of bloodshed were finally tallied, it was found that of the 816 men of the Tenth Battalion Canadian Light Infantry who had gone into the Second Battle of Ypres only 98 remained, a staggering figure, but not an uncommon one; before it was over, losses of the entire Canadian Division totaled 6,037, nearly half of its authorized strength.

The Germans had failed to achieve a breakthrough and had failed to capture Ypres; they had made some gains in the northern part of the Salient, but stiffening British and French resistance was obviously making a strategic success impossible. Perhaps it might have been better to leave well enough alone. But the Germans did not think this. Neither did the British, nor did the French. Stubbornness was a characteristic of both sides of this conflict.

French general Ferdinand Foch, charged by the French commander in chief Joseph Joffre with coordinating the Allied armies in Belgium—British, French, and Belgian—recommended immediate counterattacks to regain the lost ground. From the map room of his headquarters at St. Omer, Sir John French agreed; thus British reinforcements were hastily organized from divisions in the south sectors of the Salient—including regiments that had suffered so heavily at Hill 60—and were rushed northward immediately opposite Ypres itself and moved into position to attack. What ensued was a sort of universal slaughter, a wild and uncoordinated sacrifice of human life. And so, instead of just petering out with a growl, the battle began to roar and rage again along the entire Salient.

Meanwhile, Duke Albert of Württemberg, commander of the German Fourth Army, remained convinced that the Allies would soon abandon the Salient. Unfortunately for him, the British did not see it quite that way.

Duke Albert had been so impressed by the success of his gas attack—limited though it was—that he decided to try it again, and to some extent it worked. In the dawn hours of April 24 a German bombardment opened, followed by another great cloud of the noxious chlorine gas. By day's end, the Germans occupied St. Julian and the important high ground around it. The British regrouped to retake it, sending as the spearhead of their attack a newly arrived Indian division from Lahore. It started out dreadfully.

Someone had misinformed the Indians that the German lines were a mere 200 yards ahead of them. When they clambered out of their trenches they discovered to their dismay—and horror—that the Germans were more than ten times that distance away and, furthermore, that they had every inch of no-man's-land covered with interlocking machine guns and had already registered artillery fire down to the square foot. The Indian losses were frightful. Those who were not mown down or blown to bits clawed their way to within a couple of hundred yards of the German positions by midafternoon, where the Germans had another cruel surprise waiting. The wind again being favorable, they unleashed another gas cloud against the decimated and beleaguered Indians and with that they were forced to retire. It was becoming obvious at this early stage of the game that the primitive gas masks issued by the army during the past several days were woefully inadequate. The cotton-gauze masks—either soaked in a solution of bicarbonate of soda or urinated on—simply did not furnish sufficient protection against chlorine under any circumstances, let alone during an assault across no-man's-land.

While the Indian troops were enduring their agony, a disgraceful episode occurred in French lines adjacent to them. To provide a diversion for the Indian attack, the French commander ordered a regiment of colonial troops from Senegal to charge the Germans. According to historian Martin Gilbert, contact with the poison gas sent them into such a frenzy that they shot their own officers and ran away back to the rear areas where they proceeded to loot the supply dumps and rape the nurses at the casualty clearing stations. They were finally subdued by a brigade of British cavalry.

Over the next days many more of the futile counterattacks were made, but the results were always the same. The coffin makers were again pressed into overtime. Again and again in personal accounts men recorded how shocking and demoralizing it was—to be marched toward the battle area, guns booming in the distance, and having to pass by shops where other soldiers were busy sawing and nailing together coffin boards and wood crosses. It was beyond the bizarre.

Among those swept up in the Second Battle of Ypres was Captain Agar Adamson, of the Princess Pats, Canadian Light Infantry. From the regiment's positions in Polygon Wood, which abutted the Menin Road, he wrote to his wife Mabel on May 1 that there were 2,000 men digging at the back line trenches all night, taking shell fire from both flanks. Next day he reported that "For the last three months the regiments at rest have been building a most magnificent back line of trenches with drains, cement, bomb-proof dugouts and everything that could be devised, including wonderful wire entanglements. The army for months has been priding itself on this wonderful back line. They now find that it is not facing the right way and instead of facing the enemy, it is almost at the right angle to it. It is things like this that make one very angry and wonder how we are ever going to win the war . . . losing magnificent men for the want of a little common sense or at least judgment."

It was too true, and the British were pulling back. After the abortive counterattacks of the past week General Smith-Dorrien, British commander in the Salient, told General Foch that he was for withdrawing to a new line closer to Ypres. He suggested in the process that since it was the French who had lost the ground in the gas attack, it was up to them to regain it lest the British be forced to retire to more defensible positions. He said the same thing to his boss, Sir John French, but this perfectly reasonable assessment so infuriated Sir John that he sacked Smith-Dorrien (with whom he had been feuding ever since the British retreat from Mons) and replaced him as commander of Second Army with General Sir Herbert Charles Onslow Plumer, who was to become one of the most respected and effective generals of the war. But General Plumer quickly recognized that Smith-Dorrien had been right in the first place and ordered an immediate compression of the line by nearly three miles, to within a mile and a half of Ypres itself.

Unpalatable as a withdrawal was, considering the amount of Allied blood spilled over the lost ground, the move made good sense. First it realigned the front in concert with the new French positions in the north of the Salient; second, it eliminated at least some of the ominous "bulge" in the Salient itself, which was even more pronounced after the German attack of April 22. Finally, the new trenches, badly sited as they were in some cases, at least removed some of the helter-skelter twists and curves that had required many more men to man them than the new, straighter, and interconnected line.

In any case, Captain Adamson and the Princess Pats were ordered to hold Polygon Wood until the withdrawal could take place. This they did, but at a high cost, and then they retired themselves. "Everyone was wondering how long it would take the Germans to discover we had gone," Agar Adamson wrote, "some said a week." But at 4 A.M. next morning the Germans attacked them and thus began the Battle of Bellewaerde Ridge. It was a fast and furious fight—fast by World War I standards, since it lasted only two days. The man who had organized the Princess Pats, Hamilton Gault, had succeeded to its command but was again wounded and Adamson was put in charge.

The regiments on both sides of Adamson's were forced to retire, but the Pats kept on fighting. Under shell fire, Adamson wrote to his wife while standing in a water-filled ditch: "Fire from Maxims and artillery come from 3 different directions. I think a trapped rat would be a more accurate simile than the Knight in Alice in Wonderland. I forgot if the baseball bats did arrive. [He had asked his wife to send some to organize games for the men when they were moved back to rest positions.] They could very well be used here as a weapon of defence, when our ammunition runs out." He also reported that six of his men were in "what was called a 'state of collapse,'" and that two others "have gone mad and had to be disarmed."

The Princess Pats clung grimly and bloodily to their little piece of real estate and by the afternoon of May 8 reinforcements had been sent in and the line stabilized. However, the regiment had by then lost more than 80 percent of its men, including Captain Agar Adamson, who was shot through the shoulder. Within a few days he was evacuated to a hospital in London where he telegraphed Mabel, who was staying with relatives in London: "Arrived last night and am in Lady Ridley's Hospital, 10 Carleton House Terrace. I am only slightly wounded in the shoulder. Please bring a toothbrush and toothpaste and a package of Auto Strap Razor blades." Though he would remain on convalescent leave for five months, Agar Adamson's war was far from over.

One of the points that the Germans pressed particularly hard was Hill 60, where "2,000 British dead lay in an area the size of a large backyard garden." On May 5, after a stupendous bombardment and massed infantry charge, the Germans finally recaptured it. Among those regiments ordered to retake it were the Royal Irish Rifles. Commanding a company of the RIR was forty-two-year-old Captain Gerald Achilles Burgoyne, a descendant of the British General "Gentleman Johnny" Burgoyne, who had lost the pivotal Battle of Saratoga during the American Revolution. Captain Burgoyne had been much decorated in the Boer War and was a stern and little-forgiving officer (he was the one who described the replacements sent from England as "miserable things"). In his well-kept diary he complained bitterly of his Irishmen's sloth and penchant for drink, and even went so far as to banish their precious rum ration while in the firing trenches. To an Irishman, this was stern discipline indeed.

Burgoyne and his company were ordered forward after Hill 60 was lost, on a "hot summer day" in which "the larks were singing." Although Burgoyne had been in Flanders since December, and had endured all the daily shelling and shooting, this would be his first big fight; he describes the trek to the front lines. "As we dropped down alongside the railway embankment, we quickly came on the debris of the heavy fighting round here; for, burrowing into the embankment were, first a dressing station of the RAMC [Royal Army Medical Corps] and then a battalion of the Rifle Brigade, the litter round this latter, filthy beyond description, and I cannot understand any officers allowing their men to live in such insanitary and disgusting conditions when it was quite possible to have a camp clean and sanitary. In front of the dressing station we saw three dead bodies, awaiting burial, evidently died of wounds and, within a few yards more dead but no effort at burial. The men walking about amongst the corpses very callously. Apparently no one's job to bury them and no one cared."

As they got close to the front near Hill 60, they began to see the effects of poison gas: "All the grass and foliage around was bleached white, or a sickly yellow; all brass buttons turned black, and it even affected the bolt action of the rifles, corroding the steel apparently and making them stiff to work. A Major of the Bedfords led us into the trenches. A shell had blown in the left and he suggested we need not visit that part as there was a horrid mess there. I believe there were a number of poor fellows lying dead, horribly mutilated."

Burgoyne and his company occupied a trench designated 47; late that night he was told that his brigade was going to attack and try to retake Hill 60 at 2:30 A.M. His particular job was to recapture and secure the area between the adjoining trench, Trench 46. As long as the enemy held it, the main attack could not go forward. To accomplish this, Burgoyne and his men were presented with several boxes of "what until now we had only heard of: the 'jam tin bomb,'" and given instructions on its use.

So here Burgoyne found himself, in completely strange territory, in pitch-black dark, ordered to attack a place he'd never seen. His reaction was predictable: "So easy, so simple—in the room and over a map!" In his earlier briefing, the general commanding the brigade had informed him "that it was just wasting life to attempt Hill 60 again, as no one could hold it; but, he said, Army Headquarters wanted it re-taken and so he had to do it." Not very inspiring, and a lesser man might have gone berserk, but Burgoyne only recorded, "I often wondered how I'd feel if I was ordered to attack, but to my surprise I just felt a curiosity as to what would happen to me . . ."

As Burgoyne moved into position he encountered a lieutenant and a number of men from the Bedfordshire Regiment, which he was to relieve. His attack was a mere half hour away. The lieutenant informed him that his captain had just been killed and "I'm awfully sorry but I'm afraid I'll have to leave you to bury five of my men." Burgoyne simply stared at him: "I managed to swallow my wrath. The blighters couldn't even bury their own dead; and, by jove, they had not even removed their identity discs or papers. Told the poor fool to leave a sergeant and half a dozen men behind to collect their papers and bury them."

At precisely 2:20 A.M. Burgoyne sent a lieutenant and fifteen men to the objective, their hands and pockets full of the jam tin grenades. Immediately firing opened from the German positions. "Within a few minutes" the lieutenant returned, most of his men killed and himself wounded. "Told me the firing pins jammed in his grenades and he couldn't get them out. Had to make one more bid so I rushed out to the communication trench leading to 46 [which was open ground, since one could not navigate Trench 46 because of the bodies strewn inside it].

"The parapet which the brigadier so casually said we were to knock down loomed some eight feet high, very solid. What could I and three or four men have done, had we got up to it? My sergeant-major joined me. 'Come on, you . . .' he yelled, but there was no one to come on. I nearly cried with vexation. I was so sure we could have done it, and had promised the brigadier."

Suddenly everything turned to chaos. The main attack had started and firing broke out all along the front, including "some 17 machine guns in 46." Suddenly Burgoyne saw a flash and something hit him in the eye. He put his hand to his face and "found I was bleeding like a stuck pig." He decided to go back to the dressing station and have it attended, and then return. He took two men out with him, "one hit in the head, another with his hand blown off." As he left the trench his men said to him, "'Sure, ye are not hurt, Sorr,' and, 'Don't leave us long, Sorr,' and 'Come back to us again, Sorr.' It rather touched me."

When Burgoyne got to the dressing station a phone message came from his servant[1] saying that of the fifteen men he had sent to take the German position, six were dead and five wounded. Suddenly Burgoyne broke down. "My nerves were all on edge and just this rotten little wound brought all the winter hardships to a head and made me really break down."

---

1. British officers during the war had "servants," the equivalent of orderlies in the American army.

The doctors sent Burgoyne back to England; the wound in the eye was not very serious but he was suffering from something quite new to warfare, a phenomenon doctors had only recently begun to diagnose in the men. They classified it as "neurasthenia," first catalogued in the 1850s to describe the sometime mental derangement of railroad-wreck survivors. The soldiers had a better name; they called it "shell shock."

In 1914 there were fewer than 2,000 such cases in the British Army. In 1915 the number had grown into the tens of thousands and accounted for nearly 10 percent of all battle casualties. No one in the medical profession had seen anything like it. In past wars, battles had usually lasted a short time, a few hours or at most a day or two, and high explosives had only recently been developed. But now men were being ordered for days and weeks on end into battle areas where shells were almost constantly exploding and there exposed to all the horrors of the trenches, seeing men like themselves blown into pieces or shot to rags on a daily basis. Tennyson's spirit of the Light Brigade, "Theirs not to reason why, theirs but to do or die," might have some application to men riding bravely into artillery fire in a single cavalry charge, but it was irrelevant to men laid open to days, weeks, and months of such carnage. It was something the human mind was not equipped to handle; these men were being asked to do things that every instinct told them were unreasonable and unsafe. They did them anyway, but in a large number of cases the nerves, at some point, simply snapped.

Shell shock could take many forms: sometimes the men's motor systems just gave way, the legs or the arms would not work anymore. Sometimes their minds went blank and they could only sit or stand zombielike. Others had convulsions and had to be strapped down. Hallucinations were common and many men became incontinent. Trembling or shivering was one prevalent sign, with men clawing at their mouths and slobbering. Some went blind, some went deaf, some went dumb. Historian Denis Winter reported that sixty years after the war, in the 1970s, he visited an old veteran still confined to a mental hospital, "a man whose memory is perfect . . . up to 1917. Thereafter he can remember nothing. An explosion had wiped the recording mechanism from his life and hospitalized him from that day to this."

At first, military doctors did not consider shell shock a legitimate illness. They pointed to the small number of cases reported in 1914, when the army was composed of professional soldiers, versus the huge increase in 1915 when that army had been replaced with civilian volunteers. Medical men, let alone officers of the line, were baffled by the symptoms. Remember that Agar Adamson, before his wounding, had described how six of his men were in "what was called a state of collapse," and two others had "gone mad and had to be disarmed." But of course shell shock could strike anybody, including longtime professional officers like Captain Burgoyne, who was months in recovery.

Those who showed signs of "neurasthenia" were generally taken to recovery centers still within sound of the shelling and given large doses of physical education in hopes of snapping them out of it. Elaborate measures were put in place to ferret out faking, or "scrimshanking," as it was called. It was only later that the physicians concluded that only complete rest and sympathetic care in a proper facility far from the fighting helped many victims to recover and be returned to the front. Others never did; in fact, more than ten years after the war there were still some 65,000 former soldiers in British mental hospitals, and who knew how many others in France and Germany.

Of his own experience, Burgoyne remained bitter: "The whole of my little affair was a first rate example of bad staff management, and an example only too common. They were continually bringing men up and throwing them into an attack over ground they had never seen before, and with which they were unacquainted . . . it was a dark night and ignorant of the lay of the land I hardly knew the direction of the attack. The whole time I was out there I only on one occasion saw one of our Brigade Staff come round our trenches and I never heard of any of our Divisional Staff coming near them. The consequence was that the Staff were never in touch with the regimental officer— never in sympathy with him and appeared rather to look down on him for being shabby in appearance and at times very dirty."

Another familiar officer was also becoming disillusioned with the way things were being run. Captain Willie Fraser, who had recovered from his earlier wound during First Ypres, reappeared on the scene with his old regiment, the Gordon Highlanders. As luck would have it, they were among those sent into the fray at Hill 60 about a week after Captain Burgoyne was

wounded, quite possibily to the same trench. By now Willie had been promoted to company commander. He had recently gotten a severe shock
when, picking up a copy of the *London Daily Mail* in the trenches, he was
aghast to read that the family's great manor house in Scotland, Philorth,
had caught fire from an electrical short and burned to the ground. He wrote
his parents, "It's really too awful. We haven't had much luck in the family
the last few months, perhaps it will change soon."[2]

The trenches Fraser's company occupied were filled with bodies of
men who had been gassed the previous week, and it was the Highlanders'
unpleasant job to bury them. Furthermore, the trenches were half occupied by the Germans; the only thing separating the two was a barricade
the Germans had put up. And the only solution to that was for each side to
lob hand grenades over the barricade at the other.

On May 14, ten days before the Second Battle of Ypres began to sub-
side, Willie was going down to his trench when he was shot through the thigh.
He did not consider it a serious wound, and said so in writing to his parents,
but in fact it took nearly two months to heal. By sheer irony he was sent to
recuperate in Le Touquet, at the Golf Hotel, which had been commandeered
by the army as a field hospital. He wrote his father: "It was where Sim [his
dead brother Simon] stopped when he came over to play golf last year. How
times are changed since then, and it's under somewhat different circumstances
I am stopping here now." Like Burgoyne, Fraser was disgusted with the lack
of supervision and presence at the front of the higher headquarters personnel: "The Germans are angels compared to some of our Corps Commanders, etc. The worst of it is they are never within miles of a shell or bullet and
there is no chance of them getting killed and making way for better men. I'd
rather be dead in a ditch than on the staff of some of these fellows."

The attacks and counterattacks raged up and down the Salient until May 24,
when the Germans, behind a gas cloud, took the Bellewaerde Ridge, which
Agar Adamson and his regiment had fought so hard to defend. After that, they

---

2. This last was evidently a reference to the death of his younger brother Simon at
First Ypres and the capture of his older brother by the Germans in August.

finally called it quits and the Second Battle of Ypres, which had begun with the initial poison-gas attack, began to wind down. Since 1914 the fighting at Ypres had begun to take on the characteristics of a game of chess; the opening was fairly fluid and fast but as the game progressed moves were met with countermoves until the opposing players were reduced to sitting for long periods, pondering with their chins in their hands over what to do next. It had at last become apparent to the Germans during these spring battles of 1915 that they were not going to break through the Allied line in Flanders at this point, and were here only sacrificing more and more men who might have been more usefully employed on the Eastern Front. For their part, the British were in no position to launch any major offensive either, at least until the huge "Kitchener Army" was trained and ready to fight, which would not be for more than a year. Thus a stalemate remained, but with the disagreeable "wastage" of thousands of men every day.

The Salient, now shrunken by several miles, had assumed the shape it would take for the next two years, with the Germans occupying not only the high ground at the far edges of the amphitheater-like ridges, but also the high inner ridges close to Ypres itself. The line now ran from Ploegsteert in the south to Steenstraat in the north. In one month the Allies had given up the towns of Langemarck, Gravenstafel, St. Julian, Zonnebeck, and Westhoek, as well as Pilckem Ridge in the north and Frezenberg Ridge in the south. Nevertheless, at Allied headquarters, limited plans were already being drawn to at least retake the lost territory.

Second Ypres had cost the Allies more than 70,000 casualties and the Germans about half that amount—a combined 100,000 men shot down for less than three miles of real estate. About the best thing that came out of it for the British was the propaganda value of a poem. It was no ordinary poem. It became easily the most popular poem of the war, and after the war as well, and when it was published it swept through England and the far-off Americas like a prairie fire. It was titled "In Flanders Fields."

The poem was written by a Canadian, a physician, forty-three-year-old Major John McCrae, medical officer with the newly arrived Canadian Division. As a pastime, McCrae, like so many young men of his time, wrote poetry, and was quite good at it. He had served as an artillery officer in the

Boer War with a Canadian regiment and when the war with Germany broke out he again volunteered his services.

On May 2, at the height of the Second Battle of Ypres, a friend of McCrae's, Lieutenant Alexis Helmer, was killed. Helmer had been a popular figure in the brigade, and his death was mourned by many. The artillery shell that killed him literally blew him to bits: his remains had to be collected in sandbags and then placed in an army blanket in such a way as to resemble a human form. In the midst of booming guns, McCrae conducted the burial service himself, then went to sit on the step of a field ambulance.

Those who were present recorded that the sky was full of larks; that the poppies for which Flanders is renowned were beginning to bloom in the fields and sprout between the crosses in the growing military cemeteries. McCrae took out a pad and pencil and within twenty minutes had penned one of the immortal poems of the war.

In Flanders Fields

In Flanders Fields the poppies blow
Between the crosses, row on row,
That mark our place; and in the sky,
The larks, still bravely singing, fly
Scarce heard amid the guns below.

We are the Dead. Short days ago
We lived, felt dawn, saw sunset glow,
Loved and were loved, and now we lie,
In Flanders fields.

Take up our quarrel with the foe:
To you from failing hands we throw
The torch; be yours to hold it high.
If ye break faith with us who die
We shall not sleep, though poppies grow
In Flanders fields.

Afterward, McCrae showed the poem to several of his fellow officers, and at first did nothing else with it. At one point he submitted it to *The Spectator* but they turned it down. Somebody suggested that he send it to the English magazine *Punch,* which published it on December 8, 1915, more than seven months after it was written. It became popular immediately, and its stirring challenge to "Take up our quarrel with the foe: To you from failing hands we throw the torch" became a sort of rallying cry.

But not for everybody. In his classic book *The Great War and Modern Memory,* an examination of the poetry of World War I, the American historian Paul Fussell takes almost violent issue with the third stanza of McCrae's poem, calling it a mere propaganda ploy and a "vicious" and "stupid" argument against a negotiated peace. Fussell's reaction might have some understandable context, considering that it was written by him on the bitter heels of the Vietnam War, which he loathed. In fact, in May of 1915—with the First World War only ten months old—nobody with authority was contemplating any sort of negotiated peace, though later in the war they did. And consider this, too: that it was written almost in the heat of battle by a man who felt the Allied cause was just, and over the grave of a friend who had died for it.

"In Flanders Fields" soon became something of an emblematic image of World War I. The year after the war ended an American woman got a notion to give out cloth poppies for people to wear in remembrance of the conflict. This quickly spread into a tradition, which became known as "Poppy Day," and was celebrated every November 11 on both sides of the Atlantic well into the second half of the twentieth century. Over the years, millions have been raised for veterans' charities through poppy sales. But John McCrae never got to know this; during the last winter of the war he contracted pneumonia and died from it five days later. He was buried in a cemetery overlooking the English Channel, his grave decorated with a few winter poppies picked by members of his staff.

During this time another event had convulsed the world. Three days before John McCrae wrote "In Flanders Fields," during the height of the Second Battle of Ypres, the great Cunard liner *Lusitania,* largest and fastest in transatlantic service, was torpedoed and sunk by a German submarine off the coast of Ireland. Of the 2,000 civilians aboard, nearly 1,200 perished, including 128 American men, women, and children.

Prior to the *Lusitania*'s sailing from New York, the German embassy in Washington had taken out in American newspapers a black-bordered notice that warned that any ship coming within the territorial maritime limits of Great Britain was subject to attack and destruction. Evidently few passengers took this seriously, and the captain of the *Lusitania* himself foolishly failed to take proper zigzag measures and other precautions before the ship was struck.

At the urging of his military leaders, the kaiser had recently decided to unleash unrestricted submarine warfare against England in retaliation for the British naval blockade of Germany, which was beginning to have dark and deep consequences, not only on the importation of German war materials but on the German food supply itself. Prior to the war Germany had imported vast quantities of wheat and grains from the Ukraine breadbasket, but since that source had been shut off Germany was looking famine in the face. In fact, while the great slaughter of the Second Battle of Ypres was taking place in Belgium, a slaughter of far greater proportion was being conducted in Germany itself: the "World's Biggest Pig-Sticking."

With the realization that her foodstuffs were now severely limited by the British blockade, the Germans finally undertook to set up a rationing system for such staple commodities as grain, bread, flour, milk, fats, potatoes, and the like. Then some genius pointed out that there were upwards of 25 million hogs in Germany, which consumed more potatoes and grain than the *entire human population*; solution: kill the hogs. Thus for several months, and on into the summer of 1915, Germans binged in a gluttony of pork until they were virtually wursted and brattened to their limits.

The sinking of the *Lusitania* had immediately galvanized American public opinion against Germany. Prior to that time, many if not most Americans were ambivalent about the war and in fact there were not just a few who were actually leaning against Great Britain. It must be remembered that the American experience vis-à-vis England had not been the most cordial up until then, and there had always been a traditional mistrust of the British. It took the American Revolution of 1776 to throw off the oppressive yoke of King George III. Next came the War of 1812 during which the British set fire to the U.S. Capitol and the White House and did other reprehensible things, before finally being handed a defeat at the Battle of New Orleans. Then, during the American Civil War, Britain sided, at least tacitly, with the Southern Confederacy, selling them weapons, building them great blockade-running ships, purchasing their cotton, and holding out the threat of sending her vast fleet to lift the Union blockade of Southern ports. This last had actually been during the lifetime of many Americans.

Furthermore, the great immigrations during the last part of the nineteenth century and the first part of the twentieth had brought vast numbers of Germans into the American population, as well as huge numbers of Irish, who despised England to the core. Americans were more sympathetic to the French, who had given them Lafayette and the Statue of Liberty, as well as to the plight of the Belgians. Nevertheless, an almost endemic spirit of isolationism, spawned by the Monroe Doctrine, had permeated the United States with an attitude that Europe's problems were Europe's problems alone.

Naturally, none of this prevented the Americans, an enterprising race if ever there was one, from capitalizing on Europe's misfortune. There was money to be made. Vast stores of cotton (used in the making of explosives) and shiploads of mules and other types of quasi-military commodities embarked daily to England and France from American ports. As well, the United States was manufacturing and selling enormous amounts of ammunition and guns to the Allies. A case in point: The Bethlehem Steel Corporation manufactured ten modern submarines for the British Navy and had them transported to Canada. They might have been selling these things to the Germans, too, except for the British Navy's blockade of that country. So for these good entrepreneurs, any news of unrestricted submarine warfare by the Germans was bad.

Yet the overwhelming effect on Americans of the sinking of the *Lusitania* was outrage. Innocent women and children callously drowned in the deep, cold ocean; it did not sit well. Never mind that in all probability the *Lusitania was* carrying ammunition for the Allies. Woodrow Wilson, who had campaigned long and hard for his presidency on the slogan "Not one

American boy to the European war," declared that the sinking had "an evil effect" on the American citizenry. Newspapers decried the act as "barbarous, treacherous, inhuman," and so forth.

Taken aback by this unrewarding reaction, the kaiser quickly called off the policy of unrestricted submarine attacks, and apologized for the sinking, but it was too late. Although the United States did not enter the war for another two years, the sinking of the *Lusitania* had planted the seeds of intervention in the American psyche and, fanned by newspapers now hostile to Germany, these began to take root and sprout. Former president Theodore Roosevelt warned that if the United States did not begin to rearm, New York and San Francisco were in danger of the same fate that had befallen Antwerp and Brussels.

Not only that, but the Germans' use of poison gas had everyone in an uproar. It was, among other things, a violation of the Hague Convention of 1907, which the Germans had signed. Back in England, Lord Kitchener proclaimed that "Germany has stooped to acts which vie with those of the Dervishes," a reference to the savage practices of the Dervish army he had defeated in the Sudan seventeen years earlier. Nevertheless, next morning he asked permission of the cabinet for the British army itself to use poison gas, and received it. Furthermore, Kitchener made a plea to the women of England to produce as many protective cotton gas masks as possible; within weeks, hundreds of thousands of these were sent to the front.

Along with the sinking of the *Lusitania,* the German use of poison gas only reinforced their reputation as ruthless barbarians. They were not much helped by a letter that appeared in the *New York Times* shortly after the attack. The writer, a British officer, expressed his frustration that the public "has not the slightest idea of this damnable effort on the part of the Germans to disregard all laws of humanity and civilization," and went on to describe a visit to a hospital where gas casualties had been taken: "They are all sitting bolt upright or swaying backward and forward, gasping for breath; their faces, hands and necks a shiny gray-black color, their eyes glazed, and unable absolutely to speak or eat. It takes two days for these men to die."

The use of poison gas further dehumanized the already subhuman conditions of the war. Battle had come a long way since men went at it with rocks and clubs, slingshots, then knives and spears, swords and axes and boiling oil; then bows and arrows, then gunpowder muskets, bayonets, and cannon, then high-explosive, long-range artillery and machine guns. But now this: poisoning the very air that men breathed. It was widely condemned as cowardly and grotesque.

One of England's most promising young poets, twenty-four-year-old Wilfred Owen, was an officer in the trenches when he wrote what later became one of the most powerful poems spawned by the war.

Dulce Et Decorum Est[3]

Bent double, like old beggars under sacks,
Knocked-kneed, coughing like hags, we cursed through sludge,
Till on the haunting flares we turned our backs
And towards our distant rest began to trudge.
Men marched asleep. Many had lost their boots
But limped on, blood shod. All went lame; all blind;
Drunk with fatigue; deaf even to the hoots
Of tired, outstripped Five-Nines that dropped behind.

Gas, GAS, quick, boys!—An ecstasy of fumbling.
Fitting the clumsy helmets just in time;
But someone still was yelling out and stumbling,
And flound'ring like a man in fire or lime . . .
Dim, through the misty panes and thick green light,
As under a green sea I saw him drowning.

In all my dreams, before my helpless sight,
He plunges at me, guttering, choking, drowning.

3. Dulce et decorum est pro patria mori: "It is both sweet and good to die for one's country": a line from Horace. "Five-Nines" refers to the caliber of an artillery piece.

If in some smothering dreams you too could pace
Behind the wagon that we flung him in,
And watch the white eyes writhing in his face,
His hanging face, like a devil's sick of sin;
If you could hear, at every jolt, the blood
Come gargling from the froth-corrupted lungs,
Obscene as cancer, bitter as the cud
Of vile, incurable sores on innocent tongues,——
My friend, you would not tell with such high jest
To children ardent for some desperate glory,
The old Lie: Dulce et decorum est
Pro patria mori.

Included today in many college anthologies as a prime example of antiwar poetry, it drips irony, bitterness, and disillusionment, yet Owen was unquestionably a brave and competent officer. The previous month he had been awarded the Military Cross, "For conspicuous gallantry and devotion to duty." A week before the war ended, Lieutenant Wilfred Owen was killed in action.

There were other important developments that second year of the war. For one, at the urging of Winston Churchill, then First Lord of the Admiralty, it was decided to launch a major campaign against the Turkish empire, Germany's ally. After the vicious fighting at Ypres the previous autumn and the resulting stalemate, Churchill concluded that the best course of action would be to "knock the props" out from under Germany by conquering her allies. Following Kitchener's dictum of conducting "operations elsewhere," he proposed to steam a fleet of older battleships and other warcraft through the Dardanelles strait, then enter the Black Sea and bombard Constantinople, bringing Turkey to her knees. This did not work. The Turks let loose from upriver large numbers of mines, which either sank or incapacitated fully a third of the British battlefleet, with great loss of life. Then it was decided to take the entrance of the strait by storm and drive the Turks and their mines and land-based guns away so Constantinople could be captured. This did not work, either; furthermore, it was perhaps the most ill-executed and notorious operation of the war.

On April 25, 1915, while the Germans were unleashing their gas attack in the Ypres Salient, the first of some 400,000 Allied soldiers were landed on the Gallipoli Peninsula under heavy fire and were immediately pinned down. It seems some incompetent staff officer had wrongly loaded the ships so that weapons arrived without ammunition and vice versa. These were troops from England, Australia, New Zealand, and France. The campaign quickly degenerated into the same kind of static trench warfare that was going on in France and Belgium—the lessons of the machine gun not yet having been assimilated. By the time the Allies withdrew nine months later, more than half of them had become casualties, including more than 40,000 dead. Churchill was kicked out on his ear and, for his personal atonement, he rejoined his old regiment in the Flanders trenches. What he saw there convinced him even more strongly that they should have tried harder at Gallipoli.

Winston Churchill presents an interesting caricature of the "gentleman officer" during World War I. He had graduated from the Royal Military Academy at Sandhurst and had been posted as a cavalry lieutenant in India during the late 1890s. From there, with the help of his influential American mother, he managed to inveigle staff assignments all over the world, including the fighting in Cuba, Afghanistan, Kitchener's punitive expedition into the Sudan, and also the Boer War. He wrote about his exploits for English newspapers and gained for himself the reputation of a fearless and well-versed military correspondent, which launched his political career.

When Churchill, at age forty-two and with the rank of major, arrived on the Western Front in late 1915, however, he was in for some surprises. Naturally, he had friends in high places, including the highest of all, Sir John French, commanding general of the British Expeditionary Force, who had him met by a chauffeur and put up in his fancy château at St. Omer, "with hot baths, beds, champagne & all the conveniences." Major Churchill also arrived with a black charger, groom, and servant, piles of fancy baggage, and his own bathtub, complete with a boiler. (This kind of luxury later gave rise to the "myth of the Châteaux Generals," which tarnished many a reputation later in the war and afterward.)

Churchill had expected to be made a brigadier general and given a brigade to command, but all he got was a battalion, and he was lucky to get that. He never forgave Prime Minister Herbert Asquith for what he considered a flagrant betrayal of promise. When he got to his battalion, Churchill was not warmly received; the officers who had been fighting in the trenches for more than a year were suspicious of him as a politico. The first day he was there, Churchill wrote his wife, Clementine, asking for, among other things, "a warm brown leather waistcoat, a periscope (most important), a pair of waterproof trench wading boots . . . coming up to the thigh," and "a sheepskin sleeping bag." His interest in these practical things did not last long. A week later he was demanding that his wife send him "sardines, chocolate, potted meats, Stilton cheese, cream, hams, dried fruits," and "a big beef steak pie."

Even so, Churchill proved to be a wonderful officer. Promoted to colonel, he took his battalion, the 6th Royal Scots Fusiliers, into the trenches around Ploegsteert in the southern part of the Ypres Salient during the first week of January 1916. His motto was: "War is a game to be played with a smiling face," and he constantly chided his officers, "If you can't smile, then grin." Churchill felt it very important for the men to always see their officers as happy. His adjutant later wrote of him that "no more popular officer ever commanded troops. As a soldier he was hard-working, persevering and thorough."

Churchill was a bold and daring commander and led men himself into no-man's-land on raids. He treated his soldiers well, saw that they got hot baths and proper food, and they adored him for it. One of his great frustrations was that he was not back in England to oversee the development of the caterpillar tank, which he had helped to invent when he was running the admiralty, and he could certainly see the need of it here firsthand, from his vantage point in the frontline trenches. Finally his fertile and always calculating mind got the better of him. The war was just too big, even for a character of Churchill's stature, and he began to chafe to return to England and get back into the government. He had to run something more than a battalion.

He stayed with the Royal Fusiliers until May, then, even with an offer dangled by Sir Douglas Haig himself for the elusive brigade he had always sought, Churchill resigned his commission and went back home to run for

Parliament. According to Churchill historian Roy Jenkins, in his first campaign speeches Churchill complained bitterly about the "terrible distinction" between the "trench population" and the "non-trench population." The myth of the Châteaux Generals was about to be born.

Meanwhile, the tempest that had been brewing over the lack of artillery ammunition on the Western Front was about to burst forth. Just as the Second Battle of Ypres was reaching its most pitiless crescendo, Sir John French sent an urgent message to the British War Office saying that his supply of shells was dangerously low and that he would be unable to continue the battle unless resupplied. The response from the War Office was to order him to send more than 20,000 rounds of his precious remaining artillery rounds to Gallipoli.

Sir John was outraged, and complied with the order only under protest. In fact, he and other high-ranking commanders on the Western Front were outraged that the British had sent such a force to Gallipoli *at all*. They were of the firm opinion that the Western Front was where the Germans were, and where they must be defeated, and that every man and gun was needed there. Thus began an ongoing wrangling between the military and the highest levels of government that would last the war, between so-called Westerners, who insisted that continuous pressure on the Germans in France and Flanders was the only solution to victory, and the Easterners who, repelled by the ongoing slaughter on the Western Front, looked for solutions elsewhere, mostly in the Mediterranean and Middle Eastern theaters. In any event, the ammunition crisis had become so desperate that Sir John took the extraordinary step of confiding that information to a war correspondent, Colonel Repington of *The Times*. This was to have far-reaching ramifications, both for Sir John and, indeed, for the Liberal government.

Ignoring the army censor, Repington forthwith published a scathing series of articles in *The Times* exposing the fiasco. A wave of public indignation ensued; letters and editorials decried that Englishmen were dying in France and Flanders because they were unable to match the Germans in ammunition. The hullabaloo nearly swept aside the Liberal Party of Prime Minister Asquith and, in fact, forced him to form a coalition government with the conservatives. David Lloyd George, the charismatic Welshman and liberal, was named to head a newly formed Ministry of Munitions, and he set about to rectify the crisis.

It also sealed Sir John French's fate, though not immediately. London officials felt that he had betrayed a dangerous secret to the enemy, and before the end of the year he would be gone. So would Asquith. And for his role in it Repington did not fare very well either. He was abruptly banished from visiting the war front, on the same grounds as were held against Sir John. It was an appallingly ungrateful decision.

In any case, under Lloyd George, labor strikes in the armaments industry were immediately declared illegal and efforts were made to keep profiteering under control. But it would be nearly a year before the new arrangement began to have its desired effect. Meantime, a colossal new work program was set into motion with the passage of the National Registration Act under which every man, woman, and child in Great Britain between the ages of fifteen and sixty-five was identified as to skill: by 1918 fully three-fifths of the workers in England were employed in the military effort. For the first time in British history, the act identified men for compulsory conscription into the military. It had now become total war.

★ Chapter Eight

The French field officers had regarded the desperate British counterattacks of the past month, the Official History tells us, as their forefathers once regarded the Charge of the Light Brigade in the Crimea half a century earlier: "Magnificent, but not war." There was much truth in this; at the close of the Second Battle of Ypres there were scarcely 5,000 rounds of British artillery ammunition available for the entire Western Front. In later battles, ten times that much would easily be expended in a single hour. One thing to come out of all the sacrifice and bloodshed was the firm realization that attacks and counterattacks could not be made without overwhelming artillery preparation. The Germans had already figured this out. Where the earlier battles had been, for the most part, "soldier's" battles, Second Ypres, as the Official History points out, "was indeed the first of the new nature of battle, in which the enemy planned that his infantry should merely have to occupy ground from which his guns had driven every living creature, and in which man was not pitted against man, but against material."

In the Ypres Salient, spring drifted into summer—the hundredth anniversary of the Battle of Waterloo had come and gone—and the "wastage" in Flanders continued: hundreds and even thousands of daily casualties from bullets, bombs, shells, gas, disease, or people simply going insane. Poppies and other flowers were blooming profusely in no-man's-land, in soil fertilized by the remains of so many human and animal carcasses and enriched beyond imagination by nitrates from the high-explosive shells. The Germans still occupied Hill 60, but the British had managed to hold the town of Hooge and the stables of the vast Hooge Château. The château itself remained in German hands, although at that point it was little more than a pile of bricks and dust. To someone at British Headquarters, it did not seem right to occupy the village and the stables and not the château; after all, it was where, the previous October, a German shell had killed General Lomax and half a dozen staff officers during desperate hours of fighting in the First Battle of Ypres. Matter of fact, a plan had already been laid.

Ever since the success—albeit temporary—of the great mine explosion at Hill 60, the High Command was ever more convinced that mines were the wave of the future in breaking static warfare. Their shock value was remarkable; the problem was, after the obliterated ground had been taken, how to hold on to it? The Germans understood this, too, and had stationed ready reserves at strategic points in the line, able to move swiftly to eject an Allied advance before it could consolidate. To First Army commander Sir Douglas Haig, and others, the only solution was to keep a large ready reserve themselves, which could be rushed to the conquered ground and set up against counterattacks. Three months later, during the British offensive at Loos, twenty miles to the south of Ypres, this would lead to a rift between Haig and Sir John French that would also contribute heavily to the latter's downfall.

In mid-June the British sent to Hooge a young lieutenant named Geoffrey Cassels with a company of men who had only recently been peaceful miners in England and Wales. Cassels's job was to have the miners dig a tunnel from the Hooge Château stables across 150 feet of no-man's-land and place an explosive mine beneath the Hooge Château itself. The hitch was that to time it to the attack schedule, it must be completed within the month. The initial efforts were disastrous. The subsoil beneath the stables was a soggy, oozing sand, which kept the shaft flooded; pumps had to be manned night and day. The miners shored up the sides of the shaft but the pumps began sucking up the sand. Cassels took the kilts of some of the Scotsmen who lay dead in the area and tried to stem the flow of sand with them, but it was no use. Furthermore, Cassels was experiencing the same troubles with his miners that the tunneling company at Hill 60 had had—not being trained for the military, they were under extraordinary strain from the constant German shelling and sniping.

Finally he moved the whole operation several hundred yards away and started again. This time they succeeded, and sank a 35-foot shaft into blue clay. They were well out into no-man's-land when Cassels discovered his tunnel was badly off course. Given his time constraint, the only solution Cassels had was to increase the size of the explosive charge, and hope to bury the whole German position with it. Because of the small confines of the tunnel, Cassels realized that it could not hold enough of the bulky gunpowder or guncotton to do the job. But he seized on an idea that no one had thought of before: he would use ammonal, an explosive used in mining but new to warfare, with three-and-a-half times the strength of ordinary gunpowder.

Cassels quickly sent in a requisition for 3,500 pounds of the ammonal but, in typical army fashion, a glitch developed immediately: no one back at headquarters had the faintest idea what ammonal was. Someone assumed that it was a drug, and dispatched an inquiry to the Royal Army Medical Corps. In due time, a reply was received: "Ammonol is a compound drug extensively used in America as a sensual sedative in cases of abnormal sexual excitement."

What reaction this information elicited from the Quartermaster General is not known, but one can speculate that he must have wondered why a company of coal miners needed so much of the stuff, way out in the front lines. The confusion was cleared up after another flurry of dispatches when someone finally was able to distinguish between ammonol, the sex drug, and ammonal, the high explosive. In any case, the delay threw Cassels into a tizzy. With only three days to go before the attack, and no ammonal, he frantically began to scour every outlet for any kind of explosives at all. The only thing available was about 1,500 pounds of gunpowder—certainly not enough to achieve the desired effect. He loaded it into the tunnel anyway.

Then, at the last moment, the wagon load of ammonal arrived, in broad daylight, in full view of the Germans. Cassels was horrified and rushed to get the stuff unloaded and into the mine tunnel before some shell hit it and blew the whole position into kingdom come. It took until midafternoon next day to get the ammonal into the firing chamber and properly set up with twenty-four detonators and two long sets of wire leading back to his dugout. Then the chamber was tamped shut with sandbags and earth. The attack was set for seven. Cassels and his firing party waited tensely all through the afternoon and early evening, artillery shells crashing around them with maddening regularity. There were only a few minutes to go when a German shell suddenly exploded in the direction of the mine entrance. Cassels retested the wiring circuits, but to his dismay they were dead. He and two others dashed out of the dugout and soon found that the shell had cut the firing wires. They spliced them back together as best they could, then returned to their dugout. Another test showed that the current was flowing again.

The mine went off at exactly 7 P.M., July 19, 1915, and, at least in Cassels's mind, was a beautiful and awe-inspiring sight to behold. The blast shook everything for miles around and sent a massive cloud of debris twirling and whirling hundreds of feet into the air: earth, concrete, corrugated iron, bricks, trees, pots and pans, rifles, and, as at Hill 60, hundreds of Germans and hundreds of parts of Germans—some of which landed within the British lines. From their perspective, Cassels and his crew could not tell exactly what effect the thing had had. It was so much larger than the mine at Hill 60 that to Cassels it was conceivable the blast had actually buried alive the entire British attacking force.

In fact ten men of the Middlesex Regiment had gone too far forward and were indeed buried alive, but others, including men of the Gordon Highlanders, stormed across the battered no-man's-land and occupied the mine crater, which was 120 feet across and 20 feet deep. Among these was Captain Willie Fraser, who had recuperated from his second wound and was now back with his battalion. His disappointment in being sent to Hooge was palpable: "I don't know what the battalions will say when they are told. It will take all the heart out of the men and the officers too. It [Hooge] was the nastiest place in the Salient before, and the Ypres Salient is the worst place in the line by far."

Meantime, word had been received of the burying alive of the unfortunate Middlesex men, and Lieutenant Cassels was called on the carpet before the division commander. There, according to an account by historian Alexander Barrie, in *War Underground*, he was stripped of the symbols of his rank and told he was under arrest. Just then the corps commander, Lieutenant General Edmund Allenby, entered the room and Cassels was told to wait in the hall. When General Allenby came out, he said, "Go inside, salute the general, say thank you—then get out and get into my car." Cassels did as he was told and, according to Barrie, soon found himself the guest of honor at a fashionable luncheon party with not only Allenby but the commander in chief himself, Sir John French. That same day Cassels was awarded the Military Cross for the successful operation.

The Salient, of course, had already gained a notorious reputation as the worst place in the war, but just ten days after the Hooge Château was retaken by the British, the Germans unleashed upon them something even more diabolical—liquid fire.

For the Allies, the use of wireless communication (radio) was in its infancy, and the Germans were managing to intercept and read much of it. They learned in due time that the British trenches around the newly won Hooge crater were due to be relieved on July 29; not only that, but the relief was to be conducted by untried troops of Kitchener's New Army. Beginning in July, and into the fall, some 175,000 of Kitchener's volunteers were moved from England to the Western Front; millions would follow. The Germans knew, of course, that an attack during a relief was a most desirable tactic, especially against untested troops. And this time, they intended to assist themselves with a new and dreadful weapon, the flamethrower.

The flamethrower had been invented around the turn of the century; a mixture of carbon dioxide and nitrogen propelled a huge blast of oily fire about 75 feet in front of the operator. The device itself looked similar to a fire extinguisher with a fat hose and was strapped to the backs of flame-throwing specialists. It had not been used previously in combat.

In the early morning hours of July 29, the men manning the Hooge crater were moving into their daily morning "Stand-to" when suddenly the dark was split by a tremendous hissing sound and "a bright crimson glare over the Crater turned the whole scene red." The attacking Germans had perhaps half a dozen flamethrowers and the men in the front trenches didn't stand a chance. Most were roasted alive—about 400 of them; the others wisely fled. The Germans took the crater, and thereafter the flame-thrower became a fixture on the Western Front. Headquarters ordered an immediate counterattack, but by then the Germans were laying down an artillery barrage of the profoundest magnitude. Nothing human could have lived through it. When the attack finally got under way the Kitchener men were mown down without mercy—2,500 of them—and the effort failed. But they had had their baptism of blood, and if anything encouraging could be said of the Hooge debacle it was that the Kitchener army could and would fight with the best of them.

And so it went throughout the late summer and into early fall, killing for killing's sake over every inch of trench in the Salient. The Allies did, however, decide to give Belgian Flanders a breathing period of sorts, and launch their next big attempt twenty miles to the south, at the French town of Loos, where Sir Douglas Haig thought he saw a German weakness in troop strength. This would be England's first big offensive of the war and would have a lasting impact on its future conduct, particularly on the men in the Ypres Salient.

Haig was in charge of the Loos offensive and, after the Germans had used poison gas at Ypres, he was determined to use it also. Thus, some 5,000 cylinders of chlorine were brought to the Loos front by several thousand newly trained gas specialists, supervised by forty "gas officers." Haig was also determined to learn from at least some of the lessons of the past. The limited attack in March at Neuve Chapelle had convinced him that strong and immediate reserve reinforcements must be available to consolidate a captured position in order to hold it from German counterattacks. He therefore asked Sir John French for two full reserve divisions to be held close to the front lines. The request was granted, although the divisions would be composed of Kitchener's untested New Army and, worse, were not to be held close to the front lines as Haig had wanted, but much far-ther back. On the other hand, Haig, an old cavalryman, outlined an ex-pansive plan to have his mounted troops tear through the broken German positions and hold vital strong points as far back as thirty miles behind enemy lines. Despite much criticism, some of it deserved, Haig clung all through the war to his theory that cavalry was the way to exploit a breach in the German front.

Meantime, back in the Salient it had been decided that a "diversionary" attack would be staged so as to keep the Germans from sending reinforcements from there south to Loos. As luck would have it, Lord Kitchener himself had come to Flanders to inspect the army. Kitchener was a legendary figure not only in the military but throughout England. His face was all over Great Britain on the famous finger-pointing recruiting poster above the caption: "Your Country Needs You." The day before the attack, a company of Gordon Highlanders, Willie Fraser's regiment, was assembled to be inspected and hear Kitchener's exhortations. He put it to them plainly, according to one of the men who was there: "He told us that our attack was in the nature of a sacrifice to help the main offensive which was to be launched 'elsewhere.' For that reason, he said, no attempt had been made to conceal our preparations. He congratulated us on the position of honor and responsibility that had fallen to us as a Territorial unit and he wished us 'as much luck as we could expect,' in the course of the next few days."

Unsettling as Kitchener's words might have been to the Highlanders at Ypres, the attack at Loos got under way just after sunrise, September 25, 1915. Everything seemed to go against it. First, Loos was coal mining country and the ground around it was flat and bare as a table: there was no cover for the attackers and so an enormous smoke screen was employed. Second, Sir John French had waffled about Haig's reserve divisions and did not send them to the front until it was too late; even then, they had been exhausted by the march. Third, just minutes before Haig's planned gas attack, the wind died; although it later picked up, there were considerable troubles with the gas. Fourth, a simultaneous assault by the French to the south of Loos failed. Finally, the attack was severely hampered by a lack of artillery shells sufficient to cut the German barbed wire. And there were many other things: communications quickly broke down; because of the massive smoke screen and billowing clouds of poison gas, entire divisions marched in the wrong direction and aerial reconnaissance became impossible.

In any event, at 6:50 A.M. some 75,000 British soldiers climbed out of their trenches, some to the tune of bagpipes and others kicking soccer balls across no-man's-land, toward Loos and the Germans. Initially the attack seemed successful. They were facing no more than 11,000 Germans and these were quickly overwhelmed. But then German resistance began to stiffen. From the cellars of cottages and the rims of coal pits, German machine guns began to rattle. The reserves that Sir John had promised Haig were nowhere to be seen; when they did finally arrive, with nightfall coming on, the momentum had been lost. The British managed to take a couple of miles of ground, including the town of Loos itself, but the Germans had constructed an extremely strong second line of defense behind their first. Never content to go away and fight again another day, the British continued their assaults. After a month of these, and more than 100,000 Allied soldiers killed, wounded, or missing, the battle was brought to an unsatisfactory halt by the Allied High Command.

Aside from the appalling casualties, the most significant thing that came out of Loos was that it sealed the fate of Sir John French and marked the ascendancy of Sir Douglas Haig. The story of Sir John and Haig is a strange one—some say they despised each other; one thing that is clear is that the relationship was less than fraternal. It has been suggested that friction between the two began in 1894 when French, after being relieved and put on half pay following a sexual indiscretion with a superior officer's wife, was put in charge of revising the army's Cavalry Manual. A few years later Haig made his own mark on the manual, and it has been insinuated that his contributions made Sir John jealous. During the Boer War in 1899, however, Haig not only served amicably under Sir John in the field, but he also lent him the £2,400 to stave off bankruptcy. Haig's detractors claim that this made Sir John beholden to Haig; they suggest Haig used the loan as a vehicle for his own advancement and that Sir John resented this.

This much is true: Haig had a low opinion of Sir John when he was named to command the British Expeditionary Force. The war was just a few days old when King George, with whom Haig was on intimate terms, asked him what he thought of the new commander. Haig wrote in his diary: "I had grave doubts . . . whether either his temper was sufficiently even or his military knowledge was sufficiently thorough to enable him to discharge properly the very different duties which will devolve upon him during the coming operations with Allies on the Continent. In my own heart, I know that French is quite unfit for this high command at a time of crisis in our Nation's history. But I thought it sufficient to tell the King that I had 'doubts' about the selection."

From the outset, Haig had no confidence in Sir John, and in the coming months he repeated his concerns not only to his diary but to others on his staff and in other high places. For his part, Sir John thought Haig "would show to greater advantages a superior staff officer than as a Commander."

Loos was the straw that broke the camel's back. Haig wrote a frustrated, almost bitter letter to Kitchener complaining of Sir John's delinquency in not sending up the reserve divisions for twelve hours after the British had created "a glaring gap" in German positions. And he wrote in his diary, "It seems impossible to discuss military operations with an unreasoning brain of this kind." On October 24, as the Battle of Loos came to its melancholy close, the king visited the army. After dining with Haig he asked him to come to his room, where he candidly questioned him on French's suitability for command. Haig reiterated his distress over the tardy reserve divisions and said, "I therefore thought strongly that, for the sake of the Empire, French ought to be removed."

Others thought so too; 1915 had been a disastrous year for the Allies. The war was barely a year old, they were suffering extraordinary losses in men—including the entire army of Old Contemptibles—and they had been shoved back on many fronts, including the Ypres Salient. Furthermore, the invasion of Gallipoli was turning into a fiasco. It took the powers that be another six weeks to accomplish Sir John's demise and put Sir Douglas Haig in command of the British armies on the Western Front.

It has been suggested by a number of Haig's detractors, in particular the British historians Captain Basil Liddell Hart, General J.F.C. Fuller, and the American Leon Wolff (whose 1958 book, *In Flanders Fields,* was a positive screed against Haig), that Haig had been "intriguing" against Sir John French from the start. On the surface it certainly looked that way; after all, Haig had gone behind his commander's back to express "doubts" and to complain of him to the highest officers of the realm. These were obviously not the activities of a loyal subordinate. Yet there is another possibility, that Haig was merely expressing his honest convictions—as a Scotsman will only express them—direct and unvarnished. Whatever the case, Haig was now in charge and now upon him devolved the fate of the British empire.

As if to welcome Haig as their new adversary in chief, on the day of his appointment as commander of the Western Front the Germans upped their ante of "frightfulness" by unleashing another poison-gas attack in the Ypres Salient. What distinguished it from the earlier ones was the use of phosgene, a gas ten times more lethal than chlorine. By war's end it would account for 80 percent of all deaths by gas.

Just past midnight on December 19, the British around the ruined village of Wieltje, opposite the Frezenberg Ridge in the north part of the Salient, saw a number of strange-looking red rockets burst from the enemy line. This was followed by a loud hissing coming from the German trenches. This time when German deserters had warned of a gas attack the British went on their guard. They had already taken strong measures to protect themselves from poison gas. First, the primitive cloth masks had by now been replaced with a head-covering hood, with goggles—the so-called box respirator. Forewarned by the Russians that the Germans on the Eastern Front had killed thousands with a gas thought to be phosgene, a solution had been put in the new British gas helmet to counteract it. Officers from the meteorological department had been assigned to monitor wind conditions that would make the use of gas favorable, and so the British divisions in the north of the Salient had been on alert for several days. Furthermore, all along the line warning devices such as Klaxons and gongs had been installed—the most rudimentary alarm was to beat on an artillery-shell casing with a stick or rifle butt. In any case, when British "Very lights" were fired off, they revealed a fifty-foot-high gas cloud roiling toward them.

By the standards of the time it was huge. The cloud was eight miles wide and, before it dissipated, ten miles deep into the Salient and beyond. It quickly enveloped the British positions, but the men who had put on their masks were not injured. Those who did not, including many far behind the lines, suffered terribly. Of the more than a thousand who inhaled the gas, 120 of them died, including a man five miles in the rear.

But the Germans did not attack in force. Instead they sent forth twenty raiding parties to see what effect the gas had. In fact, according to their version, the Germans had hoped that the gas would "damage the enemy by losses and the destruction of his positions." Apparently the thinking was, according to the Official History, that the gas would have so demolished the British that the Germans "would only have to walk over and take possession of Ypres." It did not happen that way, and the German patrols were shot to pieces. The novel use of phosgene, however, added a new dimension to gas warfare. It was found that any food tainted by the phosgene caused severe illness if eaten; that the gas lingered in dugouts and caught men unawares, long after they thought the danger had passed. Furthermore, the whole countryside that was enveloped by the phosgene—nearly eighty square miles—was despoiled of vegetation; all grass, tree leaves, plants, and crops turned an ugly burned shade and died. Cows were killed in their fields as far to the southwest as Bailleul, only a couple of miles from the French border.

Thus the year closed; the bitter winter of 1915–16 foreclosed any large offensives in northern Europe, but the killing continued around Ypres and down the line in its measured and merciless way. One striking feature of the Salient, though, was its ironical proximity to peaceful civilization. A mere five or six miles back from the fighting, Belgian farmers plowed their fields and tended their livestock; children played in the grass and in the streets of villages. Shops were open and except for the pitiful refugees, the scenes were pastoral and otherwise normal. Allied soldiers who marched through these areas, listening to the growling of distant gunfire into which they were headed or from which they were leaving, must have been stricken by the bizarre contrast. Not only that, but the postal and communications systems were so organized that mail was received in the trenches only a few days after being posted in England, and the London newspapers arrived just a day or two after being published.

By now the city of Ypres had long since been abandoned by its citizens. Some had hung on through the battles of the autumn and even through the German bombardment of the early spring. But after the Second Battle of Ypres, when the Germans gained the ridges closer to the city itself and commanded almost line-of-sight artillery ranges upon them, the last of the inhabitants finally left. Ypres was still full of soldiers, though, billeting in cellars and half-blown-apart houses; the main road from the supply base at Poperinge ran through there and from the Menin Gate along the Menin Road up to the frontline trenches. A particularly loathsome spot on the Menin Road was where it dissected into a north-south junction, known as Hellfire Corner—in friendlier times, known as the Halte—the end of the streetcar line. In order to mask the movement of troops in Ypres and along the roads, the British erected gigantic tarpaulinlike cloths around the city, in hopes of preventing the Germans from calling in artillery fire at the first sign of life.

The Allies did not always get along with their Belgian neighbors. The British frequently complained that Belgians in the back areas gouged them on purchases of food and other items. For their part, the Belgians remonstrated that Allied forces looted their abandoned homes and commandeered their poultry and livestock for their own cook pots. Both of these grievances had merit.

Then there was the matter of spies. Many in the British army believed there were a large number of spies among the Belgian populace. They deduced this from the fact that German artillery was so often accurately played upon them. It was suggested that some Belgian farmers were sending secret codes to the Germans across no-man's-land by moving the sails on their windmills or the hands on clocks in the towers. One reported case concerned the killing of a Belgian teenage sniper. He was shot out of a tree, rifle in hand, and on his body were found the identity discs of half a dozen British soldiers. Or so it was said. Likewise there were continual reports of German spies having infiltrated Allied lines. One that recurred frequently involved the ubiquitous German dressed as a British officer, who came into the frontline trenches. Ranked usually as a major, he was said to speak perfect English and would appear only at night, questioning troops as to their unit strength and intentions, then, just as someone began to raise doubts about his legitimacy, he would vanish down the dark trench like a will-o'-the-wisp, and be seen no more. Though most of these episodes were merely the product of rumor, a number of German spies were in fact apprehended and summarily shot, and headquarters periodically put out bulletins for all troops to be on the lookout for impostors.

Amid all the death, horror, brutality, hatred, fear, recrimination, and confusion of battle, two weeks before the close of 1915 an institution was born in the Salient that became legendary, both during the war and in the years afterward. This was Talbot House, or Toc-H, as it was called, after the army signalers' codes used at the time.

It was the brainchild of a military chaplain, Rev. Phillip (Tubby) Clayton, a diminutive thirty-year-old vicar of the Church of England. He arrived in the Salient in November of 1915 and was assigned to the 16th Infantry Brigade, where his predecessor had been killed a month earlier. On a visit back to Poperinge, the huge British garrison and supply base six miles west of Ypres, Tubby Clayton observed that troops who had been sent out of the line for rest had no decent place to go, aside from cafés, *estaminets,* and houses of prostitution. He determined to do something about this and, with the help of his superior, Rev. Neville Talbot, managed to acquire a large three-story house in town, owned by a Belgian brewery operator who had moved to the South of France with the coming of the war.

Here he established a "soldier's house," and hung a sign out front of it that read: TALBOT HOUSE 1915____? Below this was printed: EVERY MAN'S CLUB. This was quite a remarkable convention for 1915. Britain was at the time a harsh social-class society, and each of the various pecking orders knew its place. In England, the upper classes had their London clubs; the lower classes waited upon them there. Moreover, most of the officers in the British Army were from the upper classes, and there were further strict rules about officers "fraternizing" with ordinary soldiers. Tubby Clayton chucked all that out the window and erected another sign over the door that read: ABANDON RANK, ALL YE WHO ENTER HERE.

Talbot House was named after Lieutenant Gilbert Talbot, younger brother of Rev. Talbot, who had been killed during the fighting at Hooge four months earlier. To men brutalized in the stinking trenches, it was truly a breath of fresh air. It was a house that had many mansions: there was a room for playing pool and one for playing cards; there was a library and a reading room, a writing room, a music room, and a parlor with a piano for convivial gatherings of all sorts. On the top floor was the chapel. There were also a few rooms to rent overnight, with clean sheets and a place where a man could sit on an actual toilet. A great conservatory led to a large, lovely garden; a sign pointed the way: COME OUT INTO THE GARDEN AND FORGET ABOUT THE WAR.

This they did by the tens of thousands. Practically every soldier who fought in the Salient came or went through Poperinge, and practically every British battalion fought in the Salient at one time or another. As time went on, many of the men or their families made donations of money or gifts of furniture, tableware, books, paintings, and other things to make Talbot House homey. One soldier described going there as being "like Alice stepping through the looking glass," into Wonderland.

Talbot House lasted not only the war, but so many nostalgic memories remained of it after the Armistice that a Talbot House Association was formed; on its board of trustees were some of the most notable people in England, including the Archbishop of Canterbury, field marshals, royalty, and members of Parliament. Out of this, an entire Toc-H movement was spawned, and by 1921 there were some seventy Talbot Houses in cities all around the British Isles. By World War II there were Talbot Houses around the world. In 1940, when the Germans came to Belgium again and discovered what the original Talbot House in Poperinge meant to the English, they quickly shut it down and used it for their own purposes. Its last German occupants were the staff of the German commander in chief, Karl von Rundstedt. Three months after the D-day landings in 1944, before von Rundstedt and his people fled, they tried to burn it down, but Belgian civilians extinguished the flames. Talbot House stands today. In Poperinge.

★ Chapter Nine

The eventful year 1916 opened with an air of optimism among the Allied nations. True, during the previous year they had gained little ground, and lost more, and taken casualties no one would have dreamed of before the war. But after seventeen months of struggle, a clearer picture began to emerge of what it would take to win it, and time and strength seemed to be on the Allies' side. A great sea battle had taken place in the North Sea off the coast of Denmark—the Battle of Jutland. The German High Seas Fleet had finally come out to challenge Britain's Grand Fleet and, although the British suffered more than twice the losses of the Germans, when it was over the outnumbered Germans had fled. It was now assumed that the blockade of Germany and England's command of the sea would remain unchallenged. In May, as the Second Battle of Ypres was coming to a close, Italy entered the war on the side of the Allies, putting more pressure on the German Eastern Front against the Russians, since the Austro-Hungarian armies were now also fighting in the Italian Alps. In England, the whole might of industry was now turned toward war production, and the bulk of Kitchener's armies would soon take the field for a great and, it was hoped, decisive campaign.

Meantime, there was fighting to be done in the Ypres Salient. In the middle of February, the Germans attacked a position held by the British known as The Bluff. This was a piece of high ground alongside the Ypres-Comines Canal that afforded the British one of their few decent observation points in the entire Salient. The Germans' artillery bombardment caused a platoon of the Lancastershire Fusiliers to take shelter in an old mine tunnel. Then the Germans blew off a mine of their own, burying alive the whole platoon, except for three men, after which they took possession of The Bluff.

In addition to the tactical value of securing one of the last pieces of high ground remaining in British hands, the German assault on The Bluff was a diversion for a far larger operation: the German campaign against Verdun. Before the winter closed, the German commander Falkenhayn determined that the best way to win the war was to put the much-battered French Army out of it, leaving only the British, who could then be ground up piecemeal. He selected the great French fortress of Verdun, in the southern part of the front, as his object, apparently on the theory that its capture would so demoralize the French that they would sue for a separate peace. Verdun had been perhaps the strongest of the old French border fortifications erected following the 1871 loss to Germany in the Franco-Prussian War. But ever since the autumn of 1914 it had been a relatively quiet sector manned by second-rate French troops, and had in fact been stripped of most of its armaments. It was Falkenhayn's stated intention to "bleed the French army white" there. This he almost succeeded in doing, but in the end it was his own army that was "bled white."

The British quickly organized a series of costly counterattacks to retake The Bluff, which failed. It was not until March 2 that the Germans were finally expelled. The British had thought up a trick, which led directly to their recapture of the line. For several days prior to their assault, British artillery fired a salvo onto the German positions, and followed it exactly two minutes later by another. The Germans became so used to this procedure that when the British at last attacked in between the two salvos the German defenders were found to be sheltering themselves in dugouts. Among the positions captured that day was an eminence that had become known darkly as the "International Trench," owing to the fact that it had changed hands so many times that the bodies of many different nationalities—Frenchmen, Englishmen, Irishmen, Scotsmen, Canadians, Indians, and of course Germans—were buried within it.

*   *   *

In any case, the German assault on The Bluff had been meant to keep the Allies from sending reinforcements down to Verdun once the battle had opened. General Plumer, commander of the Second Army, who was now in charge of the Ypres Salient, had other plans. First, he and other British high officers, including Haig, were alarmed that on so many sectors of the Western Front (aside from Ypres) a sort of "live-and-let-live" attitude had developed between the opposing forces—especially in French-held parts of the line. Plumer found this unhealthy and unwise and made it his intention to maintain the aggressive offensive in all cases, even limited ones. Thus Plumer decided to retaliate for the German attack on The Bluff, and his own high cost of retaking it, with an attack of his own at St. Eloi, about a mile north of it. To that end, he ordered that a number of deep (up to 100 feet) mine shafts be dug and loaded with explosives for the eventual assault.

On March 27 five mines at St. Eloi were exploded and, according to the Official History, "it appeared as if a long village was being lifted through flames into the air." The explosion was more than twice as powerful as that at Hill 60 and could be heard as far away as the southeast of England. (This was the same position that Captain Agar Adamson and the Princess Patricias had fought for so desperately the previous year.) The British then occupied the German trenches at St. Eloi without difficulty, but that was only the beginning of the problem. First, the explosions had wrecked the German drainage systems and when it began to rain the trenches were flooded; second, the mines, and the craters formed by them, and the incessant shelling had so obliterated the position that nobody could figure exactly what was where—it didn't look like the same ground anymore, and it wasn't. With relief parties confused and disoriented, the Germans began to bombard the captured trench system and eventually counterattacked it.

Here enters another character who kept a meticulous diary of his exploits during the war. He is Private Donald Fraser, who was about as far removed from the aristocratic Captain Willie Fraser of the Gordon Highlanders as it was possible to be. Private Fraser was thirty-four years old and a bank clerk in Calgary, Canada, when in 1914 he enlisted to fight for king and country. He began as a private, and he remained a private throughout the conflict—

the suggestion made by his biographer that he deliberately avoided promotion because of the risks involved. Fair or not, Fraser was particularly witty, droll, articulate, and observant in his accounts of the fighting until he was finally shot down at the Battle of Passchendaele in 1917. Private Fraser arrived in the Salient in the autumn of 1915 and, though he endured the rigors of trench warfare from the beginning, St. Eloi was his first real battle.

Private Fraser was among a company of Canadians who relieved the British troops that had been occupying the mess at St. Eloi for a week, under constant German shell fire. Guides led them by night into one of the mine craters, in the center of which was "a slimy pool of rotten, stagnant water." Fraser and his companions were terrified at being placed in this dark, obscure territory, "wrapt in gloomy mystery, with no information regarding the whereabouts of the enemy or our immediate communications. We could only look into an impenetrable darkness and conceive in our minds the general situation surrounding us."

One of the British soldiers who was being relieved had already warned them about the abominable things they would find. Fraser goes on: "When day broke the sights that met our gaze were so horrible and ghastly that they beggar description. Heads, arms and legs were protruding from the mud at every yard and dear God knows how many bodies the earth swallowed. Thirty corpses were at least showing in the crater and beneath its clayey waters other victims must be lying killed and drowned. A young, tall, slim English lieutenant lay stretched in death with a pleasant, peaceful look on his boyish face. Some mother's son, gone to glory."

As was the military custom, the trench duty of the Canadians was to last forty-eight hours, among the worst any of them would ever spend. Their first chore was to bury all the bodies of their dead English predecessors that were still in the trenches, and also to help evacuate the English wounded. Then the German artillery opened up its ritual bombardment and they began to take heavy casualties of their own. "One of the most saddening cases was a dead stretcher bearer near half a dozen dead Tommies, a little to the right of the trench, near the crater," Fraser wrote. "He was sitting with a bandage in his hands, in the very act of bandaging his leg, when his life gave out, and his head fell back, his mouth open, and his eyes gazing up to heaven, as if in piteous appeal. There he sat in a natural posture, as if in life, the bandage in his hands and the Red Cross bag by his side."

Other appalling things were encountered. Two dead men were found on the firestep of a trench, one with a cigarette still in his fingers. Neither was visibly marked and, Fraser concluded, "must have met their doom by concussion." This was not an uncommon thing, men with no bodily wounds found dead after an artillery bombardment. The mere concussion of a nearby high-explosive shell was enough to fatally stop the human heart.

Vicious fighting at St. Eloi—which by now was no more than a heap of dusty rubble—went on for two more weeks, until a sort of unspoken stalemate was reached: "Fighting over a morass of mud and in bad weather," the Official History states, "had imposed unheard of misery upon the troops and both sides were glad to bring it to a close." Several thousand men had been lost as a result, including 300 Germans who had been either atomized or buried alive when the mines blew up.

Then, on the first of June, the Germans went for one of the last pieces of high ground held by the British in the Salient. This was a position known as Observatory Ridge, near the misnamed Mt. Sorrel (which was not a mountain at all, but a hill) between Hooge and Hill 60. It was held by the Canadians, which included Private Fraser and the remains of his company. The German attack, following a terrific bombardment and explosion of German mines, was successful. Naturally, the British began to organize the inevitable counterattack, which, on June 11, drove the Germans off of the position and back to their old lines.

Sounds good, but listen to Private Fraser's account of it: "The traffic in human flesh in this region is scandalous. The Germans themselves have a dread of this front. The mention of Ypres conveyed a sort of horror to them. It had always sinister forebodings of death." He continues with a litany of those killed and wounded in his company at Mt. Sorrel, and concludes: "One has no conception of the horrors of war until he is in the midst of it."

All of these actions were relatively minor in comparison with the big battles such as First and Second Ypres, and the fighting in France at Loos and Neuve Chapelle and, of course, Verdun. The point here is that during the first six months since Sir Douglas Haig had taken command of the army, the British had suffered more than 125,000 casualties (or more than 20,000 a month) and the Germans and French about the same—in so-called minor operations or simple "wastage." It seemed to everybody that this kind of bloodletting could not keep up forever; it did so, and it got worse. For both sides, though, one thing was becoming clear: that attacks on small frontages were usually disastrous. An enemy could easily bring a preponderance of his artillery to bear over the limited area and nullify or reverse any gains made by literally blowing the invaders out of the captured trenches. These were the lessons learned.

Meantime, a profound undertaking was in progress deep in the earth beneath Flanders Fields. Just after his appointment as commander in chief in 1915, Haig had told General Plumer that he intended to launch a big attack against the Germans at Ypres, soon as he could get it ready. Plumer knew that a major attack would necessarily involve driving the Germans off of the Messines Ridge to the south. To that end in early 1916 Plumer summoned the tunneling companies and told them of a scheme of unprecedented magnitude. They were to dig twenty-one deep mine shafts beneath the ridge—some of them half a mile long—and fill them with an amount of explosives so far unheard of. The work involved in this was mind-boggling, thousands of miners tunneling night and day, with tons of soil to be disposed of, and all of it done in utmost secrecy. If nothing else, Plumer thought big; he intended to blow the entire Messines Ridge off the face of the earth with a million pounds of ammonal.

Haig's stated plan to attack at Ypres was seriously "disarranged" by Falkenhayn's attack against the French at Verdun. It was a battle of unbelievable violence and bloodshed and, for a while, the French *were* being "bled white," as Falkenhayn had threatened. In the spring of 1916 the French went to the British for relief; it was suggested that a big attack against the Germans along the Somme River might take the pressure off Verdun. Haig agreed, reluctantly (he had always wanted to attack in Flanders), but he agreed nevertheless because the French promised to cooperate with an offensive on the

Somme. Naturally, he was worried that a French defeat at Verdun could have fatal consequences if it somehow drove France out of the war. It is said by some that the Battle of the Somme was the worst British disaster of World War I. In hindsight, that is probably not true, but to many it did not seem untrue at the time. On the first of July, 1916, Haig hurled Kitchener's New Army men at the Germans on the Somme; that first day alone cost Britain 60,000 casualties, most of them in the first hours of fighting. Kitchener was not there to see it, though; a month earlier he had been drowned on his way to Russia, aboard a British battle cruiser that was sunk in the North Sea.

The fighting on the Somme went on through the summer and into autumn; 750,000 on both sides were killed or maimed. This battle also sealed Falkenhayn's fate as German commander in chief on the Western Front. The Allied attacks on the Somme had the desired effect of siphoning off German troops at Verdun and that depressing episode at last came to a close, with Verdun still in French hands. Despite the terrific losses on the Somme, the British offensive (which in five months gained barely two miles of ground) had been gradually wearing down the Germans by the grisly system of attrition. Virtually all of the German High Command admitted so after the war, but the extent to which the Somme had damaged the German war machine was generally not appreciated in England during the war itself.[1]

By the time the Battle of the Somme finally ground to a halt, it was going on 1917. Winston Churchill tells us in his history of the war, "The beginning of 1917 was marked by three stupendous events: the German declaration of unlimited U-boat war, the intervention of the United States, and the Russian revolution." Not only that, it was marked also by political shuffling among the Allies and the Germans, which would have consequences for the men in the fighting trenches, primarily at Ypres.

---

1. The Somme casualty lists were so long that most people—including those in government—felt the battle had been a waste. It was only after 1918, when German generals began publishing their memoirs, that the extent of damage done to the German army was known; namely, the loss of so many experienced and irreplaceable company-grade officers.

First, in December 1916, Henry Asquith resigned as prime minister of Great Britain and was replaced by David Lloyd George. This would
ultimately lead to serious friction between England's new chief politician, Lloyd George, and the new commander of the armies in the field,
Douglas Haig. Also, on the German end, Falkenhayn had resigned after
the beating his army took at Verdun and the Somme and was replaced by
a sort of duality of command: Erich Ludendorff, a commoner whom the
kaiser considered "crude," and Paul von Hindenburg, then in his seven-
ties. These generals had become renowned for victories on the Russian
Front, and now they would be charged with defeating the Allies in France
and Belgium.

By now, dozens of nations were at war with one another. The so-called
Central Powers consisted of Germany, Austria-Hungary, Turkey, and Bulgaria. The Allies included France, England, Canada, Australia, New Zealand,
South Africa, Russia, Belgium, Italy, Serbia, Romania, Portugal, Montenegro,
Japan, Brazil, China, and, later, America and Greece. In addition, soldiers
from various colonies fought on one side or another, men from India, Ireland, Jamaica on the British side (including a small and pitiful African tribe
called "Bastards"); also, the nations of French colonial Africa, including
Senegal and Morocco as well as French Indochina: Vietnam, Cambodia, and
Laos. In France, owing to his lack of success in expelling the Germans from
the Western Front, portly old General Joffre had been replaced by General Robert Nivelle, who took some credit for the victory at Verdun; this
selection, too, would ultimately bear directly on the coming ordeal of the
soldiers fighting in Flanders.

The German resumption of unlimited submarine warfare was a frightful prospect for England; its effect was foretold from the short period of
such action two years earlier, before the sinking of the *Lusitania* and all the
uproar that caused. By renewing it now, Germany was facing the serious
consequence of provoking America, with her huge population and resources, to come in on the side of the Allies. On the other hand, while the
Germans had only twenty-five U-boats for their 1915 campaign, by 1917
they had more than two hundred. These were enough to do major, if not
fatal, damage to England's great maritime industry, upon which she de-
pended for everything from food to war munitions. Falkenhayn, whatever

else may be said about him, had resisted the temptation to resume unrestricted U-boat war, for fear the Americans might do just what they soon did do—declare war on Germany. Ludendorff, whom the historian Barbara Tuchman described as "demonic," and fat old Hindenburg, however, had no such compunctions. They justified it on the premise that England's naval blockade of Germany was inhumanely starving the German population. It was their blunt intention to win the war before the Americans could get organized and join in, and they wanted total control of the English Channel and the waters around Britain. It was a risk and, as it turned out, a big mistake.

The beginnings of the Russian Revolution shocked everybody, including the Russians. The Red winds of change had been blowing across that vast kingdom for some time, but nobody actually expected that Lenin and the Bolsheviks could seize power in the middle of a war, dethrone the czar, and soon make a separate peace with Germany. But that is what they did, freeing huge armies of Germans to turn to the Western Front. This did not happen immediately. During the harsh winter of 1916–17, just as General Nivelle took charge of the French armies and Ludendorff and Hindenburg took charge of the German armies, riots began to break out all over Russia, as well as a mutiny by the Russian navy. On March 15, the czar, in the absence of any better idea, decided to abdicate. In his place stood Russia's war minister Aleksandr Kerensky, leading a "provisional" government riddled with soviet communists (Bolsheviks). Kerensky kept the war going for a while, but ultimately the communists under Lenin and his colleague Leon Trotsky were able to undermine Kerensky's regime.[2] In November, these two took power, defanged the Russian military establishment, demanded an immediate peace with Germany, and thus the Russian armies began to buckle. Lenin and Trotsky were devout Marxists who believed that Russia's pulling out of the war would inspire socialist uprisings all over the world and put an end to democracies and dictatorships alike, as well as to capitalism, forever. If it had not been for the United States entering the war three weeks after the beginning of Russia's collapse, who knows where or when it would have ended, or how?

2. Lenin had been exiled by the czar for his socialist activities and was living in Switzerland when the Germans found him and secretly took him by a sealed train back to Russia, where they knew he would stir up trouble.

President Woodrow Wilson hated war and what it stood for. He was an idealist who had campaigned on a promise of not bringing America into it. Not only that, he had been working both behind the scenes and onstage to bring the warring parties together. A slogan emerged from these efforts: "Peace Without Victory," under which Germany would give up the territories she had conquered, in exchange for her armies being allowed to go home unmolested—a sort of status quo ante. She ought to have jumped at the chance, too, because since the sinking of the *Lusitania* American attitudes had changed. Germany was increasingly seen as a ruthless nation that would do anything, regardless of the consequences. In the first months of 1917 Americans learned the contents of a secret message sent by Berlin to the German ambassador to Mexico—the infamous Zimmerman Telegram. It instructed the ambassador to tell the Mexicans that if they sided with Germany in the event of war, and against the United States, Germany would help them recover Texas, Arizona, and New Mexico. The American public was outraged. Then just a few weeks later the German submarines began sinking other American ships heading for England and France, killing more Americans. That was enough, even for Wilson, and on April 2 he asked for, and got from Congress, a declaration of war, "To make the world safe for democracy."

In part because of German submarine attacks, rationing had been introduced on the British home front for many foodstuffs and items such as heating coal and automobile fuel. But it was nothing compared with what was going on in Germany. There, the situation was getting downright desperate. Little or no imports were reaching the Germans and practically everything was rationed, at least if there was enough of it to ration. A kind of ersatz food was being offered. Created by chemical companies, coffee, for instance, now consisted of field grains or acorns ground up with some caffeine added. Meat was almost unheard of (after all, they had already eaten up all their pigs); bread was concocted from all sorts of things, including sawdust and ground-up straw. There was practically nothing in the shops and stores; clothing and even shoes were being made from paper or papier-mâché. In a great government program to collect materials for the war machine, German homes were virtually stripped of brass items, such as doorknobs and door knockers, which were then turned into artillery-shell casings. Church bells were melted down for metal. Crime rose dramatically, especially among teenage boys whose parents were away in the war effort. Then in the winter of 1916–17 the German potato crop failed by one half, and the citizens were forced to eat turnips—they called it the "Turnip Winter." Strikes, demonstrations, and riots broke out. Already a million German soldiers had been killed and there seemed no end in sight.

Meantime, Haig's plan for a great attack in Flanders was again "disarranged." The new British prime minister, Lloyd George, despised Haig and despised his conduct of the war. Furthermore, he was a politician with all the wit and cunning of a Shakespearean conspirator. Unlike his predecessor, Asquith, Lloyd George did not intend to meekly bow to his generals' wishes; like his fellow Liberal Winston Churchill, he was convinced it was useless to keep expending British soldiers in the fields of France and Flanders, and he was always looking for ways to win the war elsewhere, such as Italy, the Balkans, or the Middle East. For Haig, and for the chief of the Imperial General Staff, General Sir William "Wully" Robertson, this was mostly nonsense; hadn't the Allied calamity at Gallipoli proven that? To Haig in particular, like his predecessor Sir John French, the German army was in France and Belgium and it was there that it must be defeated.

Now came another opportunity that even Lloyd George couldn't resist. The French had put old General Joffre out to pasture, replacing him with the energetic and dashing sixty-one-year-old general Robert Nivelle, who was proposing to win the war immediately—by a trick. Practically everything had been tried to break the stalemate, but nothing had worked. Now Nivelle had a plan. With the assistance of the British, he said, the French would attack in an area from the Aisne River northward almost to the River Somme. The trick, according to Nivelle, was to break the German "defense in depth" by having the British feint an attack farther north so that the Germans would rush all their reserves there. Then Nivelle's French armies could surprise the Germans with a swift, deep, creeping barrage and—free of German reserves—the French army would sweep through the shattered German trenches and break out into the open countryside, outflank the Germans, and win the war. All this was to be accomplished in twenty-four or, at the most, forty-eight hours.

Haig was lukewarm on the idea, but at least the major effort would be by the French, who had somewhat recovered from their tribulations at Verdun. Still it would require yet another postponement of his big attack in Flanders, which he believed was more likely to succeed.

At the same time, another kind of struggle was brewing, which threatened to disrupt the entire war effort. After agreeing to the cooperation of the British empire in Nivelle's offensive, Lloyd George more or less conspired with the French to put the whole of the British Army under French control. From the outset, the British prime minister had believed that the French strategy for winning the war was better than Haig's. Along with his own idea of keeping down casualties on the Western Front by attacking the Germans elsewhere, Lloyd George, unlike Haig, expressed admiration for the French attitude of "live and let live" at the front. And if there had to be an attack, Lloyd George believed, it should be in the nature of some new scheme like Nivelle's, something that would surprise and trick the Germans.

In any case, at a conference shortly before the battle, the French president, Aristide Briand, presented the British with a plan to subordinate the British Army to the French command. This delighted Lloyd George because he had quietly cooked up this novel arrangement with the French politicians. As historian John Terraine has pointed out, this would have made Haig no more than "a glorified adjutant general," concerned only with his army's discipline and personnel. Haig, his staff, and the commander of the Imperial General Staff, Sir William Robertson, were naturally outraged and all agreed to resign or face court-martial if the thing was carried through. In the end, they agreed to a compromise under which Nivelle would command the British Army only for the duration of the battle he was now proposing and that, in any case, the decision could be repealed if the safety of their army was in danger. Thus the situation was defused, but the rupture between Haig and Lloyd George had begun in earnest. It must have been frustrating for Lloyd George, because he so much wanted to get rid of Haig and replace him with someone sharing his own views. But, among other things, Haig was a friend of the king, and this made it almost impossible.

For his part, Haig was "thoroughly disgusted with our Government and our politicians."

The so-called Nivelle Offensive turned out to be a tragic and epic fiasco. First, the Germans not only got wind of the plan, they got the plan itself! During a raid they managed to capture a synopsis of the whole attack order that some criminally irresponsible officer had allowed to be taken right into the trenches. Not only that, but Nivelle himself had gone around blabbing about the plan at fashionable London dinner parties, so its disclosure should have come as no surprise. Nevertheless, to the Allies' eventual astonishment, the Germans pulled their entire front line—nearly 100 miles long—back to higher, drier ground up to forty miles away, in the process both shortening it and straightening it. There they had prepared superb defenses, complete with concrete pillboxes, deep dugouts, and the like. And there they waited, on what would be called the Hindenburg Line.

So clandestine was the German evacuation (they left a skeleton force in the old positions to fire off guns and look busy) that the French did not even detect it, although the British did. Nivelle, however, was undaunted. He foolishly decided to go ahead with his attack anyway, even though his five armies would now have to trudge across nearly forty miles of territory, leaving all their carefully laid supplies and communications far behind.

Furthermore, in a carnival of mean-spirited overreaction, the Germans had completely desolated the landscape in which there were many French villages and farms that had coexisted more or less peacefully in occupation since the outbreak of war three years earlier. Upon their departure to their new positions, the Germans poisoned the wells and lakes from which they had gotten water, chopped down the orchards from which they had eaten fruit, and demolished the French homes and cottages in which they had slept when behind the front lines. Churchill fulminated that the deeds were done "with a severity barbarous because [they were] far in excess of any military requirements."

In any case, the Nivelle Offensive got under way on April 16, 1917. High-ranking government officials had tried to talk him out of it, but Nivelle threatened to quit. Haig, in fact, had told him it would be better to attack the Germans at Ypres, where they could not easily retreat, as they had done along the Somme Line. But Nivelle wasn't about to scrap all his hard months of preparations. He had originally planned to completely overwhelm the eight German divisions he thought were opposed to him, with forty divisions of his own. Knowing of the plan, though, the Germans had their own forty divisions ready and waiting. Incidentally, this went to show how dramatically warfare was changed since the last century. Commanders in years past—while they always wanted to have some superiority in numbers—had contented themselves with perhaps at most a two to one advantage and, confident of their men's fighting spirit, were rarely uncomfortable with an odds-on-even match. The high-explosive artillery, automatic weapons, barbed wire, grenades, and other implements of the new, modern warfare, had of course altered these equations drastically. Thus Nivelle felt he needed a five-to-one ratio for an attack, and he was right—except he no longer had it.

In nearly three weeks of fighting (Nivelle's twenty-four-hour limit had been extended) the French lost some 200,000 men and gained nothing of value except a few miles of front line and about 28,000 German prisoners. Ordinarily, this in itself might have been considered something of a victory, but since Nivelle had announced that his offensive was going to win the war, his shortfall became his downfall. As a consequence Nivelle was fired and General Philippe Pétain, "the hero of Verdun," replaced him. But a far greater consequence was that the episode caused a near calamity for the entire French Army.

After the battle, the soldiers were beyond furious; they had seen only too well the useless waste of life. One division suddenly refused to go back into the trenches; this mood of demoralization swept through the French armies like a wildfire. Officers were assaulted and, some say, shot by their own men. In turn, many of the mutineers were executed—nobody knows how many—while many others were exiled to Devil's Island or other French penal colonies. A division-size force of Russians who were still fighting alongside the French revolted and began to spread Bolshevik propaganda. Before they were suppressed by French artillery fire, they succeeded in starting rumors among the enlisted rank and file that Frenchmen were being sacrificed for profits for millionaire munitions makers. The mutinies at one point or another involved a very large part of the French Army, and French soldiers were seen waving red flags, shouting revolutionary slogans, singing communist songs, and sabotaging military equipment.

General Pétain put an iron-tight lid on the thing for the press, and set about to rectify the situation by visiting personally every major unit of the army. The soldiers informed him that they were willing to man the trenches to repel the enemy but would no longer take part in further senseless attacks. They demanded other things, too, such as more leave and better living conditions. Pétain realized it was going to take much time to get his army back in fighting shape and that, until then, the French were incapable of taking the offensive, a role that the British would have to perform alone.

To his profound embarrassment, it was the hero of Verdun's duty to convey this situation to the British commander, Sir Douglas Haig, but in fact Pétain did not, for more than a month, until almost the eve of the Third Battle of Ypres. Haig's intelligence system got wind of the matter anyway—at least to some extent. Haig at once recognized the dangerous implications of the collapse of French morale. If the Germans got hold of the information, a total disaster would be in the making. The whole business was treated with the utmost secrecy, but now Haig felt he had another imperative reason to bolster his big attack in the Ypres Salient—taking the pressure off of the French Army until it could regain its composure.

Back in England, from Prime Minister Lloyd George down through the various war ministries, the press, and the man in the street, the sentiment was "no more Battles of the Somme." The more than 400,000 British casualties had appalled everyone and touched so many of the homes in Britain from which the once-peaceful civilian volunteers of Kitchener's armies had come that it was almost universally felt there must be some better way. Haig did not think there was; not that he contemplated another Somme, but he believed that only a large-scale attack could crack the Germans, that all the attacks so far had been foiled by bad luck, or some misapplication of military principles. Without a big attack the war, theoretically, could go on forever. Lloyd George disagreed, and was still of the firm opinion that some distant victory in the Mediterranean theater would hobble the Germans. With this as his view and mind-set, Lloyd George was to become Haig's nemesis. However, after the embarrassing failure of the Nivelle Offensive, the prime minister went out of his way to make up to Haig, since he was aware that everyone knew Haig had not been enthusiastic about Nivelle's plan while Lloyd George had been.

A foreboding sidelight to the Nivelle affair should have been taken down by the British under "lessons learned," but it wasn't. If it had been, much of the tragedy that became Third Ypres—at Passchendaele—might have been avoided. The British role in Nivelle's scheme had been to launch an early, diversionary attack to draw the German reserves away from the French sector, which of course did not work well because the Germans knew of Nivelle's plan from the outset. This took place at Arras and the Vimy Ridge a week before Nivelle's ill-fated venture. There, the British opened up with nearly 3,000 artillery pieces—the highest concentration yet seen on their sector of the Western Front—and on the first day took all their objectives. Then it began to rain and a new and forbidding problem was encountered.

The First Army commander, General Sir Henry Horne, reported that further progress was next to impossible, mainly because they had bombarded the Germans so heavily. "It had broken up the soil so frightfully that all movement was made most difficult," Horne said. This was to become one of the great dilemmas of the offensive war Haig planned to wage. Earlier lessons learned had been that, in order to successfully attack the Germans in their trenches, a great and lengthy artillery barrage must first be laid down. But now the British found themselves victims of their own ingenuity: with the coming of the rain, the bombardment churned the landscape into a bog of water-filled shell craters that the attacking soldiers could not pass through. Mud and infantry attacks simply did not mix, an ominous sign for the days to come.

★ Chapter Ten

The road to tragedy in the Third Battle of Ypres did not begin with Haig, though he was the plan's most vehement proponent. After Nivelle's fall from grace, and the ascension of Pétain, Haig realized that the British Army would for all practical purposes now be fighting alone. The very reason for Pétain's appointment was that he advocated a defensive strategy, avoiding losses and waiting for the Americans to arrive within the next year. Haig mistrusted this idea.

A grave matter, also, was the prospect of the Germans getting wind of the condition of the French Army and attacking it in strength, with the very real probability of defeating it, a prospect too horrid to contemplate. Another thing foremost in Haig's mind was the staggering toll the new submarine war was taking on England's merchant marine—500,000 tons and more of ships were being sent to the bottom each month. At that rate, England might not be able to last until the Americans arrived, or so claimed the commander of the British Navy, Admiral Sir John Jellicoe. Also, there was the unnerving reality that the Ypres Salient continued to be a death trap for Haig's army. It was now consuming more than 1,000 casualties a day from "wastage." He was also of the opinion, given by his intelligence chief, John Charteris, that the Germans were on their last legs, and that one mighty push might break them for good. This was the information

Charteris had assembled from prisoner interrogations. All these things were on Haig's mind.

One reason Flanders was to be the site of this great battle was because they had tried it everywhere else and failed. Also, Haig wanted to fight the Germans in a place where they could not pull back to some other immensely fortified line; if they tried that at Ypres, as they had with Nivelle when they pulled back to the Hindenburg Line, they would probably have to sacrifice their Belgian North Sea ports as well as their crucial railhead at Roulers. Furthermore, Haig knew Ypres well. He had fought there from the beginning, ever since the frightening autumn of 1914. He had already concocted an elaborate and terrible scheme to drive the Germans from the Messines Ridge to the south of Ypres; so why not then use this as the springboard for the main attack? On that grim September morning when the Germans and the Allies first clashed at Ypres, Sir John French had ordered Haig's First Army to drive them from their staging areas at Thourout and Roulers, and now, two and a half years and millions of casualties later—and what must have seemed to Haig like so very long ago—this was precisely what he intended to do, and much, much more. Before anything else, though, he first needed to clear the Germans off of Messines.

By 1917 the great mining enterprise beneath the Messines Ridge was coming along well, but not without fearful obstacles. There were now more than 20,000 men in the British tunneling companies, burrowing molelike beneath the earth. They had completed or were about to complete a series of tunnels as much as 125 feet deep that reached out under no-man's-land and ended up beneath nearly half a mile of the German frontline trenches, and beyond them as well. The German line to be destroyed covered more than six miles of front, curving up from Ploegsteert Wood in the south to the wretched Hill 60 in the north. Never had such an enormous human undertaking, with so much explosive power, been seen on earth.

But there were endless problems. The mine shafts frequently flooded and had to be pumped out by hand pumps or, if available, electric pumps. Mines often caved in and buried the tunnelers alive. Gas, both natural and manufactured, was an ever-present danger. It could quickly overcome and kill a man. The presence of gas was often difficult to detect, so using an old miner's ploy, canaries were placed in the mines and near the entrances. The tiny canary felt the effects of gas much more quickly than could humans and would pass out from it and fall from its perch, giving a warning to the men. Like everything else, large numbers of canaries had to be requisitioned from the Quartermaster General, and this often gave pause to high staff officers who did not understand their use. Also, a breathing apparatus was developed, called the Proto-Mask.

Since as early as 1915 as many as 150 men at a time had been working in shifts around the clock in each of the twenty main tunnels in the Salient. It was grueling work in often deplorable conditions: cold, wet—water was sometimes knee deep—physically exhausting, and dangerous. All had to be done in the utmost secrecy, and with so much dirt, or "spoil," which needed to be removed, this required a superhuman effort, and mostly at night, when the spoil was trucked far to the rear so the Germans could not see it from their observation posts. The tunnel entrances were elaborately disguised from the outside and posted with signs such as DEEP WELL. Bad air in the mines plagued the tunnelers. Compressed air was pumped in, but sometimes it was not enough.

Even so, these new mines were a far cry from the primitive clay-kicked mines of previous years. The main tunnels were as much as six feet in height, shored up with timber and electrically lighted. Great machines that had been used to excavate the London subway system were brought over and reassembled beneath the ground, but they did not work well. One in fact is still buried deep beneath the Belgian soil.

And there were worse things, too. The Germans, as might have been expected, were not simply sitting in their trenches on the other side of no-man's-land like cardboard dummies. They not only were mining themselves, but were well aware that the British were doing so too. Crews of coal miners from the Ruhr were sinking shafts of their own and digging out from them to try to detect and intercept the British efforts. This they frequently did, and when they broke into these tunnels what ensued was a series of Battles Beneath the Earth, with men shooting, grappling, grenading, stabbing one another and going at it with picks and shovels. The British even developed a special brass dagger for this, which was strapped to the wrist. As they burrowed along, at the head was what was called a "fighting tunnel," where various armaments and bombs were stored, in case the Germans broke in.

The well-known English poet Edmund Blunden, then a twenty-one-year-old Oxford-educated lieutenant in the Royal Sussex Regiment, punctuates the irony of this grotesque subterranean dance of death in a work describing troops attending a musical concert behind the lines at Ypres. As they emerge, another type of concert is taking place in the form of an artillery barrage near St. Eloi; then

> To this new concert, white we stood;
> Cold certainty held our breath;
> While men in the tunnels below Larch Wood
> Were kicking men to death.

The primary weapon of attack against tunneling and countertunneling, however, was called a *camouflet*. It was a relatively small explosive that, when signs of enemy tunneling were detected, could be set off to cave in the enemy tunnel, without caving in your own or blowing up the ground above. There were also "torpedoes," long tubes that carried charges and could be inserted into a hole drilled in the facing, to blow in an enemy tunnel.

If they could have been seen from the air, the British mine tunnels would have looked like huge tree trunks, with smaller "branches" growing out from them. Others looked like caterpillars, with feelers. At the end of each branch, or feeler, a mine would be laid. Deep inside these caverns, night and day, dozens of men, mainly officers, sat glued to the wall facings, trying to detect the noise of enemy mining or countermining. For this they used a device called a geophone, which resembled a doctor's stethoscope and was amazingly sensitive to enemy tunneling, especially considering all the racket going on aboveground.

The engineers running the operation did not even know when Haig's big Flanders attack was to take place, and worried that the tunnels would be discovered, or be flooded, or cave in, or that the ammonal they had placed there would deteriorate. But they kept at it for almost two years, into the spring of 1917.

*   *   *

Even a synopsis of the events leading up to the Third Battle of Ypres is complicated, because it involved so many delicate negotiations between the Allies, especially the teetering French. (Germany, on the other hand, had no such problems, as all its kingdoms and principalities were united under the iron fist of the kaiser.) Since the battle itself has become so bitterly controversial, it is worth it to try to unravel at least some of the vagaries.

Late in 1916 representatives of the principal Allies, Britain and France, had met at Chantilly to decide what the future of the war would look like in 1917. The main thing that was agreed on was that the Germans should get no relief from the kind of pressure that had been put on them at the Somme and at Verdun, but instead be subjected to a constant series of "wearing-down battles," in other words: attrition. It was also agreed that Haig's plan to launch a major offensive in Flanders would be given paramount consideration. But certain powerful political forces in France disagreed with the grim notion that the war had to go on another year, and when General Nivelle presented his fantastic all-out, win-now strategy, they forced its acceptance. Hence, the Nivelle Offensive, which as we have seen derailed Haig's scheme to attack the Germans at Ypres during the months when at least reasonably good weather might be counted on.

Now that the Nivelle affair had so miserably failed, the Allies again met, in Paris in May 1917, and returned to the original design of a series of wearing-down battles. Next day another conference was held, in which General Pétain let out the first hint that his army was no longer confident in its leaders nor in its government. The admission was also expressed by the British that the all-out German U-boat campaign was exerting very serious damage to their efforts to stay in the war, and that the expulsion of the enemy from the Belgian ports just north of Ypres was a necessity. Prime Minister Lloyd George took the soapbox to tell everybody that the Germans "must not be left in peace for one moment." He further went on to say that he did not wish himself or, for that matter, other civilian officials to even know what plan of attack the military commanders contemplated. It had become his opinion that politicians tended to be loose-lipped in such matters and these secrets were too important to risk being divulged. At least that is what he said at the time.

General Pétain weighed in that he thought the so-called wearing-down battles should be conducted with limited objectives over broad fronts, and with short depths, citing figures that showed that deep penetrations of German positions only brought on unacceptable casualties due to the effectiveness of German counterattacks. He also promised that the French Army—even in its now limited capacity—would cooperate with British offensives.

Whether Haig agreed with this, or even believed it, he informed his own army commanders a day or so later that it was his intention now to bring on his big battle in Flanders to kick out the Germans and their submarines from the Belgian coast all the way up to Holland, and then drive them back eastward across Belgium toward the Rhine—hardly a limited objective. Lloyd George, for his part, was not happy with Haig's scheme—what little he knew of it—but in view of his previous support for the Nivelle fiasco, he could hardly now object. In any case, the curtains were drawn and the stage was being reset for the Third Battle of Ypres.

The man Haig picked to orchestrate the capture of the Messines Ridge was sixty-year-old Lieutenant General Sir Herbert Plumer, who was born in the year of the Great Indian Mutiny and made a general during the Boer War, while Haig was still a captain. He now commanded the Second Army and had been on the Ypres front since 1915, where his hair had turned completely white from the strain. Plumer was a short, rotund man with birdlike legs and a walrus mustache, who looked less like a general than he did a shopkeeper. In fact he was every inch a general and was perhaps the best in the British Army at that time. He was meticulous, organized, and he tried to plan his battles with the least loss of life possible. To his troops, who generally liked him, he was known as "Daddy."

Even before the Nivelle Offensive, Haig had told Plumer to prepare for him a plan for the great Flanders battle to break out and capture the Channel ports of Ostend and Zeebrugge. Plumer's response was to submit a scheme to take Messines Ridge, which, he said, was a prerequisite to any large-scale offensive. Haig was not particularly pleased with this cautious approach, and Plumer's stock therefore fell somewhat in the commanding general's estimate, though it was plain that Plumer was right. It was Plumer's contention that there simply was not enough room around the Ypres Salient to marshal all the artillery, supplies, ammunition, and men for a simultaneous assault along the entire line and subsequent large-scale breakthrough

In any event, it was Plumer's Second Army that was to attack Messines and Haig placed high hopes upon him. Plumer asked for, and received, an enormous quantity of artillery for the operation—more than 2,200 guns for its limited frontage, yet again the largest concentration during the war; in many places the guns were literally wheel to wheel. All sorts of other preparations had to take place: railroads had to be improved and scores of new ones built to transport vast amounts of munitions and equipment that would be needed for this first British offensive in Flanders; supply dumps had to be established; medical organizations had to be set up, and vast amounts of pipes and pumps laid for drinking water; pack animals, trucks, aircraft, and all that it took to keep them operating had to be put in place. Far behind the lines Plumer even had a gigantic scale model built of the whole ridge and its approaches, almost the size of a football field, and all officers and men, down to platoon commanders and privates, were taken there and shown their various roles in the attack.

One of the most vital and complex tasks during the entire war fell to the Field Surveying Companies, men who were responsible for compiling maps showing the locations of enemy artillery batteries and other critical dispositions. At the Battle of Messines they reached the zenith of their abilities.

Destruction or at least neutralization of German artillery power was an absolute necessity to a successful assault at Messines, or, for that matter, anywhere else. First the enemy batteries had to be located precisely, and that information put on a map for the Allied artillery to shoot at. Various methods were used by the Field Surveying Companies. Aerial observation by balloon or aircraft was excellent when the weather permitted, but often it did not. "Flash spotting" by ground observers using a combination of a plane table and theodolite could triangulate an enemy battery by observing its gun flashes, then, employing a complicated formula of bisection, intersection, and resection, trigonometrically place their coordinates on a map. A more advanced development was the use of intricate "sound ranging" systems, in which a series of supersensitive microphones picked up the blast of an enemy gun and transmitted its noise to a magnetic galvanometer, from which the shock wave was photo-filmed and the coordinates laid on an artillery map. A virtual army of British physicists, engineers, and mathematicians was engaged in developing and perfecting the sound-ranging equipment.

More than 30 million trench and artillery maps were printed during the war, nearly 600,000 during the weeks preceding the attack at Messines Ridge. They were immensely useful; 90 percent of the German batteries at Messines were located, and before the battle half of the enemy heavy artillery and 25 percent of his field guns were blown up by British counterbattery fire—a remarkable achievement.

Preliminaries got under way at the beginning of May with an unprecedented shelling of the German lines. During the week before the attack some 3 to 4 million shells of all description—high-explosive, shrapnel, and gas— were fired into the enemy positions. In addition, machine-gun companies saturated the German trenches with about 15 million rounds, adding to the terror. The idea was to so strain the nerves of the Germans that they would have little fight left in them.

It worked; between the unceasing blasts of artillery explosions, the rattle of machine-gun fire, and having to don gas masks all the time, the Germans were being worn out. In fact, is was so perilous to move around their battle area that dogs had to be sent up, carrying rations, but many German soldiers went hungry anyway. Many dogs died.

The new German strategy of "elastic" defense was well evolved in the Salient. The theory was that the front line would be manned lightly. The entire battle area up to half a mile and more in depth had been checkered with hundreds of pillboxes made of concrete, four feet thick, reinforced with steel rods and able to withstand a direct hit from all but the heaviest artillery. These were built with machine-gun slots and were of various sizes, the largest holding up to forty men. Unfortunately, because of the nature of the ground, when it rained they often flooded with up to several feet of water, and because the occupants could not go outside to tend to their needs the trenches became filthy-smelling and unsanitary. Likewise, dead bodies outside could not be buried and decomposed rapidly in the warm spring, adding to the foulness.

Nevertheless, the Germans believed they had the plan to repel the British. When it first became apparent that the Allies were going to attack at Ypres, General Kuhl, Crown Prince Rupprecht's chief of staff, recommended withdrawing from Messines Ridge entirely, to a new and more defensible line below and beyond the eastern slope. The crown prince concurred, but when he consulted the various corps commanders in the German Fourth Army, which was defending Ypres, he found them hard against any such evacuation. As to reports that the British had installed mines beneath the ridge, the officer in charge of countermining assured everyone that no such mines existed. In this, of course, he was wrong.

The German plan was to allow the British attack to develop into the front lines, then be met with heavy fire from the seemingly impregnable pillboxes and machine-gun nests set in the ruins of houses and farms. As the British were drawn deeper into the trap, they would be met by the strong reserves of the frontline divisions. The final blow would be struck by specially trained counterattack divisions, which by then would have arrived on the battlefield to throw the British back across no-man's-land. That was the theory.

The night before the attack the artillery barrage reached a crescendo. Zero Hour had been set for 3:10 A.M., June 7. More than 80,000 men from practically all parts of the British empire had assembled in the trenches, fixing bayonets: Australians, New Zealanders, Irish—both southern and northern—Scotsmen, Welsh, and men from every county and shire in England.

Plumer had a last-minute meeting with his commanders, then everyone went to the front to see the mines go up—except for Plumer himself, who went to his room and prayed. A moon beamed out of a clear sky as the night wore on. According to the Official History, "The British artillery fire had been normal during the night, but half an hour before dawn a calm set in, so marked that from the front lines nightingales could be heard singing in the distant woods . . ."

Then, precisely at 3:10 A.M., "Suddenly . . . great leaping streams of orange flame shot upwards, each a whole volcano in itself, along the front of attack, followed by terrific explosions and dense masses of smoke and dust, which stood like great pillars towering into the sky, all illuminated by the fires below."

Along a ten-mile front, some 10,000 Germans were instantly atomized or buried alive by the nineteen mines containing a million pounds of ammonal. Two more mines had been laid but at the last minute it was decided not to set them off, and in the ensuing years they were forgotten. This was to have consequences in the years to come long after the war was over.

It was a truly spectacular event, never before seen and not likely to be seen again. The earth shook for miles around as if in an earthquake, which terrified not only the Belgian citizens but German soldiers who, as far away as the town of Lille, in France, ran panic-stricken into the streets. The noise and shock wave crossed the channel and reached England, where it startled Lloyd George himself. There was an illusionary effect, too. Some German observers thought the explosions had occurred far behind their lines, while some British thought they had gone off behind their own lines. At the time, it was the Greatest Show on Earth.

As the mine explosions began to die out and the inevitable debris of dirt, equipment, timber, helmets, boots, pots and pans, Germans, and parts of Germans began to fall back to earth, a breathtaking artillery barrage issued from the British batteries. It exploded on the first 700 yards of the enemy front, effectively annihilating those few Germans who had survived the mines. The Official History says: "The flashes of the guns in the darkness were so close together and continuous that the whole western horizon seemed to be ablaze." At the same time, 150,000 men of three British army corps—nine divisions, with three more close behind—climbed out of their trenches and moved up the slope of Messines Ridge.

With daybreak only beginning, and the dust from the mine explosions clouding the air, some units lost direction, but this was soon sorted out. They followed a "creeping barrage," about 100 yards ahead of them, across no-man's-land. The barrage consisted of explosive and camouflage smoke, and when the men began to reach the vast craters caused by the mines, there was further confusion and problems with visibility. In many cases direction was found only by use of a compass. What they saw at the craters was astonishing. Some of the holes were 200 feet across and 20 feet deep. Huge boulders of blue clay, through which the miners had tunneled a hundred feet below, were lying about, some the size of automobiles. As they peered down into the craters German feet and arms stuck out of the rubbish; body parts were everywhere.

Of course it was not all a walk in the park. The deeper into the German lines they came, the more they began to take fire from machine guns and grenades from the various strong points and pillboxes. But in most cases the Germans had been completely shattered and demoralized. Many wept and groveled at the feet of the British soldiers, clutching their legs and pleading for mercy. By 9 A.M. the attacking force had reached the crest of Messines Ridge along most of its ten-mile front.

Now an ironic thing occurred on the ridge; the British suddenly found themselves victims of their own amazing success. It had been estimated that more than half of them would become casualties before taking the crest of the ridge. Since only a small fraction had fallen, however, there were now great numbers of soldiers bunched up and overcrowding the ridge—paradoxically, too many men had survived. They made inviting targets for German machine gunners on the opposite slope about half a mile away, which had not been affected by the mines or much by the artillery barrage. According to the Official History, at this point "casualties began to mount rapidly."

As the sun heated up the morning the British began stripping to their shirtsleeves and digging in to escape the fire and the expected counterattacks. Pack mules plodded up with rations, ammunition, and other supplies—they had been kept in dugout "mule pits" close to the front for rapid deployment. Phone lines were laid. A number of the fifty-odd tanks that had been allotted for the attack began to lumber up and heavy machine guns arrived.

From atop the ridge an extraordinary panorama revealed itself. Looking back from whence they had come, the men saw only the barren and ruined moonscape of no-man's-land and the crumbling spires of Ypres and its surrounding villages. But looking eastward, down over the German rear lines, they saw a vista of pastoral serenity: tall green trees, meadows and farmlands, and here and there villages untouched by the scourge of war. The contrast was startling, and remarked upon.

Beginning about 11 A.M. the soldiers on the ridge began to see in the distance columns of the gray-uniformed German counterattack divisions moving toward them. For any soldier anywhere, this is a chilling experience—the sight of the enemy, soon to be encountered. But as they came closer, artillery spotters—finally with perfect observation—called in for barrages, which ripped these enemy formations apart. Nearer still, the machine guns opened up. The vaunted German counterattack never developed. By nightfall, Messines Ridge was secure.

Actually the attack had spread successfully over the ridge and down to a position on the other side, known as the Oosttaverne Line, which had been the final objective set by Plumer. But owing to German counterattacks and confusion by the British this was given up and it took another week of fighting to reclaim it. Nevertheless, the Official History tells us: "With the establishment of this new line on the 14th June, the Battle of Messines ended. A great victory had been won. After two long years of patient endurance, the ambition to remove the Germans from the dominating southern face of the Ypres Salient had been realized and the aim of months of intensive labor and preparation was achieved."

More than 5,000 Germans had been made prisoners, bolstering Haig's contention that the morale of the German army was on the brink of collapse. In bringing the prisoners back to Allied lines, the British arrived at an ingenious solution to make sure their captives did not cause trouble. They cut the suspenders of the indignant Germans, so they had to use both hands to hold up their pants.

The Messines Ridge operation had cost Plumer about 25,000 casualties and the Germans about the same. Now the British held the high ground in nearly half of the Salient and were poised to launch Haig's main effort to expel the enemy from the rest of Ypres and from their U-boat bases on the Belgian coast. So far, it had been a textbook triumph, easily the most successful British operation of the war.

One of the British soldiers killed that day was not an Englishman at all, but a fifty-six-year-old Irish major named William "Willie" Redmond. He was an Irish nationalist and a member of Parliament who had fought long, hard, and eloquently for an amicable solution to the "Irish Problem," between the Catholic south and the Ulster Protestants in Northern Ireland. Though his position was condemned by the radical Irish Republican Army, his gentle personality and poetic speeches had made him beloved in most parts of that strife-torn island. Redmond's superiors had ordered him to stay behind during the Messines attack on the reasonable theory that he was too old to participate in such a strenuous enterprise, but Redmond would have none of it. His Royal Irish Regiment was set to attack that morning alongside the Protestant Ulster Division and he was determined to go.

When he finally got permission he was overjoyed. They had attacked the now ruined village of Wytschaete and just as dawn was breaking a shrapnel shell hit Redmond in the hand. He continued but soon was struck with another piece of shrapnel in the leg. His men thought the wound was slight and moved on, and Redmond was later found and carried toward the rear by a Protestant soldier from the Ulster Division. In turn that soldier was hit, but it was considered remarkable at the time that the two bitter factions of the Irish could fight side by side and help each other in time of need.

A medical officer wrote to Willie Redmond's brother that his wounds did not appear serious and that a younger man might have survived them easily. But as the sun sank over the first and victorious day of the Battle of Messines, Willie Redmond died. His funeral at a Catholic convent the next day was attended by no less than four generals and the condolences that poured in from across the world included those from practically every dignitary imaginable: the pope, the king and queen of England, the prime minister, the presidents of Ireland, Australia, Canada, South Africa, France, and the United States. It was a fitting tribute to a man who, had he lived, might conceivably have mended the fractious and violent discord that continues today between Catholic and Protestant Irishmen.

Chapter Eleven ★

A mystery that will never be solved is why General Haig did not immediately press his attack after the Messines victory, at least to move the battlefield farther east of Flanders. It appears to be the product of confusion, misunderstanding, indecision, or some combination of these.

Plumer's Second Army still had two fresh corps that had not been used in the Messines fight, and they were posted to the north of Messines, from the Gheluvelt Plateau to the far end of the Salient. This plateau, almost directly east of Ypres, was a German strong point bitterly contested since the ordeal of 1914. In order for the British to achieve Haig's great breakout, it would have to be taken because its guns enfiladed the British right flank north of Ypres and could inflict horrifying damage during an assault. Since the Gheluvelt Plateau was adjacent to Messines and Plumer already had two fresh corps opposite, it would seem perfectly logical that Plumer would be the man to carry out the attack.

But then there was the matter of Plumer's "cautious" reply to Haig back in the early spring when asked to prepare a plan for the Second Army to drive the Germans from Ypres. This now came back to haunt the rest of the campaign. Haig's displeasure at Plumer's previous "cautiousness" had led to the extraordinary step of replacing him with another commander as well as with another entire army for the "breakout" phase of the campaign. This would be the British Fifth Army, led by General Sir Hubert Gough.

Gough, like Haig, was a cavalryman, and a "thruster," as compared with Plumer, whom Haig seemed to think of as more of a "plodder." Gough was also, at forty-seven, the youngest of the British army commanders. But Gough's army had a bad reputation among the troops. One officer wrote that "no one wanted to go there." Grave mistakes had been made, mostly in staff work; in an earlier battle in France a number of tanks that were supposed to lead an assault failed to show up and the assault was crushed. By contrast, meticulous planning and staff work was Plumer's hallmark.

Gough's Fifth Army was still in the process of moving up from France when the Messines battle began. Although Haig had told Gough earlier that any exploitation of a victory at Messines would be his responsibility, Haig now wavered. Plumer was the man on the spot, a commander of proven field merit, and a few days before Plumer attacked at Messines, Haig asked him— assuming he became victorious—how long it would take to launch a further attack against Gheluvelt Plateau. Plumer had already considered the matter. He had drawn a plan for the two unused corps to attack north of Messines across the Menin Road and drive the Germans from the southern part of the plateau. All it would take, Plumer said, was three days to get his artillery moved into place. Haig apparently thought that was too long.

This, of course, was the Germans' greatest fear: a continuous series of attacks with massed artillery bombardment that would keep them off balance and drive them from the ridge. In fact Crown Prince Rupprecht considered the notion of drawing back the whole German line on the Gheluvelt Plateau, but when day after day went by with no attack Rupprecht decided to stay put.

In any case, the day after the assault on Messines, when British troops firmly occupied the ridge, Haig again asked Plumer how long it would take to get his artillery and people into position to attack Gheluvelt. Again Plumer told him three days. Haig's unexplained response was to take away Plumer's two fresh corps and give them to Gough's Fifth Army, with instructions to conduct the attack himself. Then Gough, who was completely unfamiliar with Ypres and the Salient, asked for and got six days to prepare for Gheluvelt. When the six days were up, however, Gough blinked. He told

Haig that he found the operation too dangerous and difficult and that, instead, he preferred to leave Gheluvelt Plateau unmolested for another *six weeks* until the great breakout attack in the north could be launched. Gough also got that extension from Haig.

While no one can prove that a timely attack on Gheluvelt Plateau by Plumer—or, for that matter, by Gough—would have succeeded, if it had it is certain that much later suffering would have been avoided, because Haig's armies might well have been able to move out of Flanders and the ridgelines that dominated the landscape around Ypres.

By now the war had been in progress for almost three years and the British Army had evolved into a far different creature than it had been when the first 80,000 regulars arrived in France to fight the German onslaught. The universe in which these men lived had rapidly expanded and its shapes were, if not comforting, at least now familiar.

After the regulars of 1914 were practically annihilated, they were replaced by the territorial or reserve regiments, but most of these had been annihilated too. Now the army was composed mostly of citizen-soldiers, troops from the dominions, volunteers, and, increasingly, conscripts. There were nearly 2 million of them on the Western Front in 1917.

Everything, of course, had evolved to suit the war. Battle tactics had been dramatically altered for trench warfare. By 1917 the notion of battalions "going over the top" to charge the enemy in lined waves had been replaced by a system in which every man had his job to do: some were expert grenade throwers, others machine gunners; still others composed fire-and-maneuver teams. The old soft caps had been discarded in 1916 for the new "tin hat" or shrapnel helmet. The Germans also had replaced their soft hats with an even more protective steel helmet, which looked, more than anything else, like a coal scuttle. Soldiers on both sides remarked that they could generally tell the year when a battle had been fought by the dress of corpses they discovered in no-man's-land. The British Lewis gun had been introduced the previous year, too. This was a light, handheld machine gun that fired from a circular canister-type magazine instead of being belt fed. Tens of thousands of these were issued to the troops.

Various stratagems had been developed to assist the day-to-day operations on the front. The British employed a small army of artists and painters in a vast camouflaging enterprise. They painted gigantic canvases to look like landscapes to deceive the Germans, both from the ground and from the air. One of the more curious inventions was that of the phony tree trunk. Made of bullet-proof steel, these were painted to coincide with the seasons, when the tree might be in leaf or not. After nightfall a similar natural tree trunk was removed and the phony one installed in its place. Then a sniper or an observer could safely ensconce himself in it. The engineers also developed a row of dummy British soldiers that could be taken to the trench and, at the pull of a lever, popped up over the top. When the Germans exposed themselves to fire at these, British snipers took their toll. At one point at Ypres a giant water pump was constructed, the notion being that it could be used to flood the Germans out of their trenches. But it did not work well.

Communications had always been a problem; in fact, it might have been the greatest single problem of the entire war. With such huge numbers of men fighting battles, commanders often knew nothing of their situation, progress, or lack of it. Consequently many men died from their own "friendly" artillery fire and there was agonizing confusion during attacks. Units always tried to lay telephone wire up to the forward most positions, but artillery cut it so frequently that other methods had to be employed.

Runners were used, but they were so regularly shot down that two or more men would have to be sent with the same message. Dogs were used also, but these often became panicked or disoriented by the shelling. Homing pigeons were employed by the thousands, and it was a fairly common sight in the midst of battle to see a soldier carrying a cage of eight or ten of the birds for his battalion commander. The birds, too, were susceptible to the harsh conditions of the battlefield. The poet-lieutenant Edmund Blunden described being under heavy shell fire in a captured German dugout at Ypres. "We endeavored to send off a pigeon, but the pigeon, scared by the gunfire, found his way into the dugout again, and presently a fluttering sound under the floorboards led to his discovery."

Wireless communication—radio—was in its infancy, and while both sides used it, it was considered insecure because of enemy interception. It has been suggested that if wireless had made the type of technological advances as had other innovations during the war, the outcome of many battles might well have been different. For instance, during the German gas attack at the Second Battle of Ypres, if the leading German commander had been in wireless contact with his superiors, he would no doubt have been told to push on and capture the British rear areas. As it was, by the time his runner had made known the situation to his superiors, it was too late to exploit the gain.

Ironically, but not surprisingly, the practice of medicine made important inroads because of the war. For the first time, blood transfusions were used and perfected by a more or less trial-and-error procedure. Much blood was needed because much had been spilled. Medical operations were vastly improved with the introduction of anesthetic gases instead of ether or chloroform. Mme. Marie Curie, the famous French chemist whose discoveries added so much to the practice of radiology (and which ultimately killed her), traveled often to the Ypres front in a car equipped with the new Röntgen X-ray device, developed by the German scientist who had in 1914 signed the official "manifesto" supporting his country in the war. The X ray was an immeasurable help to doctors trying to locate an embedded bullet, fragment, or broken bone. Yet soldiers still suffered terribly not only from wounds but from all sorts of dangerous diseases contracted from living in the open, unsanitary battle areas: meningitis, scarlet fever, typhus, hepatitis, pneumonia, and something called trench fever. By 1917 the Salient was a veritable sewer of human and animal excrement and the decomposing carcasses of men and animals. Little or none of the local water was safe to drink. The Royal Medical Corps was responsible for trying to suppress the contamination, but in many cases little could be done. Wounds, for instance, were particularly susceptible to potentially deadly gas gangrene, for when the bullet or fragment entered it carried with it the filth that was naturally on the men's clothing, and embedded this into the wound, a virtual injection of poison.

Lice were an ever-present plague, and the men would spend hours plucking them off themselves or their clothing and, when they had the chance, they would readily go back to a delousing station in the rear for a bath and wash of clothes. Some, in despair of everything else, even wrote that they wept when they discovered they were lousy. Everyone who went into the trenches had them.

Rats were another scourge to be endured. They feasted on corpses and carcasses in the trenches and in no-man's-land until, some said, they were as big as cats and twice as bold. Men shot them, bayoneted them, poisoned them, and beat them with clubs but in the long run to no avail. They multiplied like, well, rats. One story, perhaps apocryphal, is told of the soldier who found a cat in Ypres and brought it to his trench hoping it would get rid of the rats. Next day the cat was gone; only its tail remained, sticking out of a rat hole. Flies—mostly of the large greenbottle variety— were another bane, especially in the warm months. They invaded the trenches and pestered all and fed on the dead men and animals by the hundreds of thousands.

Discipline had become complex with an army of so many civilian soldiers thrown into desperate and terrifying situations. Young men in their late teens or early twenties huddled in trenches under shell fire, seeing their friends killed and maimed, sometimes reacted like a sane person would do and ran away, or refused to go to the front. The army dealt with this harshly. During the war more than 3,000 soldiers tried by military court-martial were sentenced to death. Of these sentences, 343 were actually carried out—more in the Ypres Salient than anywhere else. It was a horrible experience for everyone concerned. The condemned were shot by firing squad, usually at dawn. Competent legal assistance was not always provided them, and the sentence was normally carried out quickly following conviction, after being reviewed by the army commander in chief.

Parliament had bitter debates on the subject, but nothing much came of them. Most of those executed had been found guilty of desertion; cowardice was the second greatest offense. Particularly distasteful were the cases involving troops from the empire; the notion that the British could try and execute a soldier from Canada, New Zealand, India, or some other colony or commonwealth who had voluntarily come to fight for the Mother Country was abhorrent to the men. While all those nations listed above had soldiers executed, it is noteworthy that the fiercely independent Australians never had a man even sentenced to death, let alone had such a sentence carried out. As one Australian soldier put it, "They knew better. We wouldn't have stood for it." At first the British government sent a notice to the family of the dead soldier telling them he had been tried by court-martial and executed. Later they suspended this practice and simply sent a notice saying he had been "killed."

At this stage in the war both sides had captured tens of thousands of prisoners. Most of the Germans captured by the British were taken back to England where they were set to work in farm fields. In Germany, captured Allied soldiers had a more difficult time of it. Many were put to work in steel mills or, worse, salt and coal mines. Their treatment ranged from humane to brutal. In some camps packages from home and the Red Cross were permitted and the men allowed to play sports and put on theatrical skits. In others the Germans could be ruthless, allowing none of this and worse; as the British blockade squeezed the German food supply, Allied prisoners got the brunt of it. Many men reported they were half starved, their main diet consisting of "potato water," water in which the Germans had boiled their own potatoes, into which some peelings had been dropped and which they passed off for "soup." Some men reported eating grass to stay alive and not a few returned home skeletons.

By now the army had more or less accustomed itself to the strange and mournful music of the battlefield. The soldiers could easily tell the difference between the "whiz-bang" shrapnel shells that burst overhead and the black-smoking "Jack Johnson," heavy German shells, so named after a black American boxer of the era. They learned what the German flare signals meant, and the Germans knew theirs. Also by now, of course, everything in the Salient had been given a soldiers' name: Ypres was known as Wipers, Ploegsteert became Plugstreet, Wytschaete was Whitesheet, and, forbiddingly, Passchendaele became Passiondale—an eerie allusion to the Crucifixion. Bad as they were, the artillery-torn roads around Ypres were about the only way men could travel, since the rest of the ground had been torn up by shell fire. Roads were almost constantly being repaired with cordwood, metal, or duckboards, but wherever they intersected another road and there was a "corner," the Germans registered their artillery to catch congested troops in the open. Some of these areas became infamous: Shellblast Corner, Idiot Crossroads, Suicide Corner, Dead Cow Corner, Shrapnel Corner, Black Watch Corner. The most well known was Hellfire Corner, on the Menin Road.

Soldiers of both sides periodically went on leave to their home countries, a profoundly surreal experience, to be sure. One day they were in the slime, filth, and frightfulness of the trenches and the next could be walking the streets of London or Cologne, sitting at a sidewalk café or in their families' living rooms. As can be imagined, going back to the war was especially hard, but they did it anyway.

One of the things that depressed and fascinated soldiers most was the sense of the never-endingness of the war. They had been at it now, hammer and tongs, for three years; they had been told time and again by their commanders—at Loos, at the Somme, at Vimy, at Arras—that their next "big push" was going to break the Germans' backs. Now they were hearing it again at Ypres. One officer did the math on his own. He calculated that at the rate of British success in pushing the Germans back thus far, it would take 180 years to reach the Rhine. There was similar black humor among the men; one consensus was that the war might possibly be over by about 1950—the playwright George Bernard Shaw was an adherent to this timetable. Others suggested that it might actually go on forever. Our poet-lieutenant Edmund Blunden wrote: "No one here appeared to conceive any end of it."

Indeed there were good reasons to believe this; the casualty rate was such that a man could scarcely hope to escape unscathed. Death, permanent crippling, or capture were the only things that could keep him from being sent back into the line. In some divisions, by the end of the war, the casualties were two and a half times the authorized strength. (The Royal Naval Division, for instance, at full strength numbered some 19,000 men. By war's end, it had suffered 47,953 killed, wounded, and missing.)

Mary Borden was a wealthy American from Chicago, Vassar educated, who had married an Englishman and personally financed a field hospital unit near the front. She often saw the soldiers marching forward for a battle, and gave this frigid image: "They wear their caps jauntily, tilted to one side.

Their faces are bright. They smile and call out with strong voices. They throw kisses to the girls in the fields." Then:

"They come back to us, one by one, two by two in ambulances, lying on stretchers and are pulled out of the ambulances as loaves of bread are pulled out of the oven. They are carried into a shed, unclean bundles, very heavy, covered with brown blankets.

We receive these bundles. We pull off a blanket. We observe that this is a man. He makes feeble whining sounds like an animal. He lies still; he smells bad; he smells like a corpse; he can only move his tongue; he tries to moisten his lips with his tongue.

This is the place where he is to be mended. We lift him on to a table. We peel off his clothes, his coat and his shirt and his trousers and his boots. We handle his clothes that are stiff with blood. We stare at the obscene sight of his innocent wounds. We wash off the dry blood round the edges of his wounds. He says no word except that he is thirsty and we do not give him [anything] to drink.

We confer together over his body and he hears us. We discuss his different parts in terms he does not understand, but he listens while we make calculations with his heart beats and the pumping breath of his lungs. We conspire against his right to die. We plunge deep into his body and add the insult of our curiosity to the curse of our purpose, the purpose to re-make him.

He finds himself in the operating room. His mind is annihilated. He pours out his blood unconscious. His red blood is spilled and pours over the table on to the floor while he sleeps.

After this, while he is still asleep, we carry him into another place and put him to bed. He awakes bewildered as children do, expecting per-haps to find himself at home with his mother leaning over him, and he moans a little and then lies still again. He is helpless, so we do for him what he cannot do for himself, and he is grateful. We feed him, and he eats. We fat-ten him up, and he allows himself to be fattened. Day after day he lies there and we watch him. His body does not belong to him. It belongs to us for the moment, but not for long. He knows what we are fattening and clean-ing it up for; and while we handle it he smiles.

He is only one among thousands. They are all the same. They all smile as if they were grateful. And often they apologize for dying. They would not die and disappoint us if they could help it. Indeed, in their helplessness they do the best they can to help us get them ready to go back again."

As June and July wore on, vast preparations were under way for Haig's breakout from the Salient. Nearly half a million British soldiers were assembled there in the Fifth and Second Armies. Hundreds of railroad trains arrived daily with stockpiles of munitions and supplies. To free soldiers for the fighting front, the British had imported tens of thousands of Chinese coolies, as well as Zulus and other black laborers from its African colonies. They performed behind-the-lines unloading and carrying tasks, road maintenance, and other noncombat duties.

Even during this so-called quiet interval, nothing was quiet in the Salient. Trench raids, which were conducted by both sides throughout the war, were stepped up owing to the perceived need for enemy prisoners. Most prisoners taken could provide little in the way of strategic or even tactical information, but Haig's intelligence service under General Charteris wanted to know something more: what was their state of mind. All through the spring captured enemy soldiers had been telling British interrogators that they and their comrades were demoralized and this became a major factor in Haig's insistence on attacking in Flanders. So Charteris needed to know if that was still the case, and also whether the captured Germans belonged to newly arrived units, which would tell him something about enemy reinforcements. German intelligence also had things it wished to know, and so trench raids became a nightly occurrence in the Salient, some involving hundreds of men, and casualties were often stupendous.

Haig's plan to break through at Ypres was massive, expansive, and complex. Variations of it had been under study since 1915, but now the final scheme was laid down.

The first step had been the brilliant capture of Messines Ridge by Plumer, already accomplished. Next the northern ridges, including

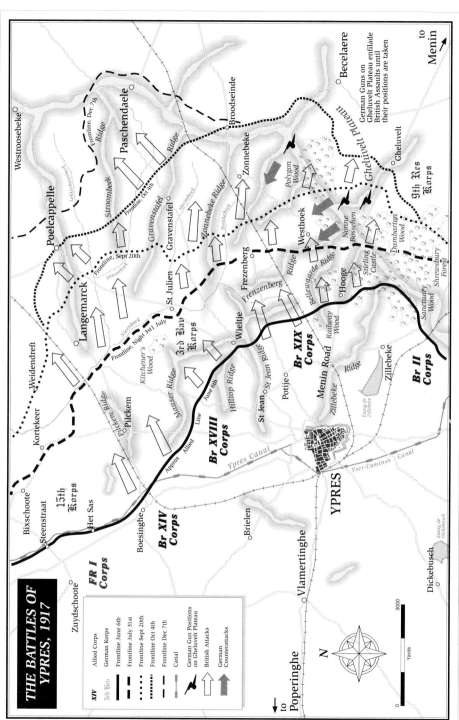

THE BATTLES OF
YPRES, 1917

XIV   Allied Corps

ℑrd ℜorps   German Korps

Frontline June 6th

Frontline July 31st

Frontline Sept 20th

Frontline Oct 4th

Frontline Dec 7th

Canal

German Gun Positions
on Gheluvelt Plateau

British Attacks

German Counterattacks

Courtesy of Eureka Cartography & Globes

to
Menin

German Guns on
Gheluvelt Plateau enfilade
British Assaults until
their positions are taken

Becelaere

Gheluvelt

9th Res Korps

Gheluvelt Plateau

Dumbarton
Wood

Shrewsbury
Forest

Zonnebeke

Broodseinde

Paschendaele
Ridge

Polygon
Wood

Nonne
Bosschen

Westhoek

Stirling
Castle

Sanctuary
Wood

Zonnebeke Ridge

Frezenberg
Ridge

Bellewaarde Ridge

Hooge

Westroosebeke

Stroombeek
Ridge

Frontline, Dec 7th

Gravenstafel
Ridge

Frontline Oct 4th

Gravenstafel

Hannebeek

Frezenberg

Railway
Wood

Frontline, Sept 20th

Poelcappelle

Langemarck

St. Julien

Stroombeek

Wieltje

St. Jean

Menin Road

Zillebeke

Br II
Corps

Br XIX
Corps

Lekkerboterbeek

Weidendreft

Kortekeer

Pilckem Ridge

Kitchener's
Wood

Mauser Ridge

3rd Bav Korps

Hilltop Ridge

St. Jean Ridge

Potijze

Zillebeke
Ridge

Etang de
Zillebeke

Frontline, Night 3rd, July

Steenbeek

June 6th

Approx Allied Line

Br XVIII
Corps

YPRES

Zuydschoote

Bixschoote

Steenstraat

15th
Korps

Het Sas

Boesinghe

Br XIV
Corps

Brielen

Ypres Canal

Yser-Comines Canal

Dickebusch

Etang de
Dickebusch

FR I
Corps

to
Poperinghe

Vlamertinghe

N

3000

Yards

0

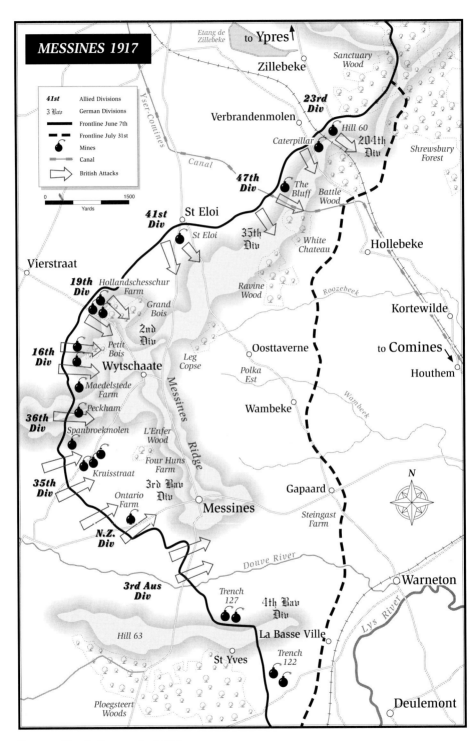

Courtesy of Eureka Cartography & Globes

The suave French general Nivelle concocted a scheme to win the war by a trick. His plan failed so miserably that the French armies mutinied. *Courtesy of Getty Images*

(*left to right*) General Erich Ludendorff, the Kaiser, and Field Marshal Paul von Hindenburg. The Kaiser was always sensitive about his withered arm and generally kept it in his pocket. In this photograph, both Hindenburg and Ludendorff, perhaps out of sensitivity to their boss, have stuffed their hands into their pockets as well. *Courtesy of Imperial War Museum*

The German Crown Prince reviewing troops. *Courtesy of Imperial War Museum*

A line of British heavy guns in the Salient.

A British soldier removing identification papers of a dead comrade near Chateau Wood during the Third Battle of Ypres. *Courtesy of Imperial War Museum*

Two artillery officers relax during a brief lull in the Third Battle of Ypres.
Courtesy of Imperial War Museum

Passchendaele 1917. A machine-gun crew in the reserve "trenches." *Courtesy of Imperial War Museum*

The dead of a Scottish regiment at Passchendaele. This photograph was taken in October 1917, near the village of Zonnebeck. *Courtesy of Imperial War Museum*

General Sir Herbert Plumer, shown here with King George V.

An advanced dressing station during the Battle of Passchendaele. The man in the center has what later became known as "The Ten Thousand Yard Stare." *Courtesy of Imperial War Museum*

A machine-gun pit near Zillebeke during the Third Battle of Ypres. Behind them a tank mired in the mud. *Courtesy of Imperial War Museum*

The tremendous British artillery bombardment during the Third Battle of Ypres reduced the ground to a swamp of shell craters that stood lip-to-lip. Thousands of men drowned in them during the attacks. *Courtesy of Robert Hunt Library*

With victory at hand, Allied leaders pose for a photograph. (*left to right*) Joffre, the French commander; French president Poincaré; King George V; Field Marshal Foch; and Sir Douglas Haig, August 1918. *Courtesy of Imperial War Museum*

A German prisoner of war captured near Passchendaele in September 1917.

German prisoners captured at Passchendaele. *Courtesy of Imperial War Museum*

A lone cross among the slop and shell craters of the Passchendaele battlefield. *Courtesy of Imperial War Museum*

German counterattack troops waiting for the call during the Passchendaele battle. *Courtesy of Imperial War Museum*

A six-inch gun in action,
softening up the Messines Ridge.
Courtesy of Imperial War Museum

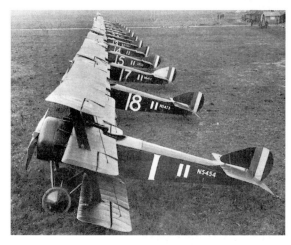

A row of British Sopwith
triplanes. At the beginning of
the war the British had only a
few dozen aircraft. By the end
they had twenty thousand,
capable of flying at altitudes of
twenty thousand feet and
bombing Berlin itself.

Aerial photo of a
British artillery
barrage. *Courtesy of
Robert Hunt Library*

A 9.2-inch howitzer and crew during the Third Battle of Ypres. *Courtesy of Imperial War Museum*

British cavalry horses during the Third Battle of Ypres. Haig had hoped to use his cavalry to break out of the Salient and drive the Germans off of the ridges, but according to the Official History, "most of the horses were shot down." *Courtesy of Imperial War Museum*

Stretcher bearers struggle with a wounded man through the morass that characterized the 1917 Battle of Passchendaele.

Plumer's attack along the Menin Road in September 1917. *Courtesy of Imperial War Museum*

German dead on Pilckem Ridge during Gough's attack in August 1917. The ridge remained in British hands until the great German offensive of 1918. *Courtesy of Imperial War Museum*

All that remained of Wytschaete (Whitesheet) during the Passchendaele battle. *Courtesy of Imperial War Museum*

The peaceful city of Ypres before the war.

Aerial view of Ypres, 1915. *Courtesy of Imperial War Museum*

One month after the war ended Pétain was made a field marshal. His role in the next German war (1939–1945) was less auspicious—he was accused of collaborating with the Nazis when he assumed leadership of the Vichy French government. In the background are Joffre, Foch, Haig, Pershing, Gillain (Belgium), Albricci (Italy), and Haller (Poland). *Courtesy of Imperial War Museum*

Field Marshal Sir Douglas Haig cuts a fine figure on a horse at the final victory march after the war. *Courtesy of Imperial War Museum*

The Menin Gate Memorial at Ypres, unveiled in 1927, contains the names of fifty-five thousand British troops whose remains were never recovered. An additional thirty-five thousand "missing and presumed dead" are carved on a memorial at Tyne Cot cemetery nearby.

Gheluvelt Plateau and Passchendaele, would be taken. At the same time, an amphibious assault would be made on the Belgian coast, which would link up with divisions of General Rawlinson's Fourth Army, posted on the narrow strip of dunes at Nieuport, some eighteen miles to the north of Ypres, marking the northernmost line of the Western Front. The amphibious assault would occur only after the taking of the Ypres ridges, including Passchendaele.

Haig calculated that the Germans would then begin to withdraw because of the danger of having their positions on the coast cut off, and at that point he had in store for them a further surprise. He would unleash his cavalry divisions to chase them down, disrupt them, disconcert them, and disperse them. Then, for the finale, the divisions of Gough's Fifth Army would come pouring through toward Bruges and the North Sea to clamp pincers on any remaining Germans on the coastal seaports of Ostend and Zeebrugge. The German defeat in western Belgium would be complete. The enemy would have to retreat from most of the rest of the country, if not all of it; their flank would have been turned, and the end of the war would be in sight. This was the way it was supposed to go, and a timetable of two weeks was contemplated.

On the face of it, Haig's scheme had much to recommend it, for only in Belgian Flanders was there any chance of turning the German flank. Everywhere else the Allies had tried a straightforward breakthrough, they had failed. The German soldiers were said to be demoralized and their home front was too, owing to Germany's massive labor strikes and the drastic food shortages. Moreover, the Germans would be kicked out of their submarine bases at Ostend and Zeebrugge and their unrestricted U-boat warfare crippled. Furthermore, the ailing French would be protected from attack.

Of course, not everyone felt that way, namely, the British prime minister, David Lloyd George. Basically, he believed in none of it, doubted the capability of the British Army to accomplish what Haig said it could, and went around mumbling "mud and blood" all the time. He predicted another grisly, drawn-out holocaust like that of the Somme, which, among other things, he feared would topple his government. Instead, Lloyd George proposed a campaign to aid the Italians in their effort to defeat the Austrians, thus to his mind hastening Germany's demise. To that end he proposed removing twelve infantry divisions and 300 heavy guns from the Western Front and shipping them to Italy. Sir William Robertson, commander of the British General Staff, declared to General Haig, "That will never happen" while he was in charge, but he also warned him not to try to persuade the recently established War Cabinet that the attack at Ypres was intended to win the war in a single stroke. Instead, he cautioned, "Argue that your plan is the best plan—as it is—that no other plan would even be *safe* let alone decisive, and then leave them to reject your advice or mine. They dare not do that."

Robertson was proved right. Instead of simply ordering Haig not to embark on the Ypres endeavor—which he certainly had the power to do— Lloyd George reluctantly deferred to the military opinion. A few weeks later, however, he announced that he and the War Cabinet would authorize only the opening stages of the Flanders offensive and, if they were unsuccessful, reserved the option of calling the operation off.

How much Lloyd George was influenced in this concession by the First Sea Lord, Admiral Jellicoe, has been much debated. Jellicoe had recently shocked the War Cabinet by informing them it was "useless to discuss plans for next spring, as we should be unable to continue the war into 1918, owing to lack of shipping, unless we could clear the Germans out of Zeebrugge before the end of the year." Even more emphatically, according to the Official History, Jellicoe stated that "if the Army cannot get the Belgian ports, the Navy cannot hold the Channel and the war is lost."

It couldn't get much plainer, or scarier, that than, although Lloyd George was highly skeptical of Jellicoe's assessment—in fact, outraged by it, since, as has been noted, he harbored a disquieting suspicion of military men. It was learned much later that fewer than a quarter of the German U-boats were operating out of the Belgian ports, the rest being launched from Germany itself. Nevertheless, and despite his misgivings, Lloyd George took no steps to interfere with Haig's Flanders attack, probably on the notion that any action by the army was better than no action at all. And so, with Haig's preparatory bombardment at Ypres already under way, the thing was finally set into motion. It was later to be memorialized as the Battle of Passchendaele, a name that became synonymous with all the suffering and futility of World War I.

Chapter Twelve ★

"The battle which all the world has been expecting has begun," wrote correspondent Phillip Gibbs of the *Daily Chronicle* on July 31, 1917. He did not add that almost from the beginning, things had begun to go wrong.

A significant part of Haig's scheme involved a combined land and amphibious attack along the Belgian coast, which was intended to sweep the Germans from their submarine pens at Ostend and Zeebrugge. Haig assigned General Rawlinson's stripped-down Fourth Army to accomplish this task. On June 20, a week after Plumer's final success at Messines, Rawlinson's divisions began relieving the French units that had established a shallow bridgehead across the Yser River, where it flowed into the North Sea.

The operation did not go smoothly, however. The British found the French positions poorly constructed—in fact, the French had intended to retreat back across the river if attacked in force. There were three floating temporary bridges across the Yser, which at that point was up to 600 feet wide. There was further confusion over artillery and in the end the British were able to bring up only a fraction of their guns. Moreover, the Germans smelled something cooking when the British began to arrive and cooked up a surprise of their own.

The plan for the amphibious assault on the Belgian coast had been well conceived. An infantry division was to be loaded on gunboat monitors at Dunkirk, which would then steam northward to Flanders. Each monitor would have in tow a huge floating pier that would allow the troops to disembark directly onto the beaches. These pontoon piers were 500 feet long, 30 feet wide, and protected by bullet-proof steel. Tanks, guns, and other heavy equipment were also to be carried on them. As the troops began to land, the plan was to have Rawlinson's corps attack up the coast as well. It was a daring but potentially fertile scheme.

But on July 10, the Germans "completely upset" the entire British design. They opened four days earlier with a furious bombardment of the bridgehead positions across the Yser. Dawn on the tenth saw the shelling become so intense that all communications were cut to headquarters on the south side of the Yser. Messenger pigeons became the only means of contact. The old French fortifications were so flimsily built that men began to die in alarming numbers. By afternoon, all three of the floating bridges were destroyed, and the bridgehead was cut off.

Then the Germans unleashed a vile new type of poison gas, delivered by artillery shells. Mustard gas may have been the most heinous of all the gases used in the war. Unlike the earlier lung gases such as phosgene, mustard gas attacked the entire body, inside and out. The results were horrifying: it seeped through clothing and caused grotesque blistering and lesions, actually peeling off layers of skin. Infection invariably set in. Victims went blind and began to cough up blood as their lungs were eaten away. Worse, unlike phosgene, it lingered, so that doctors and nurses themselves were quickly infected when they tried to remove the victim's clothes—or just from the fumes of contaminated clothes. Then they, too, began to turn yellow; even their hair turned yellow. It lingered on the battlefields, too. Whereas the previous gases evaporated within a few hours, mustard gas hung in the ground for weeks, contaminating anyone who came in contact with it. It hung especially in shell craters.

Poison-gas historian Tim Cook describes the victims: "They took on the aroma of decaying fruit, particularly trying for men and doctors who realized they were rotting both from the outside and from within." The Germans had been saving the mustard gas for the big attack they knew was coming at Ypres, but apparently they decided to try it out first on the unsuspecting British in the Nieuport sector.

In any case, when the Germans finally attacked late in the afternoon, the British units isolated in the bridgehead north of the Yser were all but annihilated. Those who could swam across to safety under cover of darkness. Rawlinson ordered an immediate counterattack, but his commanders talked him out of it on the notion that even if the bridgehead were retaken, they probably couldn't hold it. Before it was over Rawlinson's army had taken 10,000 casualties and Haig's stratagem for an amphibious attack on the coast was, for all intents, dead in the water.

Nevertheless, plans proceeded apace for the big push at Ypres. Haig had ordered diversionary attacks farther south at Lens and Lille in France to deceive the Germans into believing the main thrust would come there. But Prince Rupprecht was undeceived, and ordered ten German divisions transferred from the Lens-Lille sector to Flanders. General Gough had marshaled nine divisions of his Fifth Army for the opening assault on Pilckem Ridge alone, to the northeast of Ypres. It was the same piece of property from which the Germans had expelled the British in 1915 with their gas attack at the Second Battle of Ypres.

Lloyd George and the War Cabinet were distressed by the news that the Nieuport operation had been foiled, but Haig reassured them it did not matter. His theory was that, if nothing else, the Germans would still have to keep large numbers of troops there to face Rawlinson's army, thus making them unavailable to defend their positions around Ypres. And also, he said, the amphibious operation could always be rejuvenated at the appropriate time. The War Cabinet, consisting of six members, including Lloyd George, was evenly divided for and against Haig's Flanders offensive. In the end, they did nothing to stop it.

The total Allied force assembled for the big push at Ypres consisted of twenty-three British and six French divisions (nearly 500,000 men in all), approximately 3,000 guns, and 136 tanks. The tanks, of course, were a relatively new addition to the array of Allied battle armament, a tool to help break the stalemate of trench warfare. Tanks had first been tried at the Battle of the Somme a year earlier, where fifty of them participated in the fighting. They were not particularly successful, prompting Winston

Churchill, who had husbanded tank development early in the war, to become outraged at their being put in piecemeal and in such small numbers:
"A secret of war which well-used would have procured a world-shaking
victory in 1917 had been recklessly revealed to the enemy," was how he
put it later.[1]

In existence for only a year, the tank was already in its fourth generation, the lessons of the Somme battles and elsewhere having been applied.
The Mark IV main battle tank was made of a heavier, more bullet-proof
armor, was, roughly, 26 feet long, 13 feet wide, and 8 feet high, and weighed
28 tons. Carrying two six-pound cannon and six machine guns, it was
crewed by eight men and one officer at an average speed of two miles per
hour, powered, ironically, by an engine invented by a German engineer,
G. W. Daimler, who had pioneered the Mercedes-Benz. The Germans, for
their part, had no tanks and apparently did not wish any, after noting their
vulnerabilities at the Battle of the Somme. Yet late in the war they changed
their mind but were able to manufacture only eighteen of the monsters.
They were huge, behemoth-looking things, requiring eighteen men to man
them and looked, if nothing else, like floats in a Mardi Gras parade.

Aside from the tanks, the Allies had increased their air superiority over the
Germans by more than two to one—with 500 aircraft in the Ypres sector
alone—not only disrupting the Germans from observing preparations for
the attack, but marking for destruction the German artillery positions.
Among those Germans driven from the skies over Ypres was the famed
ace Manfred von Richthofen, the Red Baron, credited with shooting down
eighty Allied planes before being shot down and killed himself in 1918.

And so from all these perspectives it looked as if Haig's great offensive
was shaping up nicely; still, there were undertones of trouble, not the least
of which was the weather. The approaches to the German-held ridges were
in low country, crisscrossed by many streams and drainage ditches and

---

1. The tank got its name when, in an effort to keep their existence unknown, they
were labeled on railroad flatcars "tank"—as in "water tank."

canals. Over centuries the Flemish had maintained these in a delicate balance to keep the land from reverting to the swamp it once had been. Two problems now loomed. At Arras during the abortive Nivelle Offensive that spring, the British had come face-to-face with a significant dilemma. The huge preliminary artillery bombardment—which had become a sacred cow for any successful attack—had so torn up the ground that when it rained the whole battlefield became a bog in which advance was impossible. That was at Arras.

Now they faced the same problem infinitely more severe in the reclaimed swamp at Ypres, with the water table two or three feet beneath the ground surface. If the artillery barrage destroyed the infrastructure of drainage ditches and canals, if it rained the men would have to cross a morass to get at the Germans. And at Ypres, it rained.

General Charteris, Haig's intelligence chief, was responsible for predicting the weather. His meteorological section had already done a thorough study of the rainfall in Flanders going back some eighty years. Based in particular on the previous year's records, Charteris predicted a relatively normal rainfall in July, August, and September, but October was always the rainiest month. As it turned out, the August deluge at Ypres was nearly double the historical average. On the eve of the battle Charteris wrote Haig ominously, "My one great fear is the weather."

The battle had been set to open July 25—more than six weeks after Plumer's stunning victory at Messines—but owing to some artillery that did not get up to Gough's positions and a request by the French commander for more time, the jump-off hour had been postponed until July 31. Thus the preliminary bombardment continued for six more days, further destroying the ground and drainage. Worse, perhaps, was more rain and bad weather, which kept not only the Allied aircraft from flying most of the time. Aerial reconnaissance was crucial to Haig's intent of knocking out the German artillery batteries located out of ground observation behind the Gheluvelt Plateau and the Passchendaele Ridge. Flash spotting of these was a practical impossibility and strong winds severely hampered the sound-ranging method.

Other commanders were similarly concerned. The Tank Corps officers watched with growing dismay as the more than 4 million artillery shells of the preliminary bombardment inevitably churned the landscape into a continuous expanse of shell holes, which began to fill up with ground water. Tank Corps headquarters had begun distributing a "Swamp Map," denoting those sections of ground that they could not cross. As the drainage canals were destroyed and the panorama became moon-pocked with shell craters, the Swamp Map expanded until little if any of the battle area was fully navigable. Finally somebody in Haig's headquarters, probably Charteris, ordered the tankers to stop publishing it, on grounds that if Haig ever saw it he would become distressed.

Just before dawn on the morning of July 31 the artillery barrage reached its most pitiless crescendo, then abruptly stopped. The silence was startling, almost unreal. As before the Messines attack, it was reported that nightingales resumed their melancholy song. Hearts quickened, breaths caught, men spoke in whispers or with bitten breath. Some smoked, some trembled. At 3:50 A.M., which was supposed to be first light in those northern climes, hundreds of thousands of soldiers began clambering out of their trenches. Except there was no light. The skies were cloud covered, dark, low, and rain swollen.

Now a great new thundering barrage belched forth all along the Salient front, again silencing the nightingales and even shaking the railroad car that was Haig's forward headquarters, twenty miles from Ypres. This was the "creeping barrage," a curtain of iron and flame that marched ahead of the British and French attackers to protect them from fire from the German lines. At first, it seemed to be going well; in the north the French army overran German positions for more than two miles and three of Gough's corps not only captured the entire Pilckem Ridge, but they pushed on to, and in some cases across, the Steenbeck River. In addition, by noon what remained of St. Julian was now again in Allied hands. Willie Fraser, whom we first met in 1914 as a lieutenant with the Gordon Highlanders when he buried his brother during the First Battle of Ypres, was now a lieutenant colonel, commanding a battalion of Gordons in this sector. He was well pleased with the performance of his men, who took many of their objectives. However, he reported in his diary, "The state of the ground, particularly the Black Line and beyond, was indescribable. Shell holes were touching one another across the whole front for a depth of over 2,500 yards." Then it began to rain.

The rain began at first as showers, but it quickly turned into a downpour. The Germans counterattacked at St. Julian and drove the British back to their newly won positions on the Steenbeck. Still, in the northern sector of the Salient, Allied gains had been significant, if not the great "breakthrough" Haig and Gough had hoped for. It was in the center and southern sectors, however, where trouble lay.

This was the evil eminence of the Gheluvelt Plateau, bristling with German artillery and thousands of concrete pillboxes and machine-gun emplacements. As at Arras, the ground had been so torn up with mud and shell holes that navigating it was nearly impossible. Men cursed and sweated in the humid midsummer air and, as the tank commanders had warned, most of their vehicles stuck in the mud or were blown to smithereens by German light artillery. There were only three or four "tracks"—one could not dignify these by calling them roads—for the tanks to travel on, and the Germans had registered artillery on them with devastating results.

The creeping barrage, at twenty-five yards a minute, soon outran the infantry floundering in the muck-cratered landscape of Château Wood, Sanctuary Wood, Shrewsbury Forrest, and Battle Wood—which were likewise woods in name only. Instead, they had become a barely penetrable morass of shattered stumps, greasy mud, and broken tree trunks, interspersed by rusty barbed wire. Machine guns spat out from a seemingly endless concentration of German pillboxes, each located to interlock with the next, so that soldiers trying to knock them out with grenades came under immediate fire from the adjacent strong point. During this whole time they were being subjected to a continuous rain of shrapnel from the German guns. All sorts of horrors were chronicled by soldiers who went into these attacks. More than one told of seeing a man literally cut in half or having his head blown off by artillery, and yet the legs and trunk ran on for some moments before falling. Not a few of these young soldiers went berserk, throwing away their weapons and crying, "mother, mother, mother!"

As the day wore on, the rain began to fill up the shell holes that the British were fighting from, and they were forced to abandon them. Those wounded who had sought refuge in the craters began to drown in wholesale lots. Unwounded men sank sometimes up to their armpits in mud holes; one man stayed that way for four days until he was accidentally discovered and rescued. Entire battalions became lost because of the nightmarishly shattered nature of the terrain; telephone wires were cut as quickly as they were laid down and it took runners forever to pick their way back across the sea of mud and craters. Once again, homing pigeons became the main source of communication with headquarters. One officer remembered trying to send a pigeon back with a desperate message for artillery support but that the bird was too wet to fly. They toweled it off, but not well enough, and the bird flopped back down to earth and began walking toward German lines. Appalled that if the Germans intercepted the message they would be annihilated, the men of that unit, in what must have been a strange sight indeed on that ferocious battlefield, frantically began firing at the bird and finally it was killed.

A few airplanes tried to fly under the low clouds to identify where the British units were located, but they often failed and at least thirty were shot down by ground fire. Confusion reigned, both in the battalions doing the fighting and in their brigade, corps, and headquarter bases in the rear. By nightfall, the Allied advance looked on a map like a large cornucopia, with the wide-open part beginning at the northern end of the Salient and tapering down almost to nothing in the south. This posed a different sort of problem for the victors in the north, for soon they became subjected to an enfilade fire from the German guns on Gheluvelt as they lay exposed in their slimy shell holes. One particularly unpleasant feature of these bombardments was that the Germans were now using the horrible mustard gas in plentiful amounts. So distressing were the results of this that the British suppressed the details in official reports.

Meanwhile, Haig's expansive scheme to unleash his cavalry on the Germans was also set into motion. However, according to the Official History, "most of their horses were killed in a gallant effort to carry out their orders." The fact was that, while the Germans had bent, they "showed no signs of cracking; on the contrary, the reports bore out the German textbook statement that resistance would probably stiffen the deeper the attack penetrated." This "textbook" had been written by one Colonel von Lossberg, the foremost "defensive battle strategist" in the German army. It was he who had recommended that the Germans withdraw from Messines Ridge (before the British mines ultimately did it for them), but he was over-ruled. Six days after the Messines debacle von Lossberg was sent to orga-nize the German defense in Flanders, which he gleefully noted was the first time he had ever been allowed to "plan a defense from the outset." And because of the nearly two-month delay between Plumer's Messines victory and the big attack in Flanders, time had been on his side. Von Lossberg be-gan adding concrete pillboxes and strong points like a man possessed, most with walls four feet thick. These they camouflaged with earth and grass on the roofs, so they were almost invisible from the air. Everything was tacti-cally placed so that if the front line was lost, the next line became a front line just as strong, and the next back, and the next. It was he who had laid down the law that the foremost front line was to be only lightly de-fended and that for every two divisions defending, or in reserve, at the front there was to be a third "counterattack" division directly in the rear. Of these things the British knew something, but not nearly enough, and so were very unpleasantly surprised.

Among those German regiments defending Gheluvelt that day was the 16th Bavarian, Adolf Hitler's outfit. It was in the process of being re-lieved when the Allied attack was launched. Hitler left no record of his role in the battle, however. By now he was a seasoned veteran, winner of the Iron Cross and wounded the previous summer at the Somme, but still he remained a corporal. The wound took him back to Germany—which he had not seen for two years—where he became highly agitated at the state of home-front affairs. His anti-Semitism appeared in full bloom at this point; he would complain bitterly in *Mein Kampf* that "The offices were filled with Jews. Nearly every Jew was a clerk and nearly every clerk was a Jew. I was amazed at this plethora of warriors of the chosen people, and could not help but compare them with their rare representatives at the front." [2]

Hitler had become something of a loner in his unit, reading books

2. This was untrue. Contemporary statistics indicate that Germany's Jews were fighting at a rate comparable with their population numbers.

and writing political screeds while his companions indulged themselves in
the usual recreations of drinking and whoring when out of the front line.
He sometimes harangued them with stern political rhetoric, condemning
what he saw as defeatism within the army and without. Some of his comrades thought of him as a crackpot and a crank. By then he had acquired a
dog, which he named Foxl, and he became immensely attached to it. Aside
from politics, Hitler's only hobby was painting, at which he was quite good.
Many of his watercolors of ruined structures in the Ypres Salient survived
the war and in the mid-1930s a number of them were published in *Esquire*
magazine.

By the end of the day, when all the reports had filtered in, it became clear
to Gough that little more could be accomplished and, what with the
downpouring rain, he called off further attacks until artillery could be
moved forward and the weather improved. Nevertheless, Gough remained
sanguine when Haig visited his headquarters that afternoon. He called the
operation so far "a great success," and Haig reported to London that the
battle results were "highly satisfactory and the losses slight for so great a
battle." This last remark seems somewhat disingenuous, since the Fifth
Army had attained only half of its objectives and sustained more than 30,000
casualties. But Haig also might have been characterizing it as "relative" compared with some of the earlier battles—particularly at the Somme, where
he had taken nearly 60,000 casualties on the first day.

Based primarily on information supplied them by Haig's headquarters,
war correspondents began filing generally favorable stories for their papers.
They spoke once more of "The greatest battle in the history of the world," of
"Everywhere our objectives were obtained," of "Many fine and heroic acts,"
of "Powerful and expert artillery," of "casualties remarkably light."

Unlike previous press reports, however, which had been heavily censored, the correspondents also spoke of "pitiless rain," of "a horrible quag-
mire," of shell holes "flooded to the brim," of ground covered by "semi-liquid
mud." This was highly unusual, for Haig generally disliked and distrusted
the press and information of the latter sort might be construed as helping the Germans—although it is hard to see how, since the Germans had

eyes for themselves as to the conditions on the battlefield. In fact, their own counterattacks were being hampered by the weather just as much as the British attacks were.

Desultory but vicious fighting continued for the next two days, but the British advance had stalled. By August 2 it was clear that this phase of the battle had come to an end—the rain continued unabated and the German artillery fire and incessant counterattacks had made Allied occupation of the Gheluvelt Plateau seem more and more like a distant dream. Another big push was set by Gough for August 10, in hopes that the ground would by then dry out. But it didn't, and this too failed, with heavy casualties. On August 16 they tried again, and again with disappointing results, though the rubble that had been Langemarck was retaken.

The continued intensity of the fighting, and particularly the shelling, was such that even reading the accounts of quartermasters and other support troops is enough to make one shudder. These brave people night and day were compelled to bring forward all the supplies needed to keep battalions in the field: rations, water, ammunition, spare parts—everything from toilet tissue to rum and newspapers—and all under the most severe conditions, mud, rain, constant artillery fire. On their way across a mile or more of torn-up newly won terrain they encountered a horror of bodies, dead horses and mules, and grievously wounded soldiers. One quartermaster on the night of the first attack brought up all these things for a battalion of 600 men, only to be told on his arrival that the battalion no longer existed—90 percent of it had been wiped out. Not only that, but the engineer and pioneer battalions encountered the same sort of cursed predicament. It was their job to repair roads, help strengthen trenches and dig new ones, and lay forward track for the many small-gauge railways that would bring up ammunition, supplies, and troops to the newly won battle areas on different parts of the front.

Even if Haig's great offensive was not attaining all he wanted, it was nevertheless accomplishing one of its goals: namely, to kill and maim a lot of Germans. Over in the German lines near Langemarck that day was a nineteen-year-old lieutenant named Ernst Jünger who published his diary shortly after the war ended. Already wounded twenty times, Jünger's breezy yet honest account became immensely popular reading in Germany. His regiment was ordered to counterattack the British at Langemarck, and he describes the devastating effects of the Allied assault.

Going up to the jumping-off point for the counterattack under a "rain of shrapnel, as we went along half bent we were checked by a despairing voice. In the distance we could see a figure with bleeding arm-stumps raising itself from a shell hole. We pointed to the hut we had just left, and hastened on." When he reached his company Jünger found "an utterly dispirited little mob," in which all the officers had become casualties. Suddenly a British artillery barrage found them "like a wall of fire. The scene was indescribable. Faces as white as death stared at one another, and the cries of those who were hit never ceased."

Leading his men forward through the fire, Jünger finally came upon a partially smashed-up pillbox where he was appalled at being told that his brother, who he thought was still in Germany, had been seriously wounded and was lying nearby. Jünger found him at a "desolate blockhouse" that served as a dressing station. "My brother lay among a crowd of groaning stretcher-cases in a place that stank of death. He had been hit by two shrapnel bullets, one of which had pierced the lung and the other hit his right shoulder. Fever shone in his eyes; it was only with difficulty that he could move or speak or breathe."

Jünger wrapped his brother in a ground sheet and slung a pole through it so that he and five other men could carry him back to a safer aid station; then he returned to his outfit. All night they were shelled as they lay in the marshy ground by the Steenbeck with many men killed or wounded. To make things more uncomfortable they were assailed by millions of gnats from the stagnant waters. Soon they saw toward their front "the first khaki uniforms" of British soldiers, coming on for the assault. "Stern measures were necessary to persuade artillerymen and signalers, and so on that even they in circumstances like these had to take hold of a rifle and get into the firing line." At one point, Jünger noticed a canteen orderly using "all sorts of excuses to get away." When the soldier cried, "But I have no rifle!" Jünger told him, "Then wait until there's a man shot."

Jünger sums up the experience for all of them in this passage: "You cower in a heap alone in a hole and feel yourself the victim of a pitiless thirst for destruction. With horror you feel that all your intelligence, your capacities, your bodily and spiritual characteristics, have become utterly meaningless and absurd. While you think it, the lump of metal that will crush you to a shapeless nothing may have already started on its course."

Despite the torment the British were causing the Germans, for the British themselves it was maddening. First, the weather had conspired against them. Because of the rain the aircraft could not locate the German artillery batteries and call down fire on them. Because of the rain, the men had to slog through almost impassable mud to reach their objectives. A standing joke among the soldiers was that the Germans could make it rain anytime they wanted to.

Sometime during the fighting, a young American officer arrived on the scene. He was Captain George S. Patton, an aide to General John "Black Jack" Pershing, who commanded the newly arriving American Expeditionary Force, which, before the war was over, would be 2 million strong. "The Germans have a new type of gas that makes men vomit," Patton wrote his wife, Beatrice. "Then, when they remove their gas masks to spit, they send over the deadly stuff. Smart, is it not?" Possibly Patton had confused nausea gas with sneezing gas, which the Germans used for the purpose described above.

Another problem was that Gough had aimed his whole plan of operations at a breakout northward toward the Houthoulst Forest and beyond, but it had now become plain that no such thing was possible so long as the Germans held Gheluvelt Plateau on the army's right. Haig had tried to pound this into Gough as the days wore on, but to take Gheluvelt, the way he had his divisions arranged, Gough would have had to realign his entire army. On August 20 Gough made another attempt and this time, with the weather drying a little, tanks were brought up. Ground was gained— in some places up to 1,000 yards—but again the attack stalled.

Finally, Haig had had enough. He fired Gough and gave command of the overall attack back to the methodical Plumer and his Second Army. It was a shame Haig could not have fired the rain, which continued in torrents. Plumer, though he did not relish taking on a job where another army had failed, asked for and received nearly a month in which to get the Second Army realigned for the attack.

For his part, Gough seemed relieved to be off the hook. In light of his failure to achieve the great breakthrough that everybody had been talking about, Gough now actually advised Haig to shut down the campaign. What Gough had ultimately failed to realize—and it might well have been Haig's fault—was that not long after the battle had started, it soon dawned on Haig and his staff that the big breakthrough might not be possible. Therefore Haig reluctantly reverted to the notion of a "wearing-down" fight— the old doctrine of attrition—though a total, victorious breakthrough was always in the back of his mind. But somehow, probably through Haig's own taciturnity, this idea had never been impressed on Gough in a way that he understood it.

Even though strategically the offensive had so far been a failure, in fact, from a tactical standpoint, things were not quite so bad as they seemed. In three weeks of battle the British had wrested away from the Germans up to two miles of ground, including many important observation points. From Haig's point of view, he had his armies on the scene, his artillery in place, and his airplanes at the ready; with all the months of planning and training, if nothing else he intended to push the Germans off of the final ridges overlooking Ypres, in the process killing as many of them as possible. That would at least put them back where they had been in 1914.

Chapter Thirteen ★

The Battles of Pilckem Ridge and Langemarck, as they came to be styled, were only the beginning of the nine battles during the next two and a half months that defined the 1917 struggle for Ypres. For the soldiers, each fight would seem worst than the last, and, in fact, they were. These battles could almost be better characterized as major "flare-ups," since the fighting was continuous and bloody, but Haig remained confident. Just how continuous the fighting was is illustrated by the 10,000 casualties taken during the first two weeks of September before Plumer even launched his first attack—most of them by engineer and pioneer battalions repairing roads and bridges and laying forward track for the many necessary small-gauge supply railways.

Despite Haig's reassurances, Lloyd George was increasingly apprehensive over the Flanders fighting; to him it was devolving into exactly the sort of Somme-like debacle of death he had wished so earnestly to avoid. Years later he wrote bitterly that Haig and his staff had deceived him, and he accused them of "that sycophantic optimism which is the curse of autocratic power." After the first battles had ended in late August, Lloyd George threatened to shut down the Flanders battle "within ten days," and once more dusted off his old plan to ship a large part of Haig's army off to Italy, but Robertson, chief of the General Staff, was able to stave him off once again. Nothing would have pleased the prime minister more than to fire Haig and replace him with someone more akin to his own views, but he found this politically impractical: to sack Haig at this stage would have precipitated Robertson's resignation as well, and signaled to the Germans that the British government considered itself losing the war. The press would have had a field day at Lloyd George's expense and probably it would have shattered his shaky coalition government.

Instead, the prime minister settled on another plan, which he hoped would slow down the military juggernaut on the Western Front. There were nearly 75,000 officers and a million soldiers of other ranks languishing in England during this time—almost as many as in all the British armies fighting on the Western Front—and Haig was desperately calling for Lloyd George to send to him at least enough of these to replace his casualties. Granted, a large number of those soldiers in England were recuperating from wounds or had other duties to perform, but Lloyd George refused Haig's requests on the theory that if any more men were sent across the channel they would only become sacrifices to Haig's bloody war machine, a theory that he kept to himself.

Over on their side of the ridge, the Germans watched with something akin to suspicious anxiety as fine autumn weather began drying the ground and yet there was no continuation of the British attack, their most ardent fear. September had brought blue skies to northern Europe; the water in the shell holes and on the artillery-demolished landscape began to evaporate. The bursting shells began to kick up dust instead of mud. Crown Prince Rupprecht decided that the fight at Ypres was probably over and that the British were reorganizing for a larger operation farther south. Fighting of a lesser nature went on practically all the time, but as the weeks wore by no mighty Allied assault was forthcoming. And so the Germans frowned, and nervously waited and watched.

Meantime, Plumer's rearrangement of his army and artillery was being meticulously carried out. His plan crystallized around the concept that had won him victory at Messines—extraordinary concentration of force and artillery. To that end he massed more than 1,200 guns almost hub to hub on an attack front of a little more than two miles against the Gheluvelt Plateau alone. On this front 60,000 men, half of them Australians, would charge across the ground where so many of their comrades had fallen in the abortive attacks the previous month. At the same time, Gough's Fifth Army would mount similar attacks in the northern part of the Salient. This time, however, according to the Official History, the men "were inspired with more than the usual confidence." This was due to the unprecedented concentration of artillery and the support and reserve units waiting close behind to relieve them and take up the fight once they had overrun their initial objectives.

Plumer rejected the sort of grandiose timetable Gough had forecast—a huge sweep forward for three miles on opening day. Events had proven this impossible. Instead, Plumer envisioned a series of four "bite-and-hold" attacks, each pushing the Germans back about half a mile. There was to be a six-day interval between these attacks during which artillery, support and reserve troops, supplies, and communications would be brought up, the positions won would be consolidated, and then on to the next "push." By keeping the artillery right up with the attacking troops, a curtain of steel could be rained down on counterattacking Germans. If everything went according to Plumer's plan, the entire remaining ridge line overlooking Ypres would be in British hands within a month. But that would mean fighting into October. And in Flanders, in October, it rained.

Plumer opened his campaign September 20 with the Battle of the Menin Road, which ran across the Gheluvelt Plateau. But it opened on a sour note. Following a weeklong artillery barrage, the British troops were preparing to climb out of their assembly trenches at first light when a great barrage from German guns began to explode around them. This disconcerting development was due to the fact that an Australian officer had mistakenly blundered into no-man's-land an hour or so earlier and been captured by a German patrol. On his person was found a complete copy of Second Army's operation orders for the attack. The Germans immediately ordered their artillery to pummel the British lines and sent out alerts to all their defending divisions. It might have spelled catastrophe, but somehow the word got out too late and it didn't. At 5:40 A.M., behind a stupendous British creeping barrage, the English and Australian soldiers came on across no-man's-land amid a thick fog that had arisen after a midnight rain shower. To one German in his trench, they appeared "like specters out of the mist."

It was one of the most spectacular sound-and-light shows in the world. Artillery from heavy and light batteries flashed and flickered red and orange deep into the German lines in a continuous roaring, booming, thundering cacophony. Flares of all colors—red, yellow, orange, white—burst into the sky and the air hissed and sang with white-hot steel. Gray smoke swirled into no-man's-land, blending with the fog to obscure direction. Nevertheless, Plumer's divisions followed the white tapes staked out across the cutup ground, laid earlier by the Royal Engineers, and soon the Allied juggernaut began engulfing the foremost German lines.

On they went, encountering masses of shell-shocked German soldiers, "dazed and inactive, gunners sitting beside their unfired guns. Those who were still capable of action had but one idea, to surrender as soon as possible, and ran forward waving handkerchiefs or pieces of white bandage." Upon reaching their first objective lines, the Aussies and British stopped and rested and consolidated for two hours before pushing on to the next. By midafternoon, they had conquered all three objectives and stood poised to throw back the inevitable German counterattacks. The afternoon weather became crystal clear, and the troops on the plateau remarked, as those at Messines had two months earlier, of the spectacular panorama of Ypres back across the obliterated Salient, and also of the pastoral view in the opposite direction, where they now had positive observation over almost everything that moved within the German lines. "It's a wonder," one officer wrote, "that they allowed any of us at all to live."

Soon battalions of the German counterattack divisions came into sight, massing for their assaults. This time, with Plumer's enormous concentration of artillery, the Germans were screened from their mission by Plumer's impassable curtain of steel. Nothing alive could have crossed these murderous belts of fire, causing Crown Prince Rupprecht to become profoundly disturbed. He noted in his diary that in previous attacks some weak point in the British barrage could usually be found, and the counterattack set into motion, but these new tactics of Plumer's had him perfectly stymied.

Though Plumer's assault had clearly been a victory, bitter fighting continued as usual all along the lines while British divisions at the front were now being relieved by fresh divisions from the rear. The day after the Battle of Menin Road "ended," Brigadier General Francis Maxwell, who had won a V.C. in the Boer War, was shot and killed as he supervised his men in consolidating their new positions. His death belies an old myth that circulated not just in the front lines during the war but that gained much credence in England long after hostilities ended—this was the myth of the Châteaux Generals, who had become caricatures of all that was wrong with British generalship during the war: high-ranking officers in elegant châteaux far behind the lines "skulking in splendid luxury, with polished boots, eating caviar and drinking champagne," while their men suffered and died in the mud and horror of the trenches.

This accusation was basically unfair. First of all, two years earlier, in 1915, during the first week's fighting at the Battle of Loos, three major generals commanding divisions were killed, four were wounded, and one was captured. Sir John French had been so appalled that he issued instructions for his high-ranking generals not to go so near the front as to endanger themselves. This made perfect sense, given the paucity of trained senior officers, and especially because during battles the only way a general could have effective control was to be in his headquarters where there were communications with his various fighting units, and access to his artillery and other support services. For that matter, châteaux themselves were not always safe, as evidenced by the calamity at the Hooge Château during the First Battle of Ypres. Lastly, during the First World War some 232 British generals became casualties, 78 of them killed, an extraordinarily high figure.

In any event, Plumer evidently had hit on something that tactically worked and the Germans were greatly distressed. On September 26, having already dragged up his artillery and support systems nearly a mile closer to the

Germans and having replaced his original attacking divisions, Plumer now launched what would become known as the Battle of Polygon Wood.

This, too, was successful, but with the usual dreadful casualties. In the dark before sunrise, tens of thousands of men, mouths dry, teeth clenched, hands shaking, faces pallid, and each worrying about what lay in store for them, waited for the signal to climb out of the stinking shell holes that were their only cover and advance upon the malevolent morass of stumps and shell holes, which someone at headquarters still had the nerve to call a "wood."

Into one of these holes crawled Lieutenant Alfred J. Angel of a London battalion of the Royal Fusiliers; most of his men were teenagers, new conscripts and drafts from the great city. For many it was their first battle. The ground they occupied, he reported, was almost beyond description. "The stench was horrible, for the bodies were not corpses in the normal sense. With all the shell-fire and bombardments they'd been continually disturbed, and the whole place was a mess of filth and slime and bones and decomposing bits of flesh." As Lieutenant Angel crawled among these charnel pits, now under constant artillery fire, checking on his men, he came upon a young boy, a teenager, his first time in the line, "sobbing and crying. He was crying for his mother. It was pathetic really. He just kept saying over and over again, 'Oh Mum! Oh Mum! I want my Mum!'" Angel tried to reason with him, but to no avail, and became concerned that his behavior would panic the other troops. Finally he slapped him in the face, "hard as I could." This produced the desired effect, and one of Lieutenant Angel's corporals said, "I think I can manage him now, sir. Well, he took that boy in his arms, just as if he was a small child, and when I crawled back a little later to see if all was well, they were both lying there asleep, and the corporal still had his arms around the boy—mud, accoutrements and all. At zero hour, they both went over together."

The day before Plumer launched his attack on Polygon Wood, the Germans had made a substantial and ferocious spoiling attack of their own there, which nearly upset the entire plan. Although they were repulsed, several British battalions were badly cut up. Clearly, the Germans were not a beaten-down army "on their last legs," as Haig's intelligence chief had been portraying them.

The Polygon Wood operation got under way September 26 in fine, dry weather. As usual, though, it was no bed of roses. One particular spot of contention was a sinister eminence known as "Tower Hamlets," on the south side of Menin Road. There our poet-lieutenant Edmund Blunden, who had fought through the travails of the Somme with his Royal Sussex regiment, experienced an even more wretched horror. But his experience was fairly typical of life in the front lines during the battle, and is worth reporting.

When his regiment first arrived at Ypres back in the spring, Blunden remembered Tower Hamlets "through a telescope as a pretty little nook among hazy trees, with the best part of a mill and a serviceable barn still standing." Now, as a communications officer responsible for cages of messenger pigeons, telephone wire, and other signaling equipment, Blunden was led up to the front at night through a starlit carnage of dead bodies and wrecked pillboxes.

Tower Hamlets was still in dispute; only part of it was held by the British, and Blunden occupied a headquarters in a captured German pillbox filled with such bad air that his pigeons were made ill. "The men drowsed and yawned," he said. "Time went by, but no one ever felt the passage of it, for the shadow of death lay over the dial."

The Germans commenced a tremendous shelling of the place, greater than Blunden had yet experienced, and the messages he sent back were mostly about casualties. "The trenches immediately about our pillboxes were already full of bodies. One man in my headquarters died of shock from a heavy shell striking just outside."

Blunden's headquarters party actually occupied a pair of pillboxes, about thirty yards apart. During a lull in the shelling next day, Blunden ran over to the one in which the main headquarters and the medical team were located. An officer friend who had just rejoined the headquarters staff from leave in London, "as though defying this extreme fury of warfare, was in an almost smiling mood," and invited Blunden to "dinner." Not long after Blunden returned to his own pillbox, some of his telephone linesmen managed to reconnect his pillbox with another one forward, closer to the fighting.

"I was called upon the telephone [by another officer]," Blunden said. "I say, hasn't something happened at your headquarters?"

"Not that I know of—[They're] all right, I believe," Blunden replied.
"Yes, I'm afraid something's wrong; will you find out?"

Blunden sent his servant scurrying over to the other pillbox, and
he soon returned, "wild-eyed, straining. 'Don't go over, sir; it's awful.
A shell came into the door.' He added more details after a moment or
two. The doctor [a friend of Blunden's] and those with him had been
killed."

Later, Blunden would write a poem in which the event was central.

The Welcome

He'd scarcely come from leave and London,
Still was carrying a leather case,
When he surprised headquarters pillbox
And sat down sweating in the filthy place.

He was a tall, lean, pale-looked creature,
With nerves that seldom ceased to wince;
Past war had long preyed on his nature,
And war had doubled in horror since.

There was a lull, the adjutant even
came to my hole: You cheerful sinner,
If nothing happens till half-past seven,
Come over then, we're going to have dinner.

But he went with his fierce red head;
We were sourly canvassing his jauntiness, when
Something happened at headquarters pillbox.
"Don't go there," cried one of my men.

The shell had struck right into the doorway,
The smoke lazily floated away;
There were six men in that concrete doorway,
Now a black muckheap blocked the way.

Inside, one who had scarcely shaken
The air of England out of his lungs
Was alive, and sane; it shall be spoken
While any of those who were there have tongues.

So Blunden sat in his fetid, airless pillbox with machine-gun bullets and shells constantly striking it and the surrounding ground, and when he wasn't working he read poetry to calm his nerves. After three days his battalion was relieved, having suffered 30 percent casualties. Just getting back to the reserve trenches was a harrowing affair: men beside him were shot or blown up. "You could almost feel the German gunners loading for you," he remembered.

Blunden's battalion, or what remained of it, stayed in the support trenches for several more days, under constant German bombardment. "The trench around me was slowly choked and caved in by hits just outside," he wrote. "The eastern sky that evening was all too brilliant with British rockets, appealing for artillery assistance. Westward, over blue hills, the sunset was all seraphim and cherubim."

Then, at midnight, as gas shells fell on them, trucks arrived and took Blunden's men to a farm some miles back from the fighting. There they rested for several days: "baths, lectures, football . . . occasional scenery of tall guilded trees . . . a sudden break in the clouds one morning revealed as in some marvelous lens a vast extent of the country southwards, towered cities, and silver rivers, blue church spires." A further break in the clouds revealed these towering cities and spires to be nothing more than the great slag heaps in the Bethune coal fields across the French border.

And then it was time to return to the war, to the Salient, to the unreality of it all.

"There was no singing," Blunden reported. "I think there were tears on some cheeks." Blunden was just one month shy of his twenty-first birthday.

Be that as it may, General Plumer's operation was a substantial success, capturing blockhouses and pillboxes with almost all objectives attained—except the spur at Tower Hamlets where Blunden had been. The Germans counterattacked nine times, but everywhere were thrown back. The Gheluvelt Plateau was slowly falling into Allied hands, but not without a price. The fight had cost the British army more than 15,000 casualties for a gain of less than three-quarters of a mile. Among them were Lieutenant Angel's boy-soldier who had cried out for his "mum," riddled with bullets, and the corporal who had held him in his arms, shot dead.

The ferocity of the German counterattacks, though unsuccessful, should have given Haig pause about General Charteris's rosy predictions of a pending German collapse, but it did not. Lloyd George and a delegation of politicians had arrived at the front—or at least at Haig's headquarters thirty miles from it—for a look around. Haig welcomed the visit as a man might welcome a toothache. The visit was mostly perfunctory, for even by his own accounts the prime minister had little or no interest in Haig's Flanders battles; he was determined to transfer large numbers of the army's troops from the Western Front to Italy, where the Italians had just scored a great victory.

To bolster his contention that the enemy was about used up, Haig arranged for Lloyd George to visit a German prisoner-of-war cage behind the Fifth Army. There, accompanied by General Charteris, the prime minister inspected a host of bedraggled, undersized, and demoralized German prisoners. It has been charged, not beyond reason, that someone—probably Charteris, also not beyond reason—had earlier removed from the cage all German soldiers who still looked as if they were ready and able to fight.

Not only was it apparent that the Germans still had a lot of fight left in them, but more portentous was the fact that only where the ground was dry were substantial gains made by the British. In those areas of the battlefield where artillery had destroyed the drainage system, the attack bogged down with little or nothing accomplished. On the other hand, the British successes at Menin Road and Polygon Wood had thoroughly alarmed the German High Command. General Ludendorff observed darkly, "The enemy managed to adapt himself to our method of employing counterattack divisions." Hurried conferences were held and new strategies hurled about. As a result, according to the Official History, "The Germans were now returning to their pre-war axiom of field fortifications: 'One line, and a strong one.'"

It was true that Plumer had outfoxed them by organizing his series of short, bite-and-hold assaults, with the artillery moved far enough forward to lay down an impassable curtain of fire on the German counterattack divisions. So long as it did not rain and the artillery could be moved up, Plumer seemed to have found the key to breaking the German line. But in Flanders, in October, it rained and rained.

Back in London, the chief of the Imperial General Staff, Sir William Robertson, almost always a staunch supporter of Haig, wrote his gloomy assessment of continuing the fight: "I confess I stick to it more because I can see nothing better, and because my instinct prompts me to stick to it, than because of any good arguments by which I can support it."

Plumer's next "bite," nine days later, would be styled the Battle of Broodseinde Ridge. This would complete the capture of the Gheluvelt Plateau. Haig was so buoyed by Plumer's successes that he dusted off his original plan to sweep the Germans from Roulers in the north, and reinstated his amphibious operation to clear the Belgian coast. To that end he instructed the cavalry to move up and be prepared for the big breakthrough. This, he informed Generals Plumer and Gough, should occur about October 10. The two commanders were, at that point, only mildly skeptical, and suggested to Haig that another five or six days might be necessary to break the Germans' morale. But the frightening prospect of rain was on everybody's mind; the weather was good now, but what about tomorrow, next week? Plumer's assault was scheduled to push off October 6, but Haig moved it up to October 4—a race against rain.

At first light October 4, the British attacked Broodseinde Ridge, the next to last stepping-stone to Passchendaele. It was an unqualified victory, even more so than at Menin Road and Polygon Wood. Or at least that's the way the British brass saw it: victory was now measured in pushing the Germans back a thousand or so yards. True to their word, the Germans had replaced their vaunted "defense-in-depth" strategy with one in which the front line was heavily manned and the counterattack divisions brought up close behind, in the zone of fire. British artillery took a tremendous toll on these men, packed together behind the front lines, and the attack-

ing battalions of Plumer's army overpowered even the heavily fortified front
line. There were dead Germans everywhere. The four Australian divisions
of Plumer's army conquered most of their objectives, and kicked the Germans off of Broodseinde Ridge by late afternoon; Gough's four divisions
did the same in the north part of the Salient, aided especially by tanks, which
had managed to make use of macadamized roads and high ground.

The vile prominence of Tower Hamlets, where Edmund Blunden had
his near epiphany, remained, however, in German hands. The combined
losses of both of Haig's armies totaled more than 20,000; the Germans'
about the same, including nearly 5,000 prisoners. To Charteris, this last
was most important, for the "exceptionally large" number of prisoners only
reinforced his prophecy that the Germans were on their last legs. Not surprisingly, it had begun to rain.

Haig was nevertheless ecstatic, and he pressed Plumer to continue
the assault immediately to capture Passchendaele. The old walrus-faced
general wasn't so sure. His intelligence told him that the Germans had
brought up fourteen fresh divisions, and he needed time to resituate his
own artillery. Plumer resisted Haig's idea for an immediate attack.

For his part, the German commander Ludendorff remarked dismally
about the "enormous losses" to his army. "It was evident," he said, "that the
idea of holding the front line more densely . . . was not the remedy." The
German history of the battle described Broodseinde as "The black day of
October 4th." Crown Prince Rupprecht began considering whether or not
to withdraw the front to far beyond the ridges around Ypres.

Chapter Fourteen ⭑

From the day of the success at Broodseinde Ridge, the skies continued to pour. By October 7, it had blown into a gale of "cold, drenching rain," and the battleground between Ypres and the Germans on the Passchendaele Ridge became a barren swamp of millions of deep, flooded shell craters. They stood almost lip to lip as far as anyone could see in any direction, even with binoculars. Where there was not this, there was a sheet of water from overflowed streams. Such ground as could be navigated had to be laid with wooden duckboards. The battlefield was now a moonscape—worse than a moonscape—of putrid liquid mud, with the German-occupied ridges a faint, misty specter on the eastern horizon.

On the night of the seventh, with the weather still raging outside, Plumer and Gough advised Haig that the campaign should be called off for the winter, though they said they would continue if so ordered. They were so ordered, and this was extraordinary, since rarely would a commander in chief over-rule the judgment of the commanding generals of his two armies while engaged in battle. But Haig wanted the Passchendaele Ridge badly, and wanted it before the end of the year. Not the least reason was that he didn't want his soldiers to spend the bitter Flanders winter in those loathsome bogs below the ridge, with German guns frowning down on them day and night. In that sense, Haig had gotten them into a spot, because that's exactly where they were.

He was also still concerned that the French were able to do nothing; in fact, because of Pétain's liberal policies in light of the mutinies, more than 25 percent of the French Army was at home on leave. Consequently, according to the Official History—though this has been disputed—"[Haig's] opinion was strengthened by the persistent and urgent pleas of General Pétain to continue the Flanders operations in order to ensure that the flow of German reserves should be diverted from the French front."

Additionally, the Russian question loomed large. It was the time of the October Revolution, what the Allies had feared all along was finally coming true. The Russian armies were melting away and a total collapse might come at any moment, thus freeing a million and a half German soldiers to fight on the Western Front. Haig could only hope that, if this happened, it would be offset by the arrival of the Americans—he had just received a telegram of congratulations over the Broodseinde victory from General John J. Pershing, who had recently arrived in France with the first U.S. military contingents. Furthermore, Haig still clung to the notion that if Passchendaele was taken, German morale would finally crack. He wanted his last chance. Instead, Lloyd George, without consulting Haig, ordered him to send six of his fighting divisions in Flanders to take over nearly forty miles of front from the French farther south. Not only that, Haig again had begged that some of the hundreds of thousands of combat-ready replacements currently squatting in England be sent to his casualty-depleted divisions at Ypres. But the prime minister again refused him, reasoning that if he sent more men Haig would only squander them in more senseless battles.

It has been suggested by some historians that by this stage in the war Haig had become something of a religious nut, convinced it was his divine destiny to defeat the Germans with the British army before the Americans arrived in force. There is little or no evidence to support this. True, Haig was a religious man, attending regular Church of Scotland services and even making close friends with one of its pastors. But most people were religious in those days, and Haig was no spiritual kook. In fact, if anybody had a right to pray, and pray a lot, it was General Sir Douglas Haig. In any event, Haig set the next stage of the attack for October 9, with Plumer again leading the way. This was to open the first battle of Passchendaele.

* * *

The difficulties presented by the relentless rain staggered everyone's imagination, except perhaps those back at General Headquarters. It was blowing a near hurricane off the North Sea. Great inundations gave way to steady downpours and everyone almost welcomed a drizzle. All the shell craters filled to brimming with water. Engineers and pioneers continued to lay the duckboards but these quickly became slimy and any man falling off of them risked drowning—thousands did. Trying to navigate the things carrying mountains of ammunition, food, and other equipment to keep the army going was an almost superhuman task. Pack animals that fell off would simply sink out of sight; it was impossible to pull them back on. There were a number of light rail lines linking the front with supply bases in the rear, but these, too, fell victim to the rain and mud. At least one rail engine vanished entirely beneath the sea of mud. Supply runs to the front lines, which normally took an hour, now took anywhere from six to sixteen hours, according to the Official History.

Artillery, so crucial to Plumer's successful bite-and-hold tactics, posed another problem entirely. Moving it forward for the next attack was a stupendous task; it took dozens of men hauling painfully on ropes to move a field gun only a few yards. One soldier described a party of thirty men charged with moving a five-gun battery up to a new location. "The battery horses had drowned in the mire," he said, "and the wheels of the gun stuck in the mud so hauling by rope was impossible. They solved the problem by turning the wheels by hand in a Herculean effort. . . . Often we sank in mud of almost gruel thickness until the slime rose above our hips. The only thing solid underneath was a huddled dead man, and we stumbled over five or six during the morning."

Nevertheless, some guns sank up to their muzzles and were abandoned; others disappeared entirely. Material for wooden gun platforms had to be lugged forward to place the guns upon, since with the first shot the guns would sink in and disarrange the firing calculations. It was soon found that the gun platforms themselves sank in with each shot, until ranging was impossible. Because of the condition of the ground, only about half of the field guns even got into position to support the attack. It was maddening. One machine-gun officer recalled that he and his men had to stand on crates of ammunition just to keep from submerging in the mud. By the end of the day, he said, they were each standing on up to six crates of ammunition. Some enterprising soldiers got their quartermaster to bring forward a number of the tin bathing basins used for delousing the men; in these they slept, suspended in the mud. More than one soldier repeated the oft asked question, What must our officers be thinking, sending us out here in this?

This last complaint was perhaps becoming the most important. If General Headquarters believed German morale was crumbling, they had apparently not considered what the great stresses and strains were doing to their own soldiers. Time and again men recorded their hatred and detestation of fighting in the Ypres Salient. But now many were beginning to question fighting at all. The poet-lieutenant Edmund Blunden was among these. He spoke of "the grossness of the war," and the "uselessness of the offensive." "We should all die, presumably, around Ypres," he wrote. Another famous poet-officer, Siegfried Sassoon, known for his bravery as "Mad Jack," went much further, publishing similar views in an article in a British magazine. After tossing his Military Cross into the Mersey River, Sassoon wrote: "I have come to believe that the war is being deliberately prolonged . . . [it] has become a war of aggression and conquest." They could have court-martialed him, but Sassoon was a popular figure in England, and a friend of Churchill, so the authorities merely consigned him to a sanitarium.

If these were the views of many officers, then what must the men have been thinking, helpless as they were at the beck and call of commanders who ordered them into what looked like certain death. Naturally, most hated it just as much if not more; nerves wore thin, the joking stopped. To have been in Ypres at that time was as close as man will come to seeing the Infernal Regions. Picture it at night: a bleak hellish maw of mud and terror; the stench, the bodies everywhere of men and animals, since there had been no time to bury them; all of it constantly lit up by the roar and flash of artillery shells, flares, and signal rockets from both sides. It practically defies imagination that these horrors continued night and day, day and night.

Until now during the war the men had somehow gotten by with laughter and joking and singing gallows' humor ditties such as "The Bells of Hell."

"The bells of hell go ting-a-ling-a-ling
For you but not for me;
And the little devils how they sing-a-ling-a-ling
For you but not for me.
O Death, where is thy sting-a-ling-a-ling,
O Grave, thy victor-ee?
The bells of hell go ting-a-ling-a-ling,
For you but not for me."

They weren't singing anymore. What was happening now was beyond anyone's sense of humor.

Yet somehow, with the exception of those few who deserted, or feigned illness, or took themselves out with a "self-inflicted wound," the men went on. You can attribute it to some exaggerated sense of duty; to the legendary "pluck" of the British; to some indefinable sense of fate, or even fatalism that numbed the mind, so that the men simply became as automatons, with no viable alternative. But even that doesn't explain it. The Official History had this to say: "The chief cause of the great discontent during this period of the Flanders fighting was, in fact, the continuous demands on regimental officers and men to carry out tasks which appeared physically impossible to perform, and which no other army would have faced." But that still doesn't explain it; possibly the closest one can come is to suggest that the men went on because each did not want to embarrass himself before his friends.

On October 9 it suddenly stopped raining and the British armies attacked along a line that ran through the village of Poelcappelle, a couple of miles northwest of Passchendaele. The sudden letup in the weather was merely a coincidence; the attack had been scheduled anyway, rain or shine. The skies cleared bright and sunny and the high temperature was 53 degrees, but the ground remained sodden. Almost as bad, because of the weather, aircraft—the eyes of the artillery—had been unable to fly. Consequently the locations of the German artillery batteries behind Passchendaele Ridge were unknown, and so the British heavy counterbatteries had no choice but to fire blindly over the ridge, in hopes of perhaps hitting something.

Poelcappelle quickly became a disaster. German artillery crashed down on the attacking troops and the counterbattery fire was powerless to stop it. A little past 5 A.M. the tens of thousands of men who had stumbled and staggered forward across duckboards in the torrential rains for ten to twelve hours the night before now floundered sleepless out of whatever slimy shelter they had been able to find. Painfully, they began wading through the sucking mud toward the gray and misty hills in front, which were twinkling at them like a million fireflies with machine-gun and rifle fire.

They went on like men walking into a fierce storm, heads bowed, chins tucked down. After just a few dozen yards, sheer exhaustion overtook many of the Tommies; except for some advances on the north and south flanks of the line, the attack was stymied. Men simply fell into water-filled shell craters, panting, cursing, and sobbing in frustration, while the German guns rained down upon them. Isolated units made more progress—a few even reached Passchendaele village itself—but were quickly forced to withdraw by heavy German flanking fire. By sundown there had been practically no advance at all, at a cost of about 10,000 casualties.

Every man there had his tale to tell. A particularly chilling one comes from Sergeant T. Berry, of the Rifle Brigade: "Tea was all we had that night at Poelcappelle. There was no chance of getting the rations up. We'd been in the attack, come back to support, and then we were going to attack again, because in those conditions they couldn't get reliefs up. We were just crouched in shell holes waiting, and there was this one little chap. He made tea all night long, and kept nipping out and getting water out of flooded ground behind us and heating it up as best he could. Every half hour he would say, 'There you are, Tommy, a drop of tea.' It wasn't very hot, but it kept us going. The next morning when it got light he looked over the side where he'd got the water and it was a bleeding shell hole, and there was a dead Jerry in it and blood all floating around. We'd had that and all in our tea. We seemed to have no ill-effects, and we had other things to worry about.

"We heard screaming coming from another crater a bit away. I went over to investigate with a couple of the lads. It was a big hole and there was a fellow of the 8th Suffolks in it up to his shoulders. So I said, 'Get your rifles, one man in the middle to stretch them out, make a chain and let him get hold of it.' But it was no use. It was too far to stretch, we couldn't get any force on it, and the more we pulled and the more he struggled the further he seemed to go down. He went down gradually. He kept begging us to shoot him. But we couldn't shoot him. Who could shoot him? We stayed with him, watching him go down in the mud. And he died. He wasn't the only one. There must have been thousands up there who died in the mud."

Or almost worse, suffered in it, wounded. Thousands of men remained shot or torn up by artillery out in no-man's-land. The first night their cries and pleas were not only heart-wrenching but disconcerting to the soldiers back in what passed for "the line." By the second night, the cries had subsided somewhat and by the third they were feeble and far between. Soon it was time to attack again; as it turned out, too soon.

The day before the next assault on Passchendaele, Haig summoned his army commanders, Gough and Plumer, for a powwow. Gough was concerned about continuing at all. Plumer was likewise concerned about an enormous mass of barbed wire to his front that had not previously been reported, due to the grounding of aircraft. Given the sorry state of the artillery, there was no way to destroy it with shells before zero hour. About the only encouraging thing was that since the line virtually had not moved, the excruciating task of hauling up the artillery was no longer necessary. By now the usually buoyant Charteris had finally changed his tune. He spoke in his diary of the hopelessness of it all, but if he ever said that to Haig there is no record of it.

Plumer, too, seemed to have changed tunes. Always before he had insisted on meticulous and methodical preparations before sending his men into battle. Now, with time running out and winter coming on, he had agreed to launch his next assault just three days after the calamity of Poelcappelle, without sufficient artillery, without fresh troops, without being able to cut the vast entanglement of barbed wire on his front. In spite of this, he told Haig he believed his Australians and New Zealanders could take Passchendaele in one great rush on October 12. Undoubtedly he believed it, but according to the Official History, Plumer was operating under "misinformation."

Haig, for his part, blithely informed a group of war correspondents that only the mud had prevented his army from taking Passchendaele, and that his lines were now practically past the enemy defenses. That last was simply not true, for the men in the lines themselves could see plainly the squat German pillboxes menacing every yard of their front. The business about the mud was, of course, true. In fact, Crown Prince Rupprecht, who only a few days earlier had been considering retreating the German army away from Ypres, had delighted in the mud, telling his diary: "Most gratifying—rain: our most effective ally."

And rain it did the day of the attack. Just before midnight the evening before, it had begun to storm again and Gough once more telephoned Haig to ask for a postponement. But Plumer was in the mood for a fight, and he convinced Haig to carry on. When the army, exhausted and near starving—few rations or replacements had managed to get up to the front—set at it again, they were met with the same conditions of three days earlier: mud, gunfire, rain. Worse, because of the state of the ground, such artillery as could fire at all was rendered almost useless because the shells simply buried themselves in the muck and did little more than spatter the Germans with mud. A general commanding a New Zealand brigade complained bitterly that "All the attacks recently lack preparation, and the whole history of the war is that when thorough preparation is not made, we fail." He added, almost unnecessarily, "You cannot afford to take liberties with the Germans."

At the end of the day, though there were dents made here and there, the British line remained virtually where it had been, and another 13,000 men were lost. The Australians and New Zealanders bravely struggled through the swamps of mud and water; those who reached the great entanglements of wire were simply mowed down by the hundreds. At one point they found a break in the wire and floundered through it, only to be annihilated by hidden German machine-gun fire. One suspects the Germans may have deliberately cut paths in the wire to channel the unsuspecting attackers into a trap. Once more, no-man's-land was littered with the dead and wounded. Due to mud, it now took up to sixteen stretcher bearers to evacuate a single stretcher case, both because of the exertion and because so many stretcher bearers themselves were gunned down. The dead were simply left to rot, much to the dismay of the men in the next wave of attacks. The rats and crows had a field day.

Over on the German side of the line, things weren't any better. Life in the concrete pillboxes was shocking. A dozen or more men at a time were holed up in each of the hundreds of blockhouses that dotted their defense area, unable to go outside because of the unending British artillery. Dead Germans decomposed in shell craters or fighting holes outside by the thousands, and attracted flies by the millions. They crawled constantly over the skin and food of the living, who simply sat there and endured it, up to six days at a time, in the dark, waterlogged, stench—waiting for the next Allied attack. Diarrhea and vomiting were common, adding to the foulness. Because of the soil conditions, the pillboxes had not been constructed deep in the ground, so if a heavy shell landed near one it was likely to tip over. If it tipped onto its entrance hole, which often happened, those inside were trapped in a slow, horrible death, because there was no way to rescue them.

The futility of the attack at Poelcappelle dampened, but did not extinguish, the spirits of either Haig or Plumer. Yet still it did not sit well with Gough, whose army was now mired in the swamps below and to the north of Passchendaele. The failure, it was concluded correctly, was due to lack of preparation and the weather. But Haig was determined to have his army astride Passchendaele Ridge before the end of the campaign. Problem was, Plumer's Australians and New Zealanders were utterly exhausted and depleted, but for this Haig had fashioned a solution. He had ordered up from Vimy, not far away in France, the Canadian Corps, with its four infantry divisions, 70,000 strong, which had endured its baptism of fire at Ypres in 1915. The Canadians were less than thrilled to go, but go they did, arriving during the final weeks of October.

Among the first to arrive was the privately raised regiment of the Princess Patricias Canadian Light Infantry, commanded now by one-eyed, fifty-one-year-old Colonel Agar Adamson, who had been a captain and a company commander when the regiment had last fought in Flanders two years earlier. His reaction upon reentering the Salient echoed those of most who had fought there in earlier battles—disbelief: "The condition of the ground beggars description," he wrote his wife Mabel. "Just one mass of shell holes all full of water. The strongest and youngest men cannot navigate without falling down. The people we relieved tell me in the attack, a great many of their men were drowned in shell holes for want of strength to pull themselves out when dog-tired." Two days later he wrote, "Things very active, the greatest concentration of troops of the present war and in consequence, are very tightly packed. It rains or blows all the time, the condition of the ground is beyond words and of course will be much worse after the barrage." He added darkly, "This game is the biggest of big gambles and no one can foresee the future," signing off with his usual, "Ever thine . . ."

At the other end of the spectrum was another Canadian, Private Will R. Bird, who had enlisted in the kilted Canadian Black Watch after his brother was killed at Ypres in the 1915 battle. For the past year Bird had been in the trenches at Vimy, some miles to the south, with the rest of the Canadian Corps. He describes first moving up to the front lines at Ypres in October, "past waterlogged trenches, a nightmare of scummy holes, an indescribable desolation. All around the giant horseshoe of the Salient there were red flashes and winking glows, and the misty light of flares. The sky became illumined by a thousand strange flickering lights, the reflection of a thousand gun flashes, and quivered with the passage of shells." And all this while some of Bird's companions, no doubt, were still back in the saloons in Poperinge drinking beer and singing "Danny Boy."

Bird and his fellow Canadians were given the onerous task of carrying to the front sections of duckboard, which they jokingly referred to as "bath mats." As they moved forward they began to encounter the usual carcasses of mules and horses, derelict tanks, and the bodies of half-submerged soldiers in all stages of decomposition. The water in most of the shell craters, he reported, was filled with blood, and "the whole Salient had an odor beyond description."

This was in broad daylight, and the Germans watching from the ridges had calculated the Canadians' rate of progress and commenced artillery barrages on the spots forward where Bird and his companions were headed. But the Canadians outfoxed them by stopping and standing still, then moving on. In a way, the mud was a blessing, because most shells would simply embed themselves in it and explode harmlessly, if at all. Before they left on their "bath mat" expedition, the sergeant in charge of the "dump" had cheerfully told them not to worry. "He said the mud had saved at least ten thousand lives in the Salient, and was saving more every day," Bird recalled. If this was true, it was also true over on the German side of the line; ironically, of course, not a good sign for the Canadians who would have to carry on the next attack.

At about this same time, politically, not only the prime minister but the British War Cabinet as well, it seems, had for all intents written off the Ypres offensive. This would certainly have come as shocking news to the men who were fighting and dying there. It was not until the middle of October that the War Cabinet even requested an accounting of casualty figures for Haig's operation, and when they received them, no one seemed particularly concerned. Prime Minister Lloyd George, the War Cabinet, or a combination of both could have called off the battle at any time, but chose not to. In fact, it seems they more or less ignored it, apparently on the reasoning that it would soon die out on its own due to the onset of winter.

Meanwhile, the Canadian Corps commander, General Arthur Currie, informed Haig and Plumer of his plans to capture Passchendaele. He wanted the full support of his artillery, and would proceed in three steps, or "pushes," of 500 yards each to drive the Germans from the ridge. It would take two weeks to prepare for the attack. (In fact, the Canadians got only a little more than half their artillery up for the barrage.) Zero Hour was set for October 26 at 5:40 A.M. At that time the Third and Fourth Canadian divisions would have to attack on either side of the Passchendaele village. The reason was that they were separated by the impassable flood of the Ravebeck stream. Four or five days later, the other two Canadian divisions, the First and Second, would leapfrog the Third and Fourth divisions and move up 500 yards closer to Passchendaele, and so on, until the ridge was taken. At the same time, two divisions of Gough's Fifth Army would attack to protect the Canadian's northern flank, while to the south the Australians and New Zealanders would do the same.

After surveying the ground, General Currie made the foreboding prediction that it would cost his Canadians 16,000 men to pull off the operation. He missed the mark by only a few hundred.

It all went according to plan, but at a horrific cost, which has been described as a futile, useless waste of life. First of all, it rained nine of the fourteen days between the last attack on October 12 and the first Canadian attack on the twenty-sixth. Not only did this turn the ground into an even more Dantesque nightmare, but aircraft were again limited in their ability to pinpoint German batteries. Neither flank operation was successful. Gough's Fifth Army divisions found the going so atrocious it was reported that men were sinking into the mud "up to their shoulders." Most of the men's weapons quickly became jammed with the mud and the attack stalled almost immediately. The commanding generals of these divisions reported to Gough that there was simply no way their soldiers could make further progress, but Haig ordered it done anyway.

The Canadians had ultimately gained their 500 yards in the center, however, and the next attack was set for October 30. The morning before, Private Will Bird and half a dozen of his friends were ordered forward "to a spot where the mud was hard enough to make a shelter." Bird and his friend Private Mel Baillie, a big lumberjack from Saskatchewan, had just finished making their shelter when a huge shell explosion occurred some yards away. When they went to investigate, two of their friends in the squad had been buried by it, and killed. Half an hour later—and always somewhat incongruously—rations and mail arrived. Baillie received a parcel from his sister containing chewing tobacco; Bird had to read him the note that came with it, since Baillie was illiterate. Shortly afterward, Baillie began giving away the tobacco, as well as a fresh pair of socks, which he gave to Bird.

"Put these in your pack," Baillie told Bird. "I won't need them."

"What do you mean?" Bird asked, alarmed.

"Don't argue with me, Bill," Baillie replied. "I'm not coming back from this one."

Next night they were ordered to attack a German pillbox. Bird was frustrated. "Never in the war had I been so sickened and discouraged than at that moment," he said. "The whole affair was cockeyed. We were new in the sector. None knew the terrain. None knew what defences the German had or his strength. The place after dark was a swampy wilderness with nothing to use as a guide."

The attack got off to a rotten start. Both sergeants leading it were drunk on rum and nobody even knew for sure where the pillbox was. They were all floundering in the mud when machine guns opened up all around them. Bird was grazed on the head by shrapnel, dazed and sick to his stomach. Vicious hand-to-hand fighting broke out. Bird saw a group of Germans with a machine gun coming his way. He managed to throw a hand grenade, which killed them all. By this time both the drunken sergeants had been shot and killed and the platoon became leaderless. Grenades exploded everywhere and bullets snapped through the air. Bird stumbled into a crater that contained a man from another company who had been wounded in earlier fighting. His hand was blown nearly off and dangled from the wrist only by a thin strip of skin. Bird cut off the hand with his trench knife and threw it away, then bandaged the stump after emptying a bottle of iodine on it. A burst of machine-gun fire rattled out. Bird found that it had caught three of his friends, including his longtime pal, the premonitory Mel Baillie. "They were all dead, lying together, rifle in hand, all shot through the head by one sweep of the German gun."

Scenarios like this were being repeated over and over again across the battlefield, but progress was made. Another 500 yards was gained. Colonel Agar Adamson and his Princess Pats had conquered their objectives. From a shell hole, on a muddy scrap of paper, he wrote his wife Mabel: "I am still alright and hanging on. Our attack was successful, but it, and holding on, have been awfully costly." He then goes on to list nine of the officers he and Mabel knew who had been killed. The Princess Pats had gone into the fight with 600 men. They came out with 160; 150 had been killed. When he got out of the line two days later, Agar had to write the letters to the dead men's families. He, too, had now become disillusioned, and wrote to Mabel: "The higher authorities are expressing to us their appreciation of our efforts, but I cannot help wondering if the position gained was worth the awful sacrifice of life—Ever thine, Agar."

*   *   *

Meantime, Lloyd George had instigated another irritant for Haig, which he hoped would quell the bloodthirsty operations in Flanders. With the French still reeling from mutiny and the Americans beginning to arrive, the prime minister deemed it necessary to establish a Supreme War Council of all the Allied nations to coordinate the conduct of the war. This made better sense that the present arrangement, in which the warring nations simply went off and did what they thought best. The council ultimately named the French general Ferdinand Foch as Allied commander in chief. This development predictably enraged Haig and the chief of the General Staff in London, Wully Robertson, both of whom again feared the British armies would now be mere subordinates to foreign powers, as they had been during the Nivelle affair. Relations between Haig, Robertson, and Lloyd George had steadily and by now publicly deteriorated, with each side accusing the other of giving unfavorable and accusatory interviews to the press. The squabble was now common knowledge. Haig paid a visit to Lloyd George just before the last big push for Passchendaele, when the prime minister was in Paris, setting up the Supreme War Council.

Haig wrote in his diary: "At 12 o'clock he asked me to go out for a walk, and I went with him up the Champs Elysées to the Arc de Triomphe. Quite a pleasant little man when one had him alone, but I should think most unreliable."

Haig faced a wrenching conflict. With winter coming on, it was now clear even to Haig that this third great battle of Ypres was winding down, and his visions of driving the Germans from their bases on the Belgian coast had long since evaporated. But he remained determined to at least capture the Passchendaele Ridge. Savage fighting continued day and night in the slimy mire, as the Canadians and elements of the Fifth Army tried to improve their positions; naturally, the Germans responded with counterattacks. On the last day of October Haig concluded that little if any progress was possible by the Fifth Army, and he effectively shut down their operations and handed over that part of the front to Plumer. Then, on November 6, the final push to Passchendaele got off at 6 A.M. sharp. As usual, it was raining.

The Canadians struggled through mud, shell fire, and machine-gun and rifle fire, but by 8:45 A.M. they were bayoneting Germans in the rubble that had once been Passchendaele, while others of the enemy could be seen fleeing down the eastern slope of the ridge. By that afternoon the village was secured, or rather all that was left of it; what had been a quaint Belgian neighborhood consisting of a few shops and several dozen homes and cottages had been entirely pulverized by the shelling. The only recognizable feature left were the ruins of a red brick church.

Revisiting Private Will Bird, we can better see how things transpired. Bird's battalion had been relieved after their shattering attack on October 30 and they assumed they would remain behind the lines for some time. Then their ranks were replenished with new men and by a cruel twist of fate they were selected, one assumes by lottery, to represent the division (one battalion from each brigade was chosen) to hold the newly won ground at Passchendaele.

Moving up to the line, a dozen or so men were killed and then the Germans began to bombard them in earnest. A man next to Will Bird was trying to dig a shelter when a shell cut off the top of his head, "leaving only the jaw and neck." Bird and his companions began clawing at the earth to find protection; then Bird saw a dead man a little ways ahead and dragged him back to form part of a parapet. This so horrified a fellow soldier that he ran away to another spot, where he was almost immediately killed by a shell blast. The shelling continued all night and the next day, killing many more. At one point a young soldier from another outfit slithered wide-eyed into Bird's hole.

"He was so plastered with mud I could not identify his unit, and he was shaking uncontrollably," Bird said. "Soon the lad snuggled against me. I moved over and he followed." The boy was babbling over and over something that sounded like: "Yan, tean, tether, mether, pip, cesar, azar, castra, horna, dick, yan-a-dick, tean-a-dick, tether-a-dick, bumfit, yan-a-bum, tether-a-bum, mether-a-bum, jigget."

"What on earth are you saying!" Bird finally demanded.

"He shook more violently. 'I'm a shepherd boy from Hawes,' he gasped. 'That's the way we count sheep. I can't stop.'"

"It was no use to try to do anything with him," Bird recalled. "He stayed tight against me, shouting in my ear the count of the shells landing near us."

The shelling never let up. Helmets, packs, men, and parts of men were hurled into Bird's hole—men with arms and legs blown off; arms and legs themselves. Near nightfall a runner came up and told them to move forward and capture a German pillbox. Luckily, they caught the Germans by surprise during a relief and those who did not run away surrendered. The German relief party had brought up thermoses of hot coffee, which Bird and his platoon mates eagerly drank.

By next morning, Bird said, they had neither orders nor rations nor officers, and were famished. Nearby were the bodies of a number of South Wales Borderers, and Bird and his companions ransacked their packs for rations. They had just finished eating when the Germans began shelling them again, and suddenly Bird found himself buried alive. "In that split second all sound of gunfire ceased. I could not move hand or foot. There were five feet of earth piled over me. But I had one grand bit of luck."

As it happened, Bird's head had landed at the butts of several stacked rifles with bayonets attached and somehow this gave him a little air from the surface. He felt the motion of people digging and was soon pried from under the ground. Not long afterward the Germans counterattacked and, for the first time, Bird killed a man with his bayonet. They had now been there the requisite two days, but no runner or relief had reached them. Led only by a corporal, Bird and the remaining men decided to make their way back to the reserve trenches. On the way a salvo bracketed them, killing one of Bird's best friends, thirty-three-year-old Private Daniel McGillivary. Bird held him in his arms until he died, then helped another friend who had been shell shocked.

"On the duckwalk, we were just a pair on a straggling line of steel helmets and hunched shoulders, out-going units of bone-weary, shell-dazed men who had reached the walk after an exhausting struggle with the Ypres mud, treading on old dead and new dead, slipping in the foulness of slimy ditches." Afterward, he would declare: "Every man who endured Passchendaele would never be the same again; was more or less a stranger to himself."

The day that Passchendaele fell, Haig's chief of staff, Lieutenant General Launcelot Kiggell, went forward to see the battle area for the first time. Nearing Ypres in his big Rolls-Royce staff car Kiggell was first amazed, then dismayed, and finally horrified at the breathtaking morass where the battle had taken place: an almost indescribable sea of mud littered with the bloated, rotten carcasses of artillery horses, smashed guns and wagons, and other detritus of war. He is reported to have broken into tears, crying out, "Good God, did we really send men to fight in that?" His companion, an officer who had been in the battle, told Kiggell, "It's worse further on up."

★ Chapter Fifteen

Haig had finally taken the Passchendaele Ridge, which put his army back on the ridges that formed the "amphitheater" east of Ypres that the British had occupied with cavalry at the beginning, in 1914—although both the topography and geography of those ridges had been vastly altered by four years of war.

All this was accomplished at a cost of hundreds of thousands of casualties. Sixty-one Victoria Crosses had been awarded during the Third Battle of Ypres—fifteen of them posthumously. Now Haig's men would not have to spend the winter in the water and mud below, and, in places, they had shoved the Germans back up to five miles. At the same time, nearly six months of campaigning since the mines had gone up at Messines, the whole operation had only put the British into an even larger salient— though still ringed on three sides by German guns—and the bulge at Passchendaele was the most dangerous of all. Haig admitted as much to the General Staff in London.

By this time Plumer had been snatched from Haig's command by Lloyd George and sent off to fight in Italy, along with five British divisions from Haig's army. When his replacement, General Rawlinson, came to take over, Rawlinson's assessment of the Allied situation in Flanders was gloomy. "Nothing we can hope to do can make the line [that is now] held a really satisfactory defensive position," he wrote, adding that if the Germans launched a major attack at Ypres, the British must be prepared to withdraw from their newly won positions—the bitterest of notions. And a major German attack was now exactly what was being contemplated by everyone: finally, the Russians had collapsed, and division after division of fresh German troops, with all of their artillery, were now streaming westward—at the rate of more than 100,000 a week. When it thawed out in the spring, the Allies would face an entirely different German army.

Not only was Plumer gone but other heads would roll. Haig's overoptimistic intelligence chief, Charteris, was done in by a subordinate who, correctly, secretly revealed to authorities that Charteris was giving Haig bad intelligence regarding German strength and morale. This was seized on by *The Times* and Charteris became history. As well, General Kiggell, Haig's chief of staff—he of the "Did we really send men to fight in that?" remark—was forced out after *The Times* demanded an inquiry into his role in the Passchendaele affair. It was publicly suspected that the damaging information on both officers was leaked to the newspaper by none other than Lloyd George. Not only that, the prime minister succeeded in getting rid of Haig's powerful ally in London, General Robertson, chief of the Imperial General Staff. The straw that had broken the camel's back was Robertson's fierce opposition to another of Lloyd George's schemes to scale back operations on the Western Front: this time to remove troops from Haig to deliver a major attack on the Turkish army in Palestine. Finally, the prime minister managed to have Robertson sacked. To his great exasperation, however, Lloyd George was still unable to fire Haig—it remained a political hot potato. For his part, Haig publicly pronounced himself "well satisfied" with the results of the battles. Privately, and to his immediate superiors, he was less than pleased.

The debate on the wisdom of Haig's 1917 Ypres offensive continues to this day, often on caustic terms. After the war, statements and recollections from participants were solicited by historians arguing that it was a delusive, insensible, and almost criminal waste of life. The final battles for Passchendaele in particular have come under harsh attack. An argument has been made that the British Army was so depleted by the fighting that it almost cost the Allies the war in the spring of 1918, when the Germans launched their expected big attack. If Third Ypres was a victory for the Allied armies, it was certainly a pyrrhic one.[1]

The Official History, a massive twenty-eight-volume work cataloguing every battle and aspect of the war, was not completed until 1948, following the Second World War. The Third Battle of Ypres was the last in the series, and in the wake of all the controversy over the battle the Official Historian, Brigadier General Sir James Edmonds, who had been at Ypres, took it upon himself to defend Haig's plan, as well as the strategy and tactics. Many critics viewed Edmonds's work as a blatant misstatement of facts and conclusions and this, of course, led to a new spate of war books taking the opposite view. There are sensible arguments on both sides.

Haig's reasons for wanting to attack in Flanders have already been detailed here; the only alternatives were to siphon off troops to fight in Italy or some other place in the Mediterranean theater, or to have done nothing and waited for the Americans. Haig insisted, and continued to insist, that the battle was an absolute necessity, if for nothing else than to save the French from collapse.

Astonishingly, the Germans never did learn about the deplorable state of the French Army, but when you analyze this, it didn't much matter. The important point was, what if they *had*? Surely if they had known—and there was no way of knowing they didn't—they would have mounted a great crushing offensive against the French, had they not been tied down at Ypres by Haig's persistent and brutal assaults.

About the best that can be said for the battle in Flanders is that by attrition it wore down the German army. But the question arises, and continues to arise, of who attrited whom? Five years after the war, the British War Office released a document entitled *Statistics of the Military Effort of the British Empire during the Great War*. It states that British casualties on the Western Front for the six-month period July to the end of 1917, when Haig was fighting mostly in Flanders, amounted to approximately 450,000 men. Add to this the casualties during the capture of Messines and the usual

---

1. The classic Greek historian Plutarch recounted that after the defeat of the Romans at the Battle of Asculum in 279 B.C., the Greek king Pyrrhus remarked: "One more victory like this, and we are lost."

"wastage," and this totals about half a million, a staggering figure. The German losses were calculated at 270,000 for the same period. When the Official History was finally published a quarter century later, General Edmonds downgraded British casualties to almost half that figure—244,897, and ups the German casualty estimate to 400,000—almost a total reverse of the earlier report.

It has been almost impossible for either side to calculate exactly the losses, due to their sheer enormity, and the means of casualty reporting during the war. The most likely scenario is that the true figure falls approximately in between the two conflicting ones. If that is so, then by the arithmetic of adding them up and dividing by two, one arrives at a figure of approximately 350,000 British casualties versus approximately 335,000 for the Germans—horrific loses, but just about equal. If the standard World War I casualty ratio of dead to wounded and missing is applied to this number—and there is no reason why it should not be—then the Battle of Ypres in 1917 enriched the Flanders earth with the corpses of some 228,000 Englishmen and Germans, not to mention about 20,000 French, all in an area not much longer than Manhattan Island. By contrast, the Allied cemeteries in France, from D day in 1944, the Normandy invasion, till the end of the Second World War, contain the graves of approximately 10,000 American soldiers.

Mere numbers and statistics of course can never tell the story of Flanders. On both sides men fought and died for four long years in conditions that can only be described as subhuman and, to a man, they were degraded by it. It has been argued, persuasively, that *all* war is dehumanizing and degrading; that may be so, though if it is, then what further adjectives can be found to describe what those soldiers endured in the squalor of Flanders Fields? The search for "why" and "how" remains elusive and any effort to reason it out is to fashion a mirror of hell itself. Yet these *were* humans, civilized humans, men who in normal circumstance, as John McCrae pointed out in his poem, "lived, felt dawn, saw sunset glow, loved and were loved." A truly sobering thing would be a glimpse of what was actually going on in their minds during the fighting. That would not only be sobering; it would be perfectly frightening.

* * *

For their part, the Germans freely admitted that the battle had cost them dearly. Far from the theory that Haig's Ypres fight had wrecked the British Army by the time the Germans finally launched their great assault in 1918, the German Official History saw Passchendaele this way: "Divisions disappeared by the dozens into the turmoil of the battle, only to emerge from the witches' cauldron after a short period, thinned and exhausted, often reduced to a miserable remnant." Other high-ranking Germans, including Prince Rupprecht, Hindenburg, and Ludendorff, blame the Flanders fighting for their ultimate defeat in the war. (Though, on balance, generals forever blame defeat on anything besides their own ineptitude.)

Controversy continues to swirl around the battle in a frenzy of why and what-if scenarios. What if Haig had ordered Plumer, and not Gough, to conduct the operation from the start? Why did Haig continue the battle after the end of October, after the success at Broodseinde, and then on into the horrible mud? What if Haig had ordered the main battle to commence immediately after Plumer's success at Messines? Did Haig even know about the impossible conditions of the ground? These are all legitimate questions, which do not really require long answers.

In hindsight, Haig probably made a mistake in picking Gough to lead the attack; Plumer had been the man on the ground at Ypres for two years and knew it well. Gough was a "thruster," or so thought Haig, but Gough's thrusting was what did him in. Instead of first aiming for the capture of the Gheluvelt Plateau and putting the German artillery out of business, he aimed at an impossible objective miles away, and soon learned his lesson, after which he recommended the operation be shut down.

Why Haig allowed so great a time to elapse between the spectacular capture of the Messines Ridge and the commencement of the battles for Ypres six weeks later remains unclear. The Official History states that "Time was required to shift artillery from the Messines and Lens areas northward." But just before Plumer's attack at Messines, Haig had asked him how long it would require to continue the battle and Plumer had replied that he could attack the Gheluvelt Plateau within three days. Instead, Haig gave the responsibility to Gough, who had just arrived on the scene, and Gough asked for, and got, more than a month, plus another week to get up more artillery. There has never been a satisfactory explanation for this, other than to accuse Haig of being dilatory.

As to the final month of suffering during the taking of Passchendaele Ridge, there is probably more to commend Haig's detractors than his supporters. Until almost the end, Haig clung to the supposition that the taking of the ridge could lead to greater things, that the Germans would finally crack. In fact, even after the disaster at Poelcappelle on October 9, Haig instructed General Rawlinson on the coast to be prepared to put into motion the attacks on the Belgian ports. What is troublesome, though, is Haig's knowledge of the state of the ground where the attacks were to take place. The Official History states that the commander in chief was kept fully abreast of the conditions by his subordinates. But is that really so? If the shock expressed by his chief of staff, Lieutenant General Kiggell, was accurately reported ("Good God, did we really send men to fight in that?"), it would not seem so. The men and the junior officers certainly knew the state of the ground. They would have reported it to their battalion commanders, who would certainly have reported it to the brigadier generals in charge of the brigades who, in turn, would have reported it to the major generals in command of the divisions. It would have been up to them to report it to the lieutenant generals commanding the army corps, who presumably would have reported it to the two army commanders, Plumer and Gough.

With all the firsthand accounts of those who fought the battle, it is difficult to understand how Haig could not know. And if he did, and sent his army forward anyway, such a decision seems hard to justify for the capture of a piece of real estate that was defensively untenable, and at the cost of so much hopeless suffering. If he did not know—and there is no evidence that he personally visited the battlefield during this time—blame also attaches, for it is the business of a commander in chief to know these things.

A further word should be said about the Third Battle of Ypres in 1917. The Official History noted that Haig's army surmounted tasks "that no other army would have faced." If that was so—and it probably was—it was due to the morale of the British Army. Morale is one thing that distinguishes an army from a mob, and morale is a function of leadership: from the top down, to be sure, but it is especially important in the platoon, company, and battalion ranks. In the early years the army had fine professional officers, but they were soon wiped out; then they posted the newly trained officers from Britain's "public schools," but most of these had been wiped out, too, and for the first time officers were being promoted from the ranks. They were good, solid officers as well but, like most of the men in the field, they were baffled and astounded by what the High Command was telling them to do. For the first time in the war, a pall of apathy and cynicism hung over much of the army.

Men can take only so much. The combatants on all sides learned this as early as 1914; as has been demonstrated in earlier chapters: to leave men in the front line fighting for more than a few days was disastrous to their collective morale. Give the men a few days out of line and they will generally be able to restore their nerves and go back again. But the wretched and superhuman things they were ordered to do in the monthlong fight at Passchendaele had finally destroyed the morale of a great part of Haig's army, and he must bear historic responsibility for it.

Yet the gods of war were not finished with "Les Miserables" of Flanders or Ypres, not by a long shot. For a while, both armies remained opposite each other, like two great panting beasts after a fierce, gnashing contest, exhausted but still extremely dangerous. The men of both sides huddled through the long, bitter winter in their trenches, shelling and raiding and sniping at each other. The Germans were probably more miserable than the British, because their relatively comfortable longtime defenses had been captured and were now enjoyed by Allied soldiers. Both sides awaited the spring thaw, the Allies in apprehension of the great German buildup on their front and the Germans in anticipation of using that buildup to finally break out and win the war.

The arrival in Italy of Plumer and his divisions from Haig's army did not accomplish Lloyd George's fervent desire of knocking Austria out of the war following the great Italian victories on the Isonzo River. Instead, they arrived to find that their role would now be to try to keep Italy *in* the war. After the triumph on the Isonzo, a combined German and Austrian attack at Caporetto had nearly succeeded in destroying the Italian Army, and the British and French divisions desperately played their role in shoring up the front. Sixteen German-Austrian divisions had attacked fifty-five Italian divisions and drove them from their lines in the Julian Alps almost to the doorsteps of Venice itself, in the process killing 10,000, wounding 30,000, and taking nearly 300,000 prisoners. In addition, 400,000 Italian soldiers ran off into the countryside, deserters.

Meanwhile, Haig had already conceived yet another operation before the year was out, in line with his determination to give the Germans no respite. This one almost succeeded, not so much as a the fabled breakthrough everyone was hoping for but as the penultimate example of a new type of warfare about to descend upon the world in the twentieth century: the triumph of the tank. Cambrai was a French town about forty-five miles south of the Ypres Salient. During the fighting in Flanders that fall, Haig had found out that a large number of tanks would be coming available. He decided to use them, on advice from Tank Corps officers, not in the mud of Flanders but near Cambrai, where the ground was underlain with chalk and was more suitable for maneuver.

To this end nearly 500 tanks were assembled secretly in a forest behind British lines around Cambrai, in the area of the British Third Army. Everything was done with stealth. Large numbers of airplanes constantly droned above the lines to mask the noise of the highly camouflaged tanks as they moved into their assembly points. At dawn on November 20, ten days after the capture of Passchendaele, 381 of the tanks rumbled out of the woodland on a six-mile front and headed straight for the German trenches. There was no artillery barrage. Infantry followed. All considered, this was a huge number of tanks; at the Somme the previous year there had only been fifty, and at Third Ypres less than a third that number.

The operation was a smashing success. The tanks crushed the German barbed wire and crossed into the trenches, firing cannon and machine guns. The Germans fled, terrified, and by day's end the British tank assault had penetrated nearly four miles into German territory and taken 7,500 Germans prisoner. They did this with an astonishingly low casualty rate to themselves, "only" 4,000 men. Sixty-four tanks were put out of action by artillery and another 114 broke down or became stuck. But it had been a remarkable victory, and when word got back church bells were rung all over England, for the first time in the war.

The celebrating did not last long. Because of the removal of five of his divisions for the campaign in Italy, Haig did not have reserves to exploit the tank success. German reserves were quickly rushed to the battle and because the land gained had formed that old bugaboo, a salient, the Allied troops within it soon found themselves under dangerous fire and counter-attacks from three sides. A few days later they were forced to retire, giving up about half the ground gained, and then the first of the big winter storms put an end to the operation. Haig was dispirited, but the one great thing to come out of Cambrai was the realization that tanks were the weapon they had been looking for to break the stalemate of the trenches.

Before the Allied war machine could manufacture enough of these mon-strosities to make a difference, the crisis everyone had foreseen was about to burst upon them: German divisions arriving from the now defunct Eastern Front were overtaking the Allies' superiority in manpower. It was a chilling prospect, because the British and French armies had for years geared themselves to offensive warfare, and now they would definitely have to go over to the defensive. Compared with the Germans, the Allies were woefully ill equipped for it. The only bright light in all this was the steady arrival of American troops, but these men would have to spend months in training before being battle-ready.

The great German offensive began March 21, 1918, less than six months after the Third Battle of Ypres, and although they had been expect-ing it the Allies were totally unprepared for the scale and ferocity of the onslaught. What Ludendorff and the German High Command were aim-ing for was the greatest gamble of the war: the total destruction of the British Army, after which, it was assumed, the French would sue for peace. The German strategy behind this was that experience had long proven that the British would continue to fight until they were smashed beyond repair, and without them the French would have no choice but to capitulate. This theory stretched at least as far back as 1916, when, according to the Official History, "General von Falkenhayn had come to the conclusion that nothing could be gained by operations in the minor theaters, and that a decision could only be obtained on the Western Front, where the British were 'the arch enemy,' and 'the soul' of the resistance to the Central Powers."

The German secret weapon rested entirely on a new plan of assault. Thus far both sides had tried massed frontal attacks, in which men scrambled out of the trenches in human waves and tried simply to overwhelm the defenders by determination and strength of numbers. Artillery, the machine gun, and barbed wire had rendered these tactics worthless. By 1917 the Allies had developed a new kind of tactic, in which the human wave was not employed; men who were trained for specific tasks went over in teams and accomplished a particular mission, then held the ground gained until they could be relieved by fresh troops. The new German plan was different even from this, and almost cost the Allies the war.

On November 11, 1917, the day after the Third Battle of Ypres came to a close on the Passchendaele Ridge, Ludendorff announced his plans for the final offensive. To him it was the only option. The unlimited U-boat campaign, in which so many high hopes had been placed, had been foiled when the British discovered the worth of putting heavily armed convoys of destroyers around their ships. This was done only after Lloyd George forced the convoy method on the Admiralty, which up to then had resisted it. In April 1917, German subs were sinking 25 percent of British and Allied merchant shipping. After the convoys were organized, that figure was reduced to less than 1 percent, just as Haig's men were struggling in the mud of Passchendaele. Britain was no longer in danger of being starved out by sea, but Germany still was, thanks to the British naval blockade. And while Ludendorff temporarily enjoyed an edge in manpower on the Western Front, the alarming numbers of Americans arriving every month would soon put an end to that. Germany had to act quickly to secure a final, decisive victory.

The German offensive plan had been organized by a staff captain, and there was nothing particularly miraculous about it. It had been tried successfully on the Eastern Front, and perfected at Caporetto. Simply stated, it called for highly mobile warfare beginning with a huge, but short, barrage that would come crashing down on Allied front lines, followed by a great rush of infantry who would bypass Allied strong points that could be mopped up later by more heavily armed infantry. Light field guns would follow on the heels of the infantry attack to destroy rear-echelon positions. No heed was to be given to letting flanking units catch up—a great and continuous infiltration was paramount. All through the winter of 1918 these new tactics were drilled into the heads of hundreds of thousands of German officers and men who would lead the attack.

Ludendorff had wanted to try out his new scheme in Flanders, and push the British back on the channel ports, but under his tight schedule the early spring was no time to fight the British and the mud simultaneously. The scheme he came up with was to hit the British hard in the area of the Somme, where their lines joined with those of the French. If successful, it would have the effect of splitting the British and French armies and rolling them back respectively, north and south. Ludendorff correctly suspected that the French would swing back south to protect Paris and the British north to protect their ports. Only then would his armies drive north to crush the British at Ypres. Ludendorff code-named the plan "Operation Michael."

A great hush of secrecy descended over all the German armies in the days leading up to the attack. The aircraft factories had been working day and night, turning out plane after plane to give the Germans a decisive preponderance of airpower, at least in a given sector. This was so effective that during the week before the attack no British aircraft was able to reach the enemy rear lines to report the enormous concentration of infantry that was gathering there.

Chapter Sixteen ★

In the predawn hours of March 21, 1918, more than one British infantry-man must have remarked on the uncanny quiet that had fallen over the battlefield; others probably sensed that something evil was lurking behind the bank of fog that shrouded no-man's-land. In the rear areas, men were just awakening for their duties; in the misty farm fields surrounding quaint French villages, green sprouts of spring wheat wavered in a gentle morning breeze. Then, without warning, the horizon for forty miles erupted with the roar and flash of 6,000 German guns, the largest concentration yet seen in the war, or any war. During the next several hours, the front line of General Gough's Fifth Army was practically annihilated, and he received the blame for it. Then the German infantry came on.

Emerging wraithlike out of the thick mists, throwing hand grenades and gunning down any defender who remained, half a million Germans quickly overran the British trenches; next the reserve and support trenches were overrun, then the artillery positions, then headquarters and supply positions. There was disbelief on both sides. Airfields were threatened and planes began taking off for fields nearer the coast. At least one commander ordered all his planes burned. At one place the British took time to evacuate 800 inmates of a lunatic asylum.

At first the German onslaught appeared irresistible, but though the British gave up more ground than at any time during the war, their line did not break. By the end of the first week the Allies had been pushed back twenty-five miles. Haig pleaded with Foch for French troops to stem the German tide. He was refused. Foch did not know exactly what the enemy intentions were, but he wanted to keep his reserve divisions intact, to begin a counteroffensive.

In what became the greatest drama of the war, the Germans continued their attacks without letup. Everyone on both sides knew that ultimate victory or ultimate defeat hung in the balance. Plumer and his divisions were rushed from Italy back to the Ypres Salient. In April Foch was given overall command of the Allied forces, including a number of American divisions that were hastily fed into the meat grinder, five of them serving with the British armies. Following the meeting at which that was decided, the French premier, Georges Clemenceau, who did not like Foch, told him snidely, "Well, you've got what you wanted." To which Foch responded, "A fine present . . . you give me a lost battle and tell me to win it."

In the meantime, the Germans had in store for the Parisians a fearsome new weapon. This was called the Paris Gun. Actually, there was more than one; there were several. Months earlier Ludendorff had concluded that the millions of inhabitants of France's premier city had it too easy during the war. He was determined to lower their morale, much in the same way Hitler later tried to lower British morale with the London Blitz. To this end a stupendous contraption was fabricated in the great Krupp gunworks at Essen. It was a cannon, the likes of which had never been seen, before the war or since.

The barrel of the gun (known to some as Big Bertha, after the wife of Herr Krupp himself) was the height of a twelve-story building. It fired a shell weighing nearly 300 pounds into the stratosphere and had a range of eighty miles, easily enough to reach Paris itself from behind German lines. For its time, it was a most remarkable invention, requiring much complicated astrophysical technology and calculation. The barrel was so heavy that it needed an odd-looking cantilevered device to keep it from sagging. It weighed nearly 400 tons, including its own built-in rail carriage.

The Paris Gun began firing on Paris from the secrecy of the St. Gobain Forest, seventy-five miles away, on March 23, two days after Ludendorff had launched his great offensive. The gun was not particularly accurate; basically it just lobbed a shell up in the air in hopes of it landing somewhere in the large confines of the city. Six days later, on Good Friday, when all good Parisians were in church, one of the shells landed on a cathedral, killing or seriously wounding 156 people, mostly women and children.

One of those who witnessed the effects of the gun was a newly arrived American army private, Harold Ross, who would later become famous as the founder and editor of *The New Yorker*. He reported: "Last Saturday, the first day they used it, was a memorable day for me. I went to a large circle and, about eleven o'clock, was standing looking up in the air with my mouth open, when WHANGO! one of the shells dropped right behind me, so close I was spun around with the concussion. My morale was shattered. I immediately retreated to the subway station and remained there two hours. I then came up and consumed a whole bottle of 'morale.'"

These disconcerting bombardments had the effect not of undermining the Parisians' morale but of making them furious, somewhat like disturbing an ant bed. The main problem with the guns was that their barrels had to be sent back to Krupp for retooling after firing only a couple of dozen shells. Although the thing caused a certain amount of consternation among the French citizens, it did not cause the systematic destruction of Paris and it was never really effective as an instrument of terror.

On April 9, Ludendorff struck another massive blow in hopes of cutting off Plumer's Second Army, still defending the Ypres Salient. The Germans attacked with another half million men toward the town of Hazebrouck, just south in France, the vital rail center supplying Flanders with as many as one hundred trains a day. If Hazebrouck fell, it would probably have been curtains for the Second Army, which would then be left without any reliable means of resupply. Again the British lines bent but did not break, though the Germans gained an astounding amount of ground. Up in the Salient, the men in the trenches listened apprehensively to the distant thunder of the battle as the Germans rolled over a corps of the Portuguese Army, which was manning a vital sector just to the south. In the face of the ferocious odds against them, the Portuguese ran away, leaving a gaping hole in the line and, according to one wounded British soldier several months later, "are probably running still." Meantime, the situation had become so ominous that Haig ordered the dikes around his crucial and teeming ports of Calais, Dunkirk, and Boulogne to be destroyed, inundating the surrounding territory in case the Germans pushed clear to the coast.

Next day, the Germans assaulted the Ypres Salient itself. With overwhelming force they crossed the Lys River and flung the British off of their hard-won positions on the southern heights of the Ypres ridgeline amphitheater. By nightfall the Germans occupied not only the high ground but the villages of Ploegsteert, Messines, and Wytschaete, thus driving a tenmile wedge into the Allied positions. With these stunning reverses, thus opened the Fourth Battle of Ypres (also known as the Battle of the Lys), which was fought in two parts over the next six months. What the Germans were ultimately aiming at were the so-called Flanders Hills—Mt. Kemmel, Mt. Rouge, Mt. Noir, and Mt. des Cats. If these were taken, Plumer's army would be isolated from the rest of the BEF and could be destroyed in detail. The situation was growing more desperate by the hour. Haig frantically begged Foch to send him French divisions to help stem the tide, but the flamboyant old general refused, on grounds that his troops were needed to defend France, and told Haig to hang on, without help or with it. In his diary Haig wrote sourly, "I found Foch most selfish and obstinate. I wonder if he is afraid to trust French Divisions in the battle front."

That night Haig wrote out a message to all British soldiers that was to become famous. He told them that the Germans intended to destroy the British Army and went on: "There is no other course open to us but to fight it out! Every position must be held to the last man: there must be no retirement. With our backs to the wall, and believing in the justice of our cause, each one of us must fight on to the end. The safety of our homes and the freedom of mankind alike depend on the conduct of each one of us at this crucial moment." Much later, this seemed to some historians like military grandstanding, but there is little doubt that Haig meant every word of it; the situation was critical.

And fight on they did, magnificently, for the next two days when, on April 12, Plumer, in additon to running his own army, was given operational command of the First Army as well, entrenched to the immediate south. The fighting was vicious and often hand-to-hand. Next day, in resignation and disgust, Plumer deliberatly evacuated practically all the bitter, blood-soaked ground the British had won the previous spring and summer, including Passchendaele, and retired to the more defensible line of 1915, just outside Ypres. As General Rawlinson had predicted six months earlier, it had just been too much ground to hold against a determined German onslaught. Further, this would shorten Plumer's lines, thereby conserving the number of troops needed to man them.

On April 17, Ludendorff launched another brutal attack in Flanders, this time to the north of Ypres, along the shortened British line near Langemarck. This was the so-called Tannenberg movement, a pincers scheme in which Ludendorff hoped to envelope the British Army, the way he had done to the Russians during the first year of the war. But again, the British determinedly staved them off. Here is how a German regimental history described the action:

"The attacking waves were cut down by furious machine-gun fire. It was discovered that the enemy had a continuous main line with an outpost line, consisting of short lengths of trench, in front of it, and the whole intervening ground was covered by unerring machine-gun flanking fire, which made progress impossible. The foremost waves were compelled to return to their jumping-off trenches, suffering severe losses."

As Britain's own Official History recounts it, "The [German] failure very nearly led to the breaking off of the Flanders offensive."

Be that as it may, by now the British government was swept up in terrible anxiety, bordering on panic. So much so that the new chief of the General Staff, Sir Henry Wilson, recommended withdrawing the entire army to a defensive perimeter at the port of Dunkirk (an action that became a near disaster during the next war). But canny old Foch (who had finally begun to send French divisions into Flanders) was livid at such a drastic proposal: "Every foot of ground must be defended." So was Haig. Any retirement toward the coast would make it seem like they were "giving up." Nevertheless, plans had been drawn to evacuate the Salient if the need arose; Poperinge had already been evacuated of civilians and noncombatants such as labor workers.

Meanwhile, Ludendorff was beginning to realize a fatal flaw in his entire scheme, the same flaw that had led to the defeat of the Schlieffen Plan in 1914: the German army, by gaining so much ground, had outrun its means of supply. Many German soldiers were living off of food and other necessities that they had captured from the British in the huge dumps behind the lines; many others, however, made themselves useless by breaking into French wineries and cafés and getting horribly drunk. At one point the Germans captured a warehouse containing approximately a million bottles of scotch whisky, intended for the British Army, an event that may have shortened the war by who knows how many days.

The Germans attacked Ypres again at the end of April. Again they secured more ground, including many of the old place names from earlier battles: St. Eloi, Voormezel—even the eminence of Mt. Kemmel, the fulcrum of the Flanders defensive position, which was abandoned by French troops after a halfhearted fight. (Interestingly, the Germans hurled their entire "Alpine Corps" against Kemmel's less than impressive heights.) The Allies hastily regrouped, support lines held, and the Germans could not break through. Still, the fighting was fierce and deadly; the Allies suffered 116,000 casualties and the Germans 109,000. By this time the English were rushing every available soldier across the channel to the front: half trained, untrained, overaged, underaged, and, in some cases, near cripples.

Finally, Ludendorff was forced to admit he could not conquer the British and French in their new line in Flanders under the present conditions. General von Lossberg, chief of staff of the German Fourth Army (who had so brilliantly organized the German defenses before the Third Battle of Ypres), concluded that his army was exhausted and would need "ten or twelve fresh divisions" to capture Poperinge and the hills of Mt. Rouge, Mt. Noir, and Mt. des Cats. But these men were simply not available. Lossberg conveyed the distasteful news to Crown Prince Rupprecht, who passed it along to Ludendorff, and with that the great German offensive in Flanders was all but finished. Years later, the American military historian Brigadier General S.L.A. "Slam" Marshall wrote that there was "no nobler or more decisive stand [during all of the First World War] than that of the BEF in front of Ypres in 1918." Exaggerated as that might be, what the British Army did in Flanders that spring was superb. Had they caved in, the Germans might have been victorious after all.

Ludendorff was not through yet, however, even though he himself was physically exhausted and grieving over the battle death of his son a month earlier. He therefore decided to rearrange his strategy in such a way as to draw off the French divisions at Ypres by launching a feint attack aimed at Paris itself. This, he concluded, would make the French so anxious that they would pull their men out of Flanders, whereupon the Germans would pounce on the remaining British and destroy their army piecemeal. It was a gamble that almost paid off.

At the end of May, Ludendorff launched his diversionary stab at Paris. It worked beyond his wildest dreams. At least the first part did. Instead of gaining just a few miles of ground, the German assault pushed the front lines out some twelve miles in a single day. Ludendorff was exultant, and here is where he made his mistake. Convinced that his assault in the south might well capture Paris—an utter disaster to the French—he immediately ordered as many German divisions from Ypres as could be spared to entrain south to continue the Paris operation. Foch, usually a canny diviner of German intentions, decided that the German move toward the French capital was only a feint—which had been the initial intention.

Foch therefore left his own divisions at Ypres, expecting another German attack there momentarily, and was thus put in the unenviable position of being both right and wrong at the same time. Right in that Ludendorff had launched the Paris operation only to siphon off French troops from Ypres, but wrong because Ludendorff had changed his mind at the last minute. Ludendorff, likewise, was wrong because American divisions were now being thrown into the battle around Paris, and even though the Germans got within thirty miles of the city—close enough to see the Eiffel Tower, which they had last seen in 1914—they never got any farther. It was said later of Ludendorff that he had put tactics above strategy, and it was true. The German race against time to snap up a fast victory before the Americans could arrive in force had been lost.

By mid-July the immense German offensive simply ran out of steam along the entire Western Front. They had dented the Allied line—overrun it totally in many places—but were unable to break through clearly anywhere. In doing so, they also put themselves into a number of dangerous salients, bulging out from their own lines. With relish, the Allies attacked these on all three sides, causing the Germans to gradually retreat. In a counteroffensive stolen from the Germans' own new tactics, plus the use of tanks, the Allies made steady advances, shoving the Germans eastward, off their lines. The German soldiers had simply fought themselves out, much as they had in the August-September battles of 1914. They were disheartened that the promises of swift and final victory had eluded them. For the Allies, the great crisis was over. Now it was their turn.

By now there were two American divisions in Flanders, fighting with the Allies at Ypres, the 27th (New York) Division, and the 30th (Tennessee) Division, totaling more than 50,000 men, due to the enormous size of American infantry divisions. They were as shocked and disgusted as everybody else at the deplorable conditions of the lines in the Salient. "The Ypres trenches have a motion all their own," wrote Private Worth P. Stewart, a Tennessean with the 30th Division. "It is doubtful if there were ever, anywhere, since the earliest trenches dug on earth, any such trenches as those that we occupied in front of Ypres." At the end of August and in early September the Americans attacked the Germans near the village of Voormezel, which had been lost back in April, driving them eastward nearly a mile but suffering more than 2,000 casualties in the process. A monument to the American dead remains in Flanders today.

By the end of September the Allies felt strong enough to attack the Germans in force and drive them out of Flanders for good. Accordingly, they assembled an army of twenty-eight divisions, more than a quarter million men, and swept the field. The Germans' will to resist had all but evaporated; General Charteris's prediction finally came true, but a year too late, and after he was gone. The Germans offered feeble resistance; mostly they retreated in the face of the Allied onslaught. It was almost as if no one wanted to become the last man to die, and who could blame them. But now the chase was on.

Plumer's Second Army attacked astride the Menin Road, scene of so many bitter memories. Passchendaele, Messines, and all the malevolent ridgelines upon which lay the bones of so many of both sides were owned once more by the Allies. With those positions secured, the fourth, and final, battle of Ypres was concluded.

Onto and over the ridges the Allies swarmed, at last taking the elusive town of Roulers. As Haig had always predicted before the Battle of Passchendaele, with the taking of Roulers, the enemy's vital rail depot, the Germans immediately evacuated the channel ports on the Belgian coast, along with their precious submarine pens. Ironically, these had become almost useless anyway, due to the success of the British convoy system.

The demoralization of the Germans had come not because they considered themselves defeated in battle, but from the home front itself. All over Germany there had been strikes and mutinies. Munitions and factory workers by the millions refused to work and waved the red flag in the streets. The German people were going hungry and almost everyone was fed up with the war. They had to scrape the bottom of the barrel for new recruits, and these arrived at the front with tales to tell. Adolf Hitler, who had again been sent back to Ypres with his regiment, describes the mood of the men: "Yet, though the battlefield was the same, the men had changed. 'Political discussions' went on among the troops. As everywhere, the poison of the hinterland began, here too, to be effective. And the younger recruit fell down completely—he had come from home."

Hitler himself soon fell victim to the fighting at the Fourth Battle of Ypres. His regiment was holding a ridge at Wervick, beyond Passchendaele, when the British launched a barrage of mustard-gas shells at them. (After the Germans unleashed their mustard gas the year before, the British responded in kind.) Many men in Hitler's company were gassed; some died as a result. Hitler soon began to feel a terrible pain in his eyes. "My eyes had turned into glowing coals," he reported in *Mein Kampf*, "it had grown dark around me." The war was now over for Corporal Hitler.

The Fourth Battle of Ypres was fought and won by the Allies with stunning swiftness. It was especially surprising since just months before the Germans had shoved them back to the gates of Ypres itself and seemed poised to take all of Flanders and drive the Allied armies into the sea. It was not to be; the British, stubborn as ever, with their new American allies on the scene as well as Belgian and French divisions, had fought there for too long to be driven from Flanders Fields. It had become sacred ground.

Meanwhile, the Americans were finally making their presence on the battle-field felt in a significant way. At the Meuse-Argonne, St.-Mihiel, and Belleau Wood they made successful, although costly, attacks. New to the war, American "doughboys" were often mowed down like tenpins after charging in massed ranks, Civil War–style. Like the French at the beginning of the war, the effects of the machine gun and massed artillery eluded them. They soon enough learned, and by midautumn there would be a million U.S. soldiers in France, with more arriving at the rate of 300,000 a month.

By October the Germans had been pushed back so far east of Ypres that no shells from their lines could fall even as far as the old Salient. Timidly, at first, the pitiful Belgians began returning to their city and to their villages. Total ruin was all they found. Four years of war and millions of artillery shells had left scarcely one brick standing upon another.

Though German propaganda on the home front every day rejoiced in "Grand Victories," the German soldier knew the truth. The Great Ludendorff (or, as it was more commonly known in Germany, the Kaiser's) Offensive of 1918 had failed utterly, and everywhere the army was being pushed back. No one understood this more than the German High Command. Ludendorff recognized that if Germany had any hope at all, it would be to ask for an immediate armistice, then to withdraw his armies behind the Rhine, possibily to reorganize and reequip for a last stand. The spring offensive had cost him nearly a million casualties. On September 28, Ludendorff warned Hindenburg that Germany must seek a truce that very day, "or our position could only grow worse." He knew the end was near.

It had cost the Allies about the same number of casualties, but they had the Germans on the run and Haig, for one, was exuberant. He believed the war could be won in 1918, and pressed for big pushes all up and down the line. This time he did not have to convince the Supreme Allied Commander, Foch, who at this point had his Frenchmen attacking at every opportunity.

Disgracefully, almost everywhere that the Germans had lost ground in France, they returned to the scorched-earth policy of their retirement to the Hindenburg Line the previous year. French homes and buildings were looted and destroyed, water wells poisoned, and fruit trees chopped down.

At last, on October 4, elements of Plumer's Second Army reached the town of Menin, eighteen miles east down the Menin Road out of Ypres, along which there had been so much suffering during four years of war. The men must have been curious to see what the town of Menin looked like, and they were probably not disappointed. They found it a nice, tidy place of old-style brick houses and shops, undamaged by war—almost untouched by it—except for the remains of the huge German staging areas in its vicinity. Unlike the brutish behavior of their counterparts farther south, the Germans who evacuated Menin had done so in a graceful way. One British soldier even reported, "The German officers had actually left us a little food."

With Ludendorff's terrible warning about "things could only grow worse" lingering in its ears, the German government grappled with how to approach the Allies to obtain an armistice. They finally decided to go through the American president, Woodrow Wilson, who, the previous January, had laid down a proposal known as the Fourteen Points, under which Germany could obtain peace. But there had been problems with this proposal. One clause in particular, dealing with "Freedom of the Seas," was intensely annoying to the British, since they interpreted it as forbidding them from conducting naval blockades in future wars. After all, they argued, look what the British blockade of Germany had accomplished in the present war. There were other things in Wilson's program, too—including formation of a League of Nations, a notion that even some Americans were already beginning to find distasteful, reasoning it was a sop to the "One Worlders."

Over the next several days notes were exchanged between Berlin and Washington. In one, Wilson demanded that Germany renounce its monarchy and warlord system of government. This was too much for Ludendorff; he told everybody this amounted to "unconditional surrender," and that Germany should fight on to the last man. When nobody paid any attention to him, including Hindenburg, he resigned, telling the old field marshal that he was no longer speaking to him, "because you have treated me so shabbily."

The last days of October and the first in November were days of almost intolerable strain in Germany: both at Army Headquarters and within the government—its leadership now ever-changing—as well as among the population. The army knew it was on its last legs and desperately needed an armistice to regroup. The Berlin government was terrified by rioting in the streets and threats of communist revolution by large segments of the population. The revolutionaries had taken over the cities singing "The Internationale" and waving the red flag from overloaded trucks and automobiles. The sailors on the warships based at Kiel mutinied and ran up the red flag on their masts. The German government—the newest one—concluded that the kaiser should abdicate but could find no one willing to tell him so. Finally they sent a flunky, who was greeted by a defiant William II, roaring, "I have no intention of quitting the throne because of a few hundred Jews and a thousand workmen!"

Nevertheless, he did, a few days later, prompted by a deliberately false report that found its way to the German press, announcing that the kaiser had abdicated. It had been leaked by the chancellor himself. Alarmed by the general rejoicing of his subjects at the news, on November 10, 1918, Kaiser William II sneaked out of Germany on a train bound for Holland, where he remained in exile for the rest of his long life.

Meantime, the German government was positively frantic to obtain an armistice. Two days before the kaiser abdicated, a German armistice committee was formed and, on November 7, was led through the lines of the French army to a waiting train, which, with windows shuttered, took them to a remote spot in the French forest of Compiègne. There, in another railcar, plushly adorned, they met with General Foch and some of his aides. The British and Americans had not been invited.

Foch cut the Germans no slack. They tried to enter into negotiations, but the Allied commander was having none of it. "Do you ask for an armistice?" he told them sternly. "If you do, I can inform you of the conditions under which it can be obtained." They did.

The terms did not seem exceedingly harsh at first. The Allies had of course considered what would happen in the event of an armistice and were determined not to give the Germans breathing room to rebuild their armies. Immediate evacuation of all lands in Belgium and France, as well as the left bank of the Rhine—Germany territory—was a principal condition. So was the surrender of the German Grand Fleet and submarines, most of their heavy armaments, including machine guns and railroad trains, renouncement of the treaties they had made with the communists that had ceded parts of Russia and Poland to the Germans, and the return of all property stolen in the occupied countries. This, in effect, would put the German war machine out of business. Foch gave them seventy-two hours to think it over. Meantime, the Allies intended to continue the war, as well as the blockade.

The German negotiators countered that within seventy-two hours Germany might have already fallen to communist revolution, but Foch was unmoved, replying that if such happened the Allied armies could deal with that, too.

Couriers came and went from the railcar to Berlin and back and finally the German government agreed to the Allied terms. Mention was not made at that point of German "war guilt," or of "reparations" for damages done. The laying down of arms was set by someone in Allied High Command, with a certain sense of irony, for 11 A.M.: the eleventh hour of the eleventh day of the eleventh month of the year. Finally, peace was at hand.

Orders were issued by Allied headquarters that there would be fighting as usual up until the final minute. For the millions of soldiers, most of them, anyway, it was a strange, almost unearthly experience. French troops were said to have festooned their uniforms with what flowers they could find but, for a time, the mood was subdued. From the British part of the line little noise was heard, aside from an occasional rendition of "God Save the King" by a regimental band. After the penultimate moment had passed, the men in the trenches poked up their heads in wonderment; a few shook hands. At last the storms were over. Only from the Americans, who had suffered but a few months of the bitter struggle, was cheering immediately reported. It was said that for a while an eerie silence settled over the great battle line, nearly 500 miles long. Larks and other birds wheeled in the sky. On the German front there was some weeping, and much ugly muttering. Up in Flanders, in the Salient at Ypres, naturally, it was raining.

Chapter Seventeen ★

The Great War did not end neatly; there was too much squabbling to do.

First, in Germany a near revolution was going on, which might have handed the country over to the Soviets. Despite routine political assassinations and general bloodshed for several years, a communist overthrow was averted, and something approaching a parliamentary democracy was established. As bad if not worse for Germany was the internal rancor caused by the terrible conflict. The Allies, against the advice of the Americans, demanded war reparations from the Germans in billions of dollars in gold, to be paid out over twenty years. The Germans naturally squawked to anyone who would listen, branding the notion "Unbearable," "Barbarous," "Impossible," "Unspeakable," and so forth. But in the end they were forced to sign the final surrender, the Treaty of Versailles, seven months after the armistice. That was because the Allies still had not let up their strangling naval blockade, which, it was asserted by the Germans, had starved to death hundreds of thousands of citizens since the armistice. (This was an exaggeration, but the German citizens were suffering badly.)

Also, as ordered by the armistice terms, the German Navy sailed its magnificent fleet of battleships, cruisers, and destroyers to the main British naval port in Scotland where they were to be handed over to the Allies. Instead, in what is possibily the world's most spectacular example of sour grapes, the German sailors scuttled the entire fleet in 120 feet of water at the entrance to Scapa Flow, the famous British naval station. To date, no one has been able to identify who actually gave the orders for this immoderate deed.

After the Soviets had signed a separate peace treaty with the Germans in the autumn of 1917, horrible fighting broke out all over the vast reaches of Russia. White Russians, Red Russians, and various other Russian factions, some aided by American troops, instigated a bloodbath that lasted until the 1920s, when the communists finally consolidated their control and established a totalitarian state. The czar, whom the Germans always blamed for starting the world war, was murdered, along with his entire family, by the communists.

The Germans forfeited all their foreign colonies and possessions to various Allied countries, as well as the French provinces of Alsace and Lorraine, which went back to France.[1] Austria-Hungary was divided up and the nation of Czechoslovakia created within its old borders. In the Balkans, Bosnia and Serbia, where the whole thing had ignited in the first place, were combined into the nation of Yugoslavia. The Baltic countries of Lithuania, Latvia, and Estonia were also created from the old Russian empire. Turkey lost her empire in the Middle East, and the state of Palestine was created, to be administered under a British mandate; many European Jews began to migrate there. For reasons somewhat obscure, the Turks changed the name of their ancient Ottoman capital of Constantinople to Istanbul.

The League of Nations was duly formed, guided by the principles in President Wilson's Fourteen Points, but without the membership of the United States. Politicians in Washington had quickly reverted to their creed of isolationism and wanted no part of being dictated to by any so-called New World Order.

---

1. Among the German possessions forfeited were a number of island chains in the southern and mid-Pacific Ocean. These were ceded to Japan as "mandates," a reward for Japan's declaration of war against Germany, even though the Japanese did not actually fight. During World War II these islands became important Japanese bases in its fight against the United States and her allies.

Twenty-six major nations and many smaller ones—including even an army of Arab Bedouins commanded by Lawrence of Arabia—had been at war with one another for more than four years. Among them they suffered some 9 million military dead on the battlefields and on the seas. For the Central Powers, these included about 1,800,000 Germans, 1,300,000 Austro-Hungarians, 300,000 Turks, and 100,000 Bulgarians. On the Allied side, 1,700,000 Russians were killed, 950,000 subjects, or former subjects, of the British empire, 1,400,000 Frenchmen, and 615,000 Italians. Nearly 50,000 Americans died as well. Militarily—excluding civilian deaths—no war in history has matched it—not even World War II (if you adjust the latter's casualty figures given out by the Soviets, which remain suspect). When it was over, the vast empires of Germany, Austria-Hungary, Russia, and the Ottoman empire had been erased from the map. Millions of civilians were also killed, including the still inflammatory massacre of a million Armenians by the Turks.

The war was fought from the steaming jungles of equatorial Africa to the slaughterhouses of France and Belgium, as well as on the Eastern Front with Russia. It was fought in the icy Italian Alps and the shifting sands of the Middle East. It was fought in Asia Minor and in strange, distant places like Persia and Mesopotamia. It was fought on the high seas all over the world, and practically no human living on earth at the time escaped at least some of its consequences.

These consequences could be far reaching. One was a social upheaval in England, mild, perhaps, in view of the effects of the war itself, but nevertheless significant. Many of the millions of men who had fought were no longer content with the stern prewar class society from which they had been hurled into the trenches. This was true, too, for the millions of British servants, plowmen, gardners, hod carriers, and other menial workers who had joined the war effort. During the victory celebrations in London, thousands gleefully broke out in a novel song:

> *"What shall we be . . .*
> *When we aren't what we are?"*

For many soldiers, the experience had been so bitter that they instilled into others the notion that war for any reason was too horrible to contemplate. This led to the now infamous resolution by the prestigious Oxford Union in the 1930s that they would henceforth "Not Fight for King and Country." Hitler and the Nazis used this flimsy information to bolster their belief that England had lost its stomach for war. It turned out, of course, that both were wrong.

For his part, Hitler returned to Germany disillusioned and venomous. He subscribed to the popular theory that the war had been lost only because Germany had been "stabbed in the back" by its politicians, who allegedly had caved in to what was essentially an unconditional surrender, when there still might have been room for negotiations. In for special malediction in his powerful orations were Germany's Jews, whom Hitler asserted were behind all profiteering, socialist uprisings, and factory strikes during the war. In the coming years Hitler and his like-minded cronies would exact an unimaginable vengeance upon them. Out of the prostration of Germany following the war would grow the Nazi movement and the onset of a war yet more vast in scope.

France, which lost nearly 1.4 million of her sons, clearly no longer had the stomach for war. This became evident twenty years later with their milquetoast performance when the Germans attacked them again. The Germans once more came through Belgium, through all the old familiar places; this time, with the hard lessons of the First World War behind them, they came with an army of tanks. In a matter of days the French surrendered, and who should be put in as their new leader but the gallant Philippe Pétain, the hero of Verdun, who had commanded the French armies in the perilous days of 1918. By now, though, Pétain was old and had lost his fire, and at the end of World War II he was accused of treason for collaborating with the Nazis.

America, which had turned the tide in favor of the Allies at the last minute, had not suffered in comparison with them. The war had made some Americans rich and others reckless; various economists trace the roots of the Great Depression to World War I. The war had also vexed strong political emotions in the United States, which resulted in women for the first time being given the right to vote.[2] General John J. Pershing faded into retirement but several other officers who fought on the Western Front would play vital roles in the next war: Douglas MacArthur, Dwight Eisenhower, George Marshall, and Harry S. Truman.

Among the Allies there had been much talk of hanging the kaiser, but nothing came of it. The Allies declared him a war criminal but the Dutch refused to extradite him. Much blame was put on him for starting the war, and much of it sticks. He had installed around him a clique of Prussian militarists and, when he could have called a halt to things, he didn't. To his death, the kaiser believed that he was not at fault, that it was his cousin, the czar, who bore the responsibility for mobilizing the Russian armies in the summer of 1914. He also blamed England, and his other cousin, the king, for interfering with his war plans, maintaining that if England had not come in on the side of Belgium and France, the war would have been a short one, with a swift and equitable settlement. The most charitable thing that can be said in the kaiser's favor is that, although he was reckless, he neither wanted, contemplated, nor enjoyed what he and his military cabal had unleashed. If Germany had been a democracy, things probably would have turned out quite differently, but it wasn't. In any case, the old German ruler died in Holland in 1941, at age eighty-two, in time to see Hitler and the Nazis lead his former country down another road to ruin.

Erich Ludendorff, defiant to the end, took part in Hitler's Nazi uprising in 1923. He was elected to the German parliament (Reichstag) as a member of the right wing, advocating the rearming of Germany. He saw the beginnings of this with the rise of Hitler but died in 1937.

Paul von Hindenburg, supreme commander of the German armies, along with Ludendorff went also into politics after the war and was elected president of Germany in 1925. He retained that position until his death in

---

2. The first thing they voted for was Prohibition, the nationwide ban on alcohol, an unhappy experiment.

1934. Meanwhile, the Nazis developed a stranglehold on the country and in 1933, while in his late eighties, Hindenburg finally acquiesced to Hitler's growing popularity and named him chancellor, thus paving the way for the former army corporal's totalitarian dictatorship.

Crown Prince Rupprecht of Bavaria, the suave bon vivant and commander of the German forces in Flanders, exiled himself after the war when Bavaria declared itself a republic and resumed his world travels. According to *The Dictionary of World War I,* Rupprecht was a direct descendant of Charles I of England, which, some historians asserted, made him rightful heir to the English throne. Clearly that would have been ridiculous. He died in 1955, at the age of eighty-six.

Lieutenant Ernst Jünger, the German storm trooper at the Third Battle of Ypres, who had been wounded fourteen times during the war, wrote a memoir, *The Storm of Steel,* in which he extolled the virtues of the German fighting soldier and German superiority in general. It became immensely popular among his countrymen. In the 1920s Jünger flirted with Nazism but soon left the political scene. During World War II he served as a captain in the German Army, but when he was very distantly linked with the plot to kill Hitler he was dismissed from the army. He went on to a long life as a novelist, essayist, and lecturer and died in 1998, at the age of 103.

General Sir Hubert Gough, commander of the British Fifth Army, who had performed poorly at the Third Battle of Ypres, performed poorly again during the great German onslaught of 1918 when his positions were overrun, or so it was charged. Though his 1918 actions were staunchly defended by Haig, Gough was sacked by the War Cabinet, although a subsequent investigation exonerated him. He lived to the ripe age of ninety-three.

General Sir Herbert Plumer, commander of the Second Army, the hero of Messines, was showered with accolades after the war. He was made a baron in 1919, as well as appointed a field marshal. He later served as governor of Malta, and died, much beloved, in 1937 at the age of seventy-five.

Sir Douglas Haig, unlike most of his subordinates after the war, was never given another job. Many attribute this to Lloyd George's hatred of him. So Haig invented a job for himself. Recognizing the need for some kind of meaningful organization that would aid the millions of ex-service-men and their families, he created the British Legion, in which he was active until the day he died, in January 1928, at home, following a game of cards. Even before his death, grumblings about Passchendaele began to find their way into the newspapers and magazines but Haig never responded to them; his dignity was authentic. Since then, many critics have lambasted Haig for his conduct of the war. They point to the awful slaughters on the Somme and especially at Passchendaele and accuse him of being "unimagi-native" and "callous," even "stupid." One thing most of the critics seem to overlook is that when the war was finally over, Haig and his army were the winners.

David Lloyd George, the British prime minister, was made an earl and published his memoirs during the 1930s. They were filled with invectives against Haig and other military leaders. Expressions abounded, such as "insane offensives," "hopeless slaughter," "ghastly butchery," and "incompetence." Even though he won reelection after the war, Lloyd George's own Liberal Party soon began to distrust him, and a few years later he was thrown out. As World War II loomed there was talk of bringing him back to some sort of power, but that did not happen, since he was considered an appeaser and defeatist. He died in 1945, at the age of eighty-two, at least with the satisfaction that England once more stood victorious over the Germans.

Of the other individuals included in this drama: William "Willie" Fraser, who had been a mere lieutenant at the First Battle of Ypres, where he had buried his brother, was promoted to colonel and at war's end was a member of the force occupying Germany. In time he became a general and was wounded during World War II. He died in 1964.

Colonel Agar Adamson also went with the occupying force, and served as a court-martial officer in Bonn. Afterward, he divided his time between Canada and England and took up flying. In 1929 his plane crashed into the Irish Sea, contributing to his death that same year, at the age of sixty-four. Until then, he still signed his letters to his wife, Mabel, "Ever thine . . ."

Captain Gerald Burgoyne, descendant of "Gentleman Johnny" Burgoyne, who suffered shell shock at Ypres in the battles of 1915, went on to government work. He was killed by an Italian aircraft bomb in 1938 during the Italian-Ethiopian war, while leading a team of Red Cross pack mules.

Private Donald Fraser, who had fought with the Canadians in both the First and Second Battles of Ypres, returned to Calgary and found a job with the Civil Service. He died in 1946, age sixty-four.

The poet-lieutenant Edmund Blunden went on to become a highly respected author, lecturer, and teacher of English literature. Toward the end of his life he was named Oxford Professor of Poetry. Blunden died in 1974, at the age of seventy-eight.

Private Will Bird, who had remarked, "I mentioned Ypres and he cursed the place. Rumors of what waited ahead of us had disturbed everyone," also returned to his native Canada. He settled in Nova Scotia where he became a well-known journalist and author. In 1944 his only son was killed in France, fighting another generation of Germans.

In the 1950s Bird was visiting with a wealthy Scottish industrialist whose hobby was collecting and cataloguing the curious language that shepherds used when counting sheep. The Scotsman regretted that his one failure had been with the shepherd boys of Hawes in North Yorkshire, whom he said were too difficult to understand.

"Get you a paper and pencil, sir," Bird told him, "and I will give you the count in Hawes!" He then proceeded to tick off what still haunted his memory forty years after the war: "Yan, tean, teather, meather, pip, cesar, asar, castra, horna, dick, yan-a-dick . . . jigget."

Private Will Bird, Canadian Black Watch, died in 1984, age ninety-three.

Ypres and all the towns and villages around it, of course, had been obliterated by four terrible years of fighting. The returning Belgians could scarcely believe what they saw: a vast treeless sea of mud, slop, craters, and ruins as far as the eye could behold. At first there was talk of not rebuilding it at all. Winston Churchill, for one, thought the wreckage itself should be preserved, declaring, "I should like to acquire the whole ruins of Ypres. A more sacred place for the entire British race does not exist in the world." The

London Times reported, "Ypres is to remain unrestored, as a monument to what Belgium has suffered in the war."

That was news to the Belgians. Those forced out during the fighting had suffered badly all through the war, living in tents and hovels and often without proper food. They wanted their homes and businesses back. The main question was how the rebuilding was going to be paid for. Eventually, the Belgian government, with the assistance of funds from many nations, set up a program. Then another furor broke out over just what was to be rebuilt. During the first part of the twentieth century, a school of "Modernist" architecture had come into vogue, exemplified by the buildings of Frank Lloyd Wright and Mies van der Rohe. There was considerable pressure put on the Belgians to employ these cheaper and more utilitarian designs rather than to try to rebuild the city and its surrounding towns in their original architectural styles, which went back many centuries. But the citizens of Ypres and its environs were having none of that, either. They wanted it back the way it was, and in the end they got it.

One of the most stupendous tasks was simply cleaning up the battlefield. First the drainage system had to be completely restored. This was difficult enough in itself, but in order to do so it would be necessary to remove from every inch of the battleground hundreds of tons of the vulgar debris of war: millions of unexploded shells, carcasses of dead animals and humans, wrecked wagons, smashed artillery pieces and tanks, crashed aircraft, carts, rail track, concrete pillboxes, thousands of miles of barbed wire, splintered timbers, shattered trees, and seas of other equipment from both sides. For years to come, the scrap-metal business was the main engine that drove the Flanders economy. Henry Ford, the American pacifist, sent over a number of tractors, fresh off his assembly line. Painstaking and often repugnant work began. The Yprians even rebuilt their magnificent Cloth Hall, though it took them until the 1960s.

Within months of war's end, visits to the Salient became popular. Tour companies were set up. The Michelin tire company put out a guidebook in 1920, the one that I found on my grandfather's bookshelf. The Belgians began a brisk cottage trade selling souvenirs to British tourists: uniform buttons, caps, revolvers, mess kits, helmets, gas masks, badges, boots—even human bones. For a time a twenty-acre section of the old battlefield near the Ypres-Comines Canal and Hill 60 was roped off and maintained for tourists in its wartime condition, with its trenches, duckboards, dugouts, guns, barbed wire, periscopes, sandbags, and other implements of war. Subsequently it, too, was reclaimed.

It was clear long before the war was over that some arrangement had to be made for formal, permanent cemeteries. As reconstruction began the ground was yielding thousands of corpses and pieces of corpses, which were brought in daily for teams to try to identify. Eventually nearly two hundred British cemeteries were established in the Salient, neatly laid out with stone crosses, and the men were buried, or reburied, for the most part without regard "to military or civil rank, race or creed." These cemeteries contain the graves of more than 200,000 British soldiers. (If you add to these the list of British soldiers "missing and presumed dead," the fighting in Flanders alone, which includes the Ypres Salient, cost the British Army more battle deaths than the entire number of Americans killed in action during all of World War II.)

Americans have their own cemetery in the Salient, laid out in four plots. Among the graves is that of Lieutenant Kenneth MacLeish, brother of the Pulitzer Prize–winning poet Archibald MacLeish. On Memorial Day, 1927, Charles Lindbergh, who had in March flown solo over the Atlantic Ocean, flew *The Spirit of St. Louis* up to the Ypres Salient and flung a handful of red poppies over the site.

The Germans have their cemeteries as well, though many of their dead had been shipped back to Germany. Nevertheless, more than 126,000 Germans lie under Belgian soil. Flanders is one of the most vast graveyards on earth, and monuments abound, many of them quite striking.

Today Belgian farmers are still plowing up tons of old shells and explosives each year. These are collected and detonated by special demolition teams. Especially dangerous are the gas shells, which tend to leak. Even today there is an average of thirty deaths per year from shell accidents along the old Western Front. In 1955, thirty-seven years after the war ended, one of the two huge unexploded mines under the Messines Ridge finally blew up, set off during an electrical storm. It alarmed everyone for miles around, but fortunately no one was injured. The last mine is still down there, somewhere.

As work on the British cemeteries continued, it became apparent that a great many of those killed would never be found; their bodies had simply been blasted into nothingness by four years of constant shelling. Accordingly, a great memorial to these missing soldiers was commissioned—the reconstruction of the old Menin Gate at the eastern edge of Ypres, through which millions had marched on their way to the battlefield. In the summer of 1927 the memorial was unveiled: a massive stone archway, set with marble, facing the once merciless ridges of Messines and Passchendaele. It had taken four years to build. On its walls were carved and gold-plated the names of 55,000 British soldiers whose remains could not be found. Construction of the Menin Gate memorial had been well under way when it was determined by the British War Records office that there were an additional 35,000 dead forever unlocatable, and their names were ultimately inscribed into a memorial at Tyne-Cot cemetery, a few miles away, the largest British cemetery in the world.

All morning on July 24, 1927, a line of ferries crossed the English Channel to the Flanders coast. Aboard were thousands of relatives of those killed and missing at Ypres, come to witness the unveiling of the Menin Gate monument. Many were mothers, widows, sweethearts, and orphans. They came from London and Manchester, Edinburgh and Cardiff, Belfast and Dublin. More still came from the smaller cities, towns, and quaint countryside villages of the United Kingdom. It was reported that some came from as far as Canada and Australia. Many of the women had brought summer flowers grown in their own gardens or window boxes to leave as meager memorials to their sons or husbands or fathers.

It was a warm day in Flanders and for a change the sun was shining. The war-worn, heartbroken British mums in their funny little hats clutched their flower bouquets to their breasts and watched with trembling lips as a man stepped smartly up to the podium.

He was white-haired and pudgy, with little, birdlike legs and a white walrus mustache but dressed in the regalia of a full British field marshal.

It was Plumer.

He surveyed the crowd in the hot afternoon sun and the women misty-eyed beneath their black veils, then swept his arm back toward the great memorial arch with its thousands of golden names carved inside.

"They are not missing!" he told them. "They are here!"

Bibliographical Notes
and Acknowledgments ★

The fighting in Belgian Flanders can be better understood in context by studying the whole of World War I. There are many fine books on the subject, including Basil Liddell Hart's *History of the First World War, 1914–1918,* Winston Churchill's *The World Crisis, 1911–1918,* C.R.M.F. Cruttwell's *A History of the Great War, 1914–1918,* Cyril Falls's *The First World War,* John Terraine's *The Great War, 1914–1918,* Sir Martin Gilbert's *The First World War,* and John Keegan's *The First World War,* among others.

Any detailed investigation of the battles of Ypres must begin with appropriate sections of the indispensable twenty-eight-volume *History of the Great War* (or the "Official History," as it has come to be known), compiled by Brigadier General Sir James Edmonds. This monumental work has come under scrutiny and occasionally been called into question as to its conclusions by later historians, especially over Edmonds's defense of Haig's strategy at the Third Battle of Ypres, or Passchendaele. On balance, it seemed to this writer that the Official History tried hard to present the facts as amassed from official reports—as well as interviews and excerpts from the German histories and autobiographies of the major German participants—and that its conclusions were, at the least, heartfelt. But the old maxim "history belongs to the winners" seems at times to apply.

There are any number of instructive and detailed books on the various campaigns in Flanders currently in print in Great Britain: notably, those from Leo Cooper, Pen & Sword Books, the Cameos of the Western Front series, and The Battleground Europe series. Also, Osprey Military has numerous handsome and useful World War I imprints. I would like to thank Ray Westlake of Westlake Books Ltd. for his help in researching this project. Some of the most useful and certainly a most enjoyable series are the many works, published by Penguin Books Ltd., of historian Lyn Macdonald, who managed to interview hundreds of actual participants, beginning many years ago. As all of those remaining soldiers would be in their hundreds by now, her work is invaluable for painting the scenes of battle from the actual memories of those who lived it. Likewise, Denis Winter's works *Death's Men* and *Haig's Command: A Reassessment* are highly readable and of great importance.

In sorting out the vagaries of various campaigns and controversies, historians Peter Liddle and Hugh Cecil have produced *Facing Armageddon,* a compelling compilation of essays by leading contemporary historians and experts, which is well worth its 500-plus-page read. Liddle also published a similarly constructed work in *Passchendaele in Perspective: The Third Battle Ypres,* which examines in minute detail all aspects of that terrible fight. Others have written equally well on the Third Battle of Ypres, notably Robin Prior and Trevor Wilson in *Passchendaele in Perspective* and John Terraine in *The Road to Passchendaele.* Terraine also wrote a fine biography: *Douglas Haig: The Educuated Soldier.* There are other useful biographies and compilations on Haig, including *Haig: A Reappraisal 70 Years On,* edited by Brian Bond and Nigel Cave. For the battle of Messines, Ian Packingham's *Pillars of Fire* is a fine appraisal.

Practically all the major players wrote their memoirs after the war: Ludendorff, Hindenburg, Rupprecht—even Kaiser William. On the Allied side, Foch, Joffre, Lloyd George, Churchill; only Haig opted out, although his diaries, as well as those of Charteris, his intelligence chief, subsequently became available.

It occurs to me now that I undertake too much here. The list of World War I books—histories, biographies, atlases, appraisals, and reappraisals— is almost limitless, and it would take page after page for me to list only those I have read or referenced. But there is an indispensable Internet site called Trenches on the Web that, for anyone interested in the Great War, will lead you with links to practically anything you would wish to read or see.

As well, the great Imperial War Museum in London is a vast storehouse and wealth of knowledge on the war, with fascinating exhibits as well as firsthand documents and photographs of the action; so is the

National Museum of Canada. And up at Ypres in Belgium there is the In Flanders Fields Museum.

I owe an invaluable and profound debt of thanks to all those dogged historians who have gone before, including of course those listed above. In addition I would like to thank those publishers from whose books I have quoted portions of memoirs, diaries, and poetry: CEF Books (Canada)— and in particular Norm Christie—for *Ghosts Have Warm Hands,* the memoir of Private Will Bird, *The Letters of Agar Adamson,* and *The Journal of Private Fraser;* Howard Fetig, publisher, for Ernst Jünger's *Storm of Steel;* Thomas Harmsworth Publishing, for *The Burgoyne Diaries;* Penguin Books for Edmund Blunden's *Undertones of War;* Michael Russell Ltd., for *In Good Company: The Letters and Diaries of the Hon. William Fraser;* Tom Donovan Publishing, for Alexander Barrie's *War Underground;* The Feminist Press, for the excerpt from Helen Zenna Smith's *Not So Quiet;* The Calgary Highlanders Regimental Funds Foundation, for excerpted quotes from *Gallant Canadians, The Story of the Tenth Canadian Infantry Battalion, 1914–1919;* and Heinemann, for the excerpt from Mary Borden's *The Forbidden Zone.*

Moreover, I owe a profound debt of gratitude to Morgan Entrekin, publisher and president of Grove/Atlantic, for seeing the worth of this book, and, as emphatically, to its editor, Daniel Maurer, for his painstaking and patient work on the manuscript and assistance locating photographs and permissions. Donald Kennison, who did the copyediting, saved me from myself more times than I wish to mention. My old friend Dr. Hugh Cecil, one of Britain's most eminent historians of both world wars, gave invaluable advice on the manuscript throughout, and to him I owe a very special thanks for this particular labor of kindness. Also Dr. John Strange, who helped immeasurably in ironing out computer glitches. And last, but of course not least, a huge debt of gratitude goes to my wife, Anne-Clinton Groom, and to her mother, Wren Murphy, not only for all their technical assistance: copying, laying out photography, identifying captions, mailings, faxes, and computer support, but also, most important, for their unflinching moral support during this lengthy enterprise.

Winston Groom
Cashiers, North Carolina, February 2002

✯ Source Notes

43: "Big guns they are... one horse wounded too." General Sir David Fraser, ed., *In Good Company: Letters and Diaries of the Hon. William Fraser* (Norwich: Michael Russell Publishing Ltd., 1990). © Fraser Publications. Used by permission.

52–53: Quotes from the diary of Hon. William Fraser. Ibid.

55–56: "Shortly afterwards . . . it's one of our officers!" Ibid.

77: "Debrett's *Peerage* . . . made very sorry reading." Lyn Macdonald, *1914: The Days of Hope* (London: Penguin Books Ltd., 1989), p. 421. Used without authorization.

78: Oh come with me . . . A most unfortunate occurrence!" Helen Zenna Smith, *Not So Quiet: Stepdaughters of War* (London: A.M. Heath & Co., Ltd., 1930).

81: Quotes from the diary of Father Camille Delaere. Macdonald, *1914,* pp. 403–5, 408. Used without authorization.

92–93: Quotes from the diary of Agar Adamson. Norm Christie, ed., *Letters of Agar Adamson* (Ontario, Canada: CEF Books, 1997). Used by permission of CEF Books.

108–10: Quotes from the diary of Agar Adamson. Ibid.

110–12: Quotes from the diary of Captain Gerald Achilles Burgoyne. Gerald Achilles Burgoyne, *The Burgoyne Diaries* (London: Thomas Harmsworth Publishing, 1985). © 1985 by Claudia Davison. Used by permission of Thomas Harmsworth Publishing.

115: Quotes from the diary of William Fraser. General Sir David Fraser, ed., *In Good Company.*

117: "In Flanders Fields," by John McRae. (First appeared in *Punch* magazine, 1915.)

122: "Dulce et Decorum Est," by Wilfred Owen, from *The Collected Poems of Wilfred Owen.* © 1963 by Chatto & Windus, Ltd. Reprinted by permission of New Directions Publishing Corp.

131: "I don't know what . . . in the line by far." General Sir David Fraser, *In Good Company.*

145–46: Quotes from the diary of Donald Fraser. Donald Fraser, *The Journal of Private Fraser* (Ontario: CEF Books, 1997). © 1997 Norm Christie. Used by permission.

161: Selection from "Concert Party: Busseboom," reproduced from *Undertones of War* by Edmund Blunden (London: Penguin Books Ltd., 1925). © 1928 by permission of PFD on behalf of the Estate of Mrs. Claire Blunden.

178–80: "They wear their caps . . . to go back again." Mary Borden, *The Forbidden Zone* (London: Heinemann Ltd., 1929). Used without authorization.

194–95: Quotes from the diary of Ernst Junger. Ernst Junger, *The Storm of Steel: The Diary of Ernst Junger* (New York: Zimmermann & Zimmerman, 1985).

202: Quotes from Alfred J. Angel. Lyn Macdonald, *They Called It Passchendaele* (London: Penguin Books Ltd., 1993), p. 178. © 1978 Lyn Macdonald. Used without authorization.

203–5: Quotes from Edmund Blunden, including "The Welcome." Blunden, *Undertones of War.*

214–15: "Tea was all we had . . . who died in the mud." Macdonald, *They Called It Passchendaele,* p. 206. Used without authorization.

218: "The condition of . . . can forsee the future." Adamson, *Letters of Agar Adamson.*

218: Quotes from the diary of Will R. Bird. William R. Bird, *Ghosts Have Warm Hands: A Memoir of the Great War* (Ontario: CEF Books, 1997). © 1997 Norm Christie and The Estate of W. R. Bird. Used by permission.

220–21: Quotes from the diary of Will R. Bird. Ibid.

221: Quotes from the diary of Agar Adamson. Adamson, *Letters of Agar Adamson.*

223–24: Quotes from the diary of Will R. Bird. Bird, *Ghosts Have Warm Hands.*

258: Quotes from the diary of Will R. Bird. Ibid.

★ Index

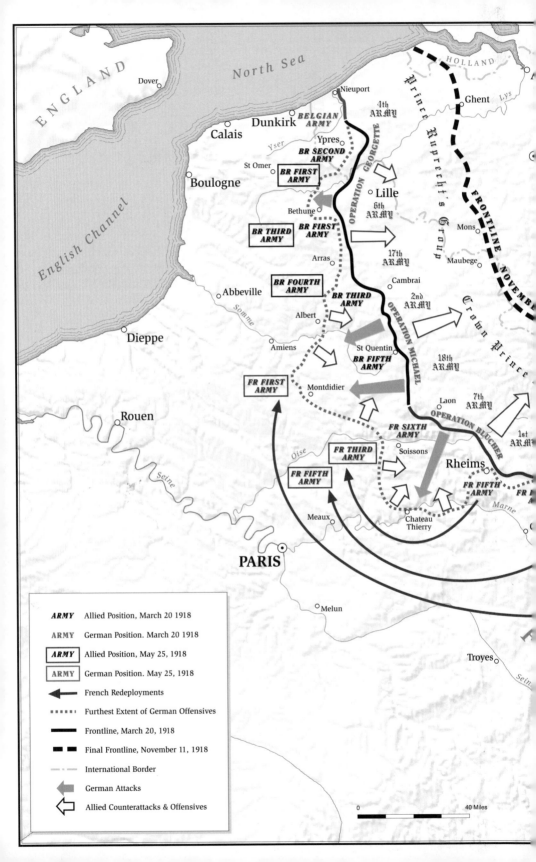

ENGLAND

North Sea

HOLLAND

Dover

Dunkirk

Calais

Boulogne

English Channel

Dieppe

Rouen

Nieuport

4th ARMY

Ghent

Lys

BELGIAN ARMY

Ypres

BR SECOND ARMY

St Omer

BR FIRST ARMY

Yser

Bethune

Lille

6th ARMY

Mons

BR THIRD ARMY

BR FIRST ARMY

17th ARMY

Maubege

Arras

Cambrai

BR FOURTH ARMY

2nd ARMY

Abbeville

Somme

Albert

BR THIRD ARMY

St Quentin

BR FIFTH ARMY

18th ARMY

Amiens

FR FIRST ARMY

Montdidier

Laon

7th ARMY

Rheims

1st ARMY

FR SIXTH ARMY

FR THIRD ARMY

Soissons

Oise

FR FIFTH ARMY

Meaux

Chateau Thierry

FR FIFTH ARMY

Marne

FR A

Seine

PARIS

Prince Rupprecht's Group

Crown Prince

OPERATION GEORGETTE

OPERATION MICHAEL

OPERATION BLUCHER

FRONTLINE NOVEMB

Melun

Troyes

Sein

ARMY — Allied Position, March 20 1918

ARMY — German Position. March 20 1918

ARMY — Allied Position, May 25, 1918

ARMY — German Position. May 25, 1918

French Redeployments

Furthest Extent of German Offensives

Frontline, March 20, 1918

Final Frontline, November 11, 1918

International Border

German Attacks

Allied Counterattacks & Offensives

0   40 Miles